Key management models

FT Prentice Hall
FINANCIAL TIMES

In an increasingly competitive world, we believe it's quality of thinking that gives you the edge – an idea that opens new doors, a technique that solves a problem, or an insight that simply makes sense of it all. The more you know, the smarter and faster you can go.

That's why we work with the best minds in business and finance to bring cutting-edge thinking and best learning practice to a global market.

Under a range of leading imprints, including *Financial Times Prentice Hall*, we create world-class print publications and electronic products bringing our readers knowledge, skills and understanding, which can be applied whether studying or at work.

To find out more about Pearson Education publications, or tell us about the books you'd like to find, you can visit us at **www.pearsoned.co.uk**

MARCEL VAN ASSEN
GERBEN VAN DEN BERG
PAUL PIETERSMA

Key management models

The 60+ models every manager needs to know

2nd edition

FT Prentice Hall
FINANCIAL TIMES

An imprint of **Pearson Education**

Harlow, England • London • New York • Boston • San Francisco • Toronto • Sydney • Singapore • Hong Kong
Tokyo • Seoul • Taipei • New Delhi • Cape Town • Madrid • Mexico City • Amsterdam • Munich • Paris • Milan

PEARSON EDUCATION LIMITED

Edinburgh Gate
Harlow CM20 2JE
United Kingdom
Tel: +44 (0)1279 623623
Fax: +44 (0)1279 431059
Website: www.pearsoned.co.uk

First edition published in 2003
Second edition published in Great Britain in 2009

© Berenschot BV 2003, 2009

ISBN: 978–0–273–71910–6

British Library Cataloguing in Publication Data
A CIP catalogue record for this book can be obtained from the British Library

Library of Congress Cataloging in Publication Data
A CIP catalog record for this book can be obtained from the Library of Congress

10 9 8 7 6 5 4 3 2 1
12 11 10 09 08

Set by 3
Printed and bound in Great Britain by Ashford Colour Press Ltd, Gosport, Hants

The Publisher's policy is to use paper manufactured from sustainable forests.

Contents

PART THREE Operational models 193

About the authors

Marcel van Assen (1969) is a senior consultant within the operations management group at Berenschot, and assistant professor of manufacturing management at the department of management of technology and innovation of RSM Erasmus University. He has a deep understanding of the issues that affect manufacturing, supply chain and strategic management, resulting from his extensive consulting experience, which encompasses operational excellence, outsourcing and contract manufacturing and value-innovation, using tools such as strategic conversation, road-mapping and foresight.

He holds an MSc in mechanical engineering from the University of Twente, an MSc in business administration (strategy and organisation) from the Open University, and a Ph.D. in business administration from the Erasmus University Rotterdam. As an associate member of ERIM (Erasmus Research Institute of Management), his research interests focus on both strategic innovation management and operations management in knowledge-intensive (high-tech) manufacturing firms, clusters and networks. In addition, he is co-author of several books and articles on operations and innovation management.

Gerben van den Berg (1979) is a senior strategy consultant for the business strategies group at Berenschot. He advises the boards of directors and management of start-ups and established companies industry-wide on strategic business planning and organisational restructuring issues, such as M&A, reorganisation and outsourcing. An alumnus from the University of Groningen, where he read business administration (with two majors), he is also a co-author of *Excellence = Optimisation and Innovation*; and co-author of *The Strategy Book II*, a leading title on strategy published in Dutch. He has also published several articles on strategy and business planning.

Paul Pietersma (1965) MSc, BA, is a senior strategy consultant and managing director of Business Strategies at Berenschot. He has more than 10 years' experience in the consultancy business, during which time he has advised many CEOs and boards of directors on various strategic issues. He won the Dutch Professionals Award for Management Consultancy in 2006. He has published several articles on strategy and is the co-author of two leading books on strategy – *The Strategy Book I* and *The Strategy Book II*, both published in Dutch.

Publisher's Acknowledgments

We are grateful to the following for permission to reproduce copyright material:

Figure 1.1 and Figure 1.2 reproduced with permission of the Ansoff Family Trust; Figure 2.1 from the *Product Portfolio Matrix*, © 1970, The Boston Consulting Group; Figures 3.1 from *Blue Ocean Strategy: How to Create Uncontested Market Space and Make Competition Irrelevant* by W. Chan Kim and Renée Mauborgne. Harvard Business School Publishing Corporation, Boston 2005. With permission of Berenschot; Figure 4.1 and Figure 4.2 reprinted with the permission of The Free Press, a Division of Simon & Schuster Adult Publishing Group, from *COMPETITIVE STRATEGY: Techniques for Analyzing Industries and Competitors* by Michael E. Porter. Copyright © 1980, 1998 by The Free Press; all rights reserved.; Figure 5.1 from Jay Barney, *Journal of Management* (Volume 17, Issue 1), pp. 99-120, copyright © 1991 by (Southern Management Association) Reprinted by permission of SAGE publications; Figure 6.1 reprinted by permission of Harvard Business Publishing. From "Evolution and Revolution as Organizations Grow" by Larry E. Greiner, *Harvard Business Review*, issue 5/1/98. Copyright © (1998). All rights reserved; Figure 8.1 and Figure 9.1 with permission of Berenschot; Figure 18.1 from Treacy, M. and Wiersema, F. (1995) *The Discipline of Market Leaders: Choose your customers, narrow your focus, dominate your market*. New York: Perseus Books. Reprinted by permission of Basic Books, a member of Perseus Books Group; Figure 22.1 and Figure 22.2 from *Operational Excellence*, nieuwe stijl, Marcel van Assen, Roel Notermans, Joes Wigman. Academic Service, The Hague 2007. With permission of Berenschot; Figure 26.1 from *The 7 Habits of Highly Effective People*, The Free Press, (Covey, Stephen R., 1989); Figure 27.1 reprinted with the permission of The Free Press, a Division of Simon & Schuster Adult Publishing Group, from *CUSTOMER MARKETING METHOD: How to Implement and Profit from Customer Relationship Management* by Jay Curry with Adam Curry. Copyright © 2000 by The Customer Marketing Institute BV. All rights reserved.; Figure 30.1 from Henderson, J.C. and Venkatraman, N. (1991) 'Understanding strategic alignment'. *Business Quarterly* 55 (3): 72. Copyright © (1991) Ivey Management Services. One time permission to reproduce granted by Ivey Management Services on October 2008; Figure 31.1 is based on Geert Hofstede and Gert Jan Hofstede, *"Cultures and Organizations: Software of the Mind"*. Revised and Expanded 2nd Edition. New York: McGraw-Hill USA, 2005, ISBN 0-07-143959-5. Reproduced with permission from the authors and copyright holder; Figure 32.1 from The House of Purchasing and Supply, Copyright A.T. Kearney, Inc, 2002. All rights reserved. Reprinted with permission.; Figure 33.1 from *Van kiem tot cash*, Marcel van Assen, Joost Krebbekx, Wilma Schreiber. Berenschot, Utrecht 2006. With permission of Berenschot; Figure 34.1 from KOTLER, PHILIP; KELLER, KEVIN LANE, *MARKETING MANAGEMENT: ANALYSIS, PLANNING, IMPLEMENTATION AND CONTROL*, 12th Edition, © 2006, p.27. Reprinted by permission of Pearson Education, Inc., Upper Saddle River, NJ.; Figure 35.1 reprinted with the permission of The Free Press, a Division of Simon & Schuster Adult Publishing Group, from *A FORCE FOR CHANGE: How Leadership Differs From Management* by John P. Kotter. Copyright © 1990 by John P. Kotter, Inc. All rights reserved.; Figure 36.1 from reprinted by permission of Harvard Business Publishing. From "Purchasing Must Become Supply Management" by Peter Kraljic, *Harvard Business Review*, issue 9/1/83. Copyright © (1983); all rights reserved.; Figure 39.1 from *Compensation* by Milkovich, G.T. and Newman, J.M. (New York: McGraw-Hill, 2007) © The McGraw-Hill Companies, Inc; Figure 40.1, MINTZBERG, HENRY; *STRUCTURE IN FIVES DESIGNING EFFECTIVE ORGANIZATION*, 2nd Edition, © 1992, p.154. Reprinted by permission of Pearson Education, Inc., Upper Saddle River, NJ. Reprinted with kind permission from Henry Mintzberg; Figure 41.1 from "The Global Procurement and Supply Chain Benchmarking Initiative", Monczka, Robert M., Michigan State University, Unpublished. With kind permission from Robert M. Monczka, Ph.D., Michigan State University; Figure 43.1 from *QUICK RESPONSE MANUFACTURING: A COMPANYWIDE APPROACH TO REDUCING LEAD TIMES* by Rajan Suri. Copyright 1998 by Taylor & Francis Group LLC – Books. Reproduced with permission of Taylor & Francis Group LLC – Books in the format Tradebook via Copyright Clearance Center.; Figure 44.1 from *THE FIFTH DISCIPLINE* by Peter M. Senge, copyright © 1990, 2006 by Peter M. Senge. Used by permission of Doubleday, a division of Random House, Inc; Figure 46.1 from *The EFQM Excellence Model for self-appraisal*. EFQM: Brussels, Belgium; Figure 49.1 from reprinted by permission of Harvard Business Publishing. From "The Balanced Scorecard: Measures That Drive Performance (HBR Classic)" by Robert S. Kaplan; David P. Norton, *Harvard Business Review*, issue 7/1/05. Copyright © (2005); all rights reserved.; Figure 55.1 and Figure 55.2 reprinted with kind permission from Henry Mintzberg

In some instances we have been unable to trace the owners of copyright material, and we would appreciate any information that would enable us to do so.

Preface

Management models are not only tools for professionals and managers but essentially they are a way of communicating. Management models bridge differences in abstraction and provide comprehensiveness. Berenschot has a long lasting tradition of both application and development of management models. This started in 1938. The year our company was founded and continued over the years. The models show the variety of academic disciplines from which they originated. Elements of the early engineers approaches as just as much visible as influences of social sciences.

This new edition of *Key Management Models* reflects the scope of Berenschot and its consultants. And it shows the necessity of keeping on track when it comes to new developments.

I thank all our consultants who provided input for this *Key Management Model* edition and extend these feelings to the authors of the previous edition, Frans Stevens, Wouter ten Have and Steven ten Have. I'm confident that we will continue this tradition in the future.

Prof. Dr. Theo Camps
Chairman Berenschot Group

Management models are designed to resolve common problems and challenges in business. At best they will provide a new way of seeing a situation that will result in positive change. The models may be applied strategically, tactically or operationally; some are problem-solving tools, designed to improve efficiency and effectiveness; most are designed to solve specific problems arising out of a specific situation. Unfortunately, no management model, or group of models, can guarantee that a manager or consultant will deal with an organisational problem objectively and to the best of their ability; and the vast array of management models on offer can be bewildering, for managers and consultants alike. Models can none the less provide valuable insights and a sound framework for making appropriate business choices. Management models and theories can help managers and consultants to gain clarity in business by reducing the complexities and uncertainties involved – nothing more, but definitely nothing less.

The first edition of *Key Management Models* was published in 2003. At that time our highly respected colleagues (Steven ten Have, Wouter ten Have and Frans Stevens) rose to the challenge of imposing some sense of order on the range of models available, and drew up an overview of the most frequently used and quoted management models. In the present edition, we have revised and further developed their overview. We have revisited the world's classic and best-known models, and have discovered that not all of them are used as frequently in daily practice as we had thought. Some are too theoretical or outdated; whereas other, lesser-known or new models are now in common use. We have therefore updated the previous edition with up to 60 of the management models that are in most frequent use. In addition to a brief description of each model and suggestions as to its application, we include a description of how to use it. For the 'diehards' among our readers, we have added recommended reading and, where appropriate, have drawn attention to the potential limitations or shortcomings of each model.

We arrived at the final selection of management models by asking managers and consultants from various disciplines which models they use in their work. For this purpose, we defined a model as a tool that can be employed (either for process and / or analytical purposes) to enhance the daily functioning of the business, by improving both management methods and the performance of the organisation; or to solve related problems. As a result, our compilation reflects ideas and insights that are 'proven technology' and is largely the result of practical rather than literary research. The criterion for inclusion, therefore, was not whether the models selected are scientifically or technically profound, but whether they actually work.

This book is intended neither as a 'top 60' of popular or 'hyped' management models, nor as a prescription for 'good' management and organisation. In order to identify more clearly the variety and function of the models and the differences in their scope, we have grouped the models into six distinct and sometimes overlapping categories (see 'Using the book'); in this way we aim to put each individual model into perspective, and into the context of management models in general. Descriptions of each model, and an overview of how and when to use it has also been included, to reduce the risk of managers being tempted to view the next popular model that happens to be 'hyped' as being the ultimate solution for their organisational malfunctions.

Some of the models stand up to a high degree of scientific scrutiny, but many are simply memory aids. The majority provide useful ways of ordering reality. They offer a common language with which to compare performances and challenges, and solve problems. They contain inspiring characterisations, but above all, they are of great practical value (and are used on a daily basis) when it comes to analysing situations and identifying possible courses of action.

It is with both pleasure and pride that we present this compilation. We are confident that the managers and consultants who use it will possess the necessary maturity, intelligence and discernment to place the models we have included into perspective, and will use them to act on sound, creative, consistent management and advice. It was never our intention to produce a comprehensive overview of all management models; our aim is rather to supplement the readers' existing knowledge by providing additional ideas and insights, and sound, easily comprehensible descriptions of actual and frequently used models. Thus enriched, managers and consultants will be able to determine quickly which model is most appropriate for a given situation, while also recognising its limitations. This ties in neatly with our daily field of work, where we face the extremely difficult task of successfully managing, changing and providing contingent advice simultaneously. We view this book as a means of not only giving expression to this complexity, but also of making it more manageable, by providing models to reduce complexity and visualise reality, so that management issues can be discussed based on a 'common language'.

It is impossible to thank personally all of those who have been involved in the publication of this book. Invaluable work was carried out behind the scenes by Catherine Zijlstra, Noortje de Lange and Charlotte van der Heyden. Without their efforts, getting this book to publication would have been a very different story. Bart Koops, Jeroen Nijzink, Karin Stalenhoef, Klaas de Gier, Laurens Friso, Lotte van der Veer, Luddo Oh, Maartje Elderhuis, Marijke ten Have, Mark Nijssen, Michiel Baldal, Rob de Groot, Tim Krechting, Titia Tamminga, Vera van Vilsteren and Wouter de Wolf have also helped to describe some of the models. We would like to thank these colleagues for their valuable efforts and commitment. Special thanks go to Luc Steenhorst for his support. Finally, we would like to thank our employer, Berenschot, for the time and support given to revise *Key Management Models*. The company has remained the innovative front-runner among Dutch consultancy firms since its foundation in 1938.

We wish all who read this book, much energy and many constructive results from applying the models. Use the models wisely in your own specific context: structuring reality is completely different from managing reality.

Marcel van Assen
Gerben van den Berg
Paul Pietersma

Using the book

Key Management Models describes 60 contemporary management tools and practices and explains how each can be used and applied in business management. There are many different ways in which business models could be categorised; we have chosen two broad classifications that focus on their use and function, namely: management decision-making (strategic, operational, tactical), and business function (e.g., finance or marketing). For the purposes of the book we have grouped the models into three sections, according to the area of management where their use is most appropriate:

- Part 1: Strategic (positioning / aims). These models are valuable when analysing and planning the strategic position of a company and help to answer strategic questions.
- Part 2: Tactical (design / organisation). These models can be used to organise company processes, resources and people. They address important 'how to' questions when analysing and designing excellent organisations.
- Part 3: Operational (implementation / execution). These models can be used to change organisations and help to implement best practices. They address the 'who, what, when' questions that are asked when analysing and improving implementation in excellent organisations. Models that help to optimise the effectiveness of operational processes and activities are included in this category.

The models in each section are listed alphabetically and marked with one or more icons that represent six functional areas and levels of management decision-making:

Strategy and organisation. Models used for formulating strategy and designing organisational structures.

Finance and governance. Models used to design governance mechanisms and related performance metrics, including financial instruments.

Marketing and sales. Models used to formulate marketing and sales policies, to structure marketing and sales departments, and to develop operational marketing and sales instruments.

Operations, supply chain management and procurement. Models used to formulate operations, supply chain and procurement policies, and methods to design, optimise and implement best practices for operations, supply chains and procurement.

 Innovation and technology management. Models related to innovation management. Models used to formulate R&D and technology policies, to align R&D technology objectives with corporate strategy, to develop R&D instruments.

 HRM, leadership and change. Models used to formulate HR policies, and to design and implement HRM practices and instruments. Models and methods related to change management are also included in this category.

For ease of use, each entry is divided into:

- **The big picture** – the essence and purpose of each model.
- **When to use it** – its usefulness and applicability.
- **How to use it** – a description of how to apply the model using a step-by-step approach.
- **The final analysis** – the models' limitations and the potential pitfalls with regard to their use.

Should you require more information on a specific management model, please refer to the reference section at the end of each section. Each entry includes one or more examples of how to apply the model and, where useful, includes case studies to describe how the models can be used in a specific situation. Where relevant we also refer to alternative, but equally applicable models.

[PART ONE]

Strategic models

hese models help to analyse and plan a company's strategic
position and provide answers to strategic questions.

Ansoff's product / market grid

The big picture

The Ansoff product/market grid offer a logical way of determining the scope and direction of a firm's strategic development in the marketplace. The firm's strategic development consists of two related types of strategy: portfolio strategy and competitive strategy.

The portfolio strategy specifies the objectives for each of the firms product / market combinations. It points the dots on the horizon. The competitive strategy specifies the route to reach those objectives.

In the Ansoff product / market grid setting the objectives (portfolio strategy) was introduced as choosing a *growth vector*, specifying the ultimate future scope of business. The growth vector is expressed on two dimensions: products and markets.

Later, Ansoff introduced the *geographical growth vector*, replacing the growth vector from his product/market grid. The geographical growth vector has three dimensions, which the firm can use to define its desired future business scope:

- **the market need** (such as need for personal transportation or need for amplification of electric signals)
- **the product/service technology** (such as integrated circuit technology)
- **the market geography** (such as regions or nation states)

Product / Mission	Present	New
Preset	Market penetration	Product development
New	Market development	Diversification

Figure 1.1 Ansoff's growth vector components products and markets

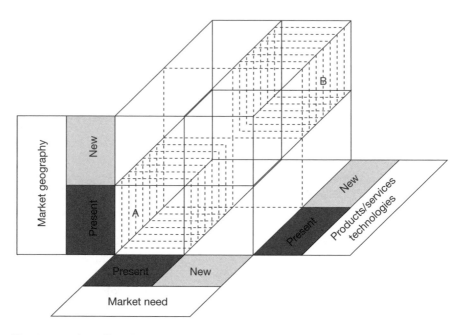

Figure 1.2 Ansoff's dimensions of the geographic growth vector: market need, product/services technology and market geography

These three dimensions together form a cube. They offer a variety of combinations and strategic directions for a firm. Extreme choices are on the one hand to continue serving current regions with existing technologies to fulfil traditional needs or on the other hand to enter new regions with new technologies to fulfil new needs.

When to use it

Deciding a direction and a strategy for corporate growth depends upon a number of factors, including: the level of risk involved, the current set of products and markets, and whether the organisation wants to develop new or existing products or markets. In order to plan for the future in a systematic way, it is vital that managers understand the gap between the firm's current and desired position. The Ansoff product / market grid and the Ansoff cube can be used as a framework to identify the direction and opportunities for corporate growth.

Ansoff introduced four components that cover the portfolio strategy and help specify the desired future business scope:

1 Geographical growth vector
2 Competitive advantage;
3 Synergies;
4 Strategic flexibility.

The geographical growth vector can be determined with Ansoff's cube, by connecting the current scope of business with the desired future business scope.

A competitive advantage is needed to both to enable the chosen scope, but also to be able to sustain en route towards it. The competitive advantage can be anything from a core competence or a patented technology to offering better after sales service to clients than your competitors.

As a third strategy component, Ansoff suggests taking account of the synergy between the firm's competencies. This not only enables economies of scale but also can strengthen the firm's competitive position.

The fourth, and final, strategic component is the strategic flexibility. It is aimed at minimizing the impact of unforeseen events and seeks to discard all unnecessary 'ballast'.

The four components are interlinked. Optimizing one of the components is likely to depress the firm's performance on the others. In particular, maximizing synergies is very likely to reduce flexibility. The process of selecting and balancing the strategic objectives is a complex matter.

How to use it

To use the product / market grid in practice, an organisation must first assess its existing product–market combinations and corresponding levels of competitive advantage. Then, its desired future business scope is to be chosen as the geographical growth vector within the Ansoff cube.

Next, the feasibility of the chosen scope and direction should then assessed with an analysis of the combination of the intended direction and extent of corporate growth and the firm's distinctive competitive advantages (core competences). Not only should there be the means that enable the chosen scope, those means should also provide the firm with a sustainable competitive advantage.

Then, synergies have to be found and/or created either by making use of an existing outstanding competence (aggressive synergy strategy), or by developing or acquiring the necessary competence (defensive synergy strategy).

Finally, strategic flexibility has to be attained. This can be attained externally to the firm though diversifying of the firm's geographic scope, needs served and technologies so that a surprising change in any one of the strategic business areas does not produce a seriously damaging impact on the firm's performance. Alternatively, it can be attained by basing the firm's activities on resources and capabilities which are easily transferable.

A shortcut in determining the strategic objectives is by deriving them from the strategic requirements of three archetype firms:

- An operating company will focus on synergies and a relatively narrow focused geographical growth vector. Its investments are often irreversible, have long lead times and will often be into R&D or physical assets. It must be able to anticipate change and minimize the changes of making bad decisions. Synergies often will be created around core competences

- A conglomerate firm will focus on flexibility. Its strategy would have no synergy nor geographical growth vector. Instead it would include enough flexibility to be protected from strategic surprises or discontinuities in the environment of one or more of its subsidiaries.

- An investment fund can only focus on flexibility. It will have widely diversified holdings Such firms seldom have the depth of knowledge of individual industries to enable to seek a specific competitive advantage.

In actuality these 'pure form' firms do not exist. There are no stereotypes as there are numerous shadings of characteristics. There are different degrees of integration in synergistic companies, some companies act as conglomerates in some parts and are synergistic in others, and some investment firms do have specialized knowledge of certain industries. Each firm will have to determine its own strategic objectives (portfolio strategy).

Next a competitive strategy is to be chosen to determine the distinctive approach to succeed in reaching the chosen objectives in the strategic portfolio strategy (the path forward).

Based on the original product/market grid, four generic competitive strategies were identified:

- Market penetration. (Current product / current market.) Sell more of the same products and services in existing markets. This growth vector indicates growth through increase of market share for the present product-markets.

- Market development. (Current product / new market.) Sell more of the same products and services in new markets.

- Product development. (New product / current market.) Sell new products and services into existing markets. This growth vector means growth by developing new products to replace or complement existing products.

- **Diversification.** (New product / new market.) Sell new products and services into new markets.

And depending on how 'different' the new product and the new market are, a variety of more specific growth vectors were identified within the diversification quadrant:

- **Vertical integration** – An organisation acquires or moves into suppliers' or customers' areas of expertise to ensure the supply or use of its own products and services.

- **Horizontal diversification** – New (technologically unrelated) products are introduced to current markets.

- **Concentric diversification** – New products, closely related to current products, are introduced into current and / or new markets.

- **Conglomerate diversification** – Completely new, technologically unrelated products are introduced into new markets.

In actuality there are different ways that lead to Rome. The generic competitive strategies can only do little to answer the question of which competitive strategy would be most beneficial. Each firm will have to determine its own strategic objectives (portfolio strategy) and its own strategic direction (competitive strategy).

Final analysis

Despite its age, Ansoff's work remains valid and is used a great deal in practice. Although mostly the product/market grid is used in its original form, it still offers good framework for describing product-market opportunities and strategic options. It forms a good basis for further exploration and strategic dialogue.

Groundbreaking however are the amendments Ansoff himself made to his own work. With the perspective of more than twenty years' experience he has concluded that his own, very well known product/market grid did not reflect reality enough and he introduced a different approach to corporate strategy. Revisiting all of Ansoff's work makes clear that some of today's most favourite management models originate from his models.

Reference

Ansoff, H. I. (1987) *Corporate Strategy* (revised edition), London: Penguin Books

Ansoff, H. I. (1988) *New Corporate Strategy*, New York:John Wiley and Sons

Ansoff, H. I. (1984) *Implanting Strategic Management*, Englewood Cliffs: Prentice Hall

2

The BCG matrix

The big picture

The Boston Consulting Group designed the BCG matrix in the 1970s. It is one of the best-known methods for product portfolio planning, based on the concept of the product life cycle. It takes account of the inter-relation between market growth and market share. The underlying assumption is that a company should have a portfolio of products that contains both high-growth products in need of cash inputs and low-growth products that generate excess cash to ensure long-term success.

The use of the BCG matrix helps to identify and assess the priorities for growth in a product portfolio. The matrix comprises two dimensions: market share and market growth. Products are assessed, based on these dimensions, and each is then classified in one of four different categories: stars, cash cows, question marks and dogs. The basic premise of the model is to invest in (economic) growth opportunities from which the company can benefit.

When to use it

The BCG matrix can be used as a strategic tool to identify the profit and growth potential of each business unit of a company. By defining a strategy for each business unit (determining whether to 'hold', 'harvest', 'divest' or 'build') the overall portfolio of an organisation can be maintained as a profitable mix.

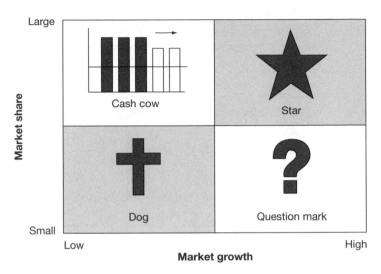

Figure 2.1 The BCG matrix

How to use it

First, determine a measure or rating of expected market growth for each product or service in the portfolio. Next, apply a percentage of the rating to each product to define its relative market share. Finally, plot each of the products in the portfolio into the four quadrants that are defined by two dimensions: relative *market share* and relative rate of *market growth*. Although this is generally arbitrary due to small differences, it must be carried out consistently. This is the most difficult part, but using predetermined criteria may help. For example, a company's market share can be indicated as being small if it is less than one-third of that of its largest competitor. The growth rate of a market can be indicated as high when annual revenues grow by more than 10 per cent after correction for inflation. It is important to maintain the predetermined criteria and change them only during the product assessment phase. Otherwise, 'pet' projects and products will be shifted into a more favourable position, thereby defeating the object of the exercise.

- **Stars** are products that enjoy a relatively high market share in a strongly growing market. They are (potentially) profitable and may grow further. It is therefore advisable to invest in these products.
- **Cash cows** are products that are extremely profitable, and no extra effort or investment is needed to maintain the status quo. A product becomes a cash cow when the growth of a product's market decreases but the company's market share remains high and stable.
- **Question marks** are products that have high market growth but small market share, and so their growth rate is uncertain. Investments to generate further growth may or may not yield big results in the future. Additional investigation into how and where to invest is advised.

- Dogs should be dropped or divested when they are not profitable. If profitable, do not invest in them, but make the best of their current value. This may even mean selling the product's operations and / or brand.

Do's
- **Analyse your current business portfolio periodically and decide which products require investment.**
- **Pay attention to market changes and your competitors.**

Don'ts
- **Do not hesitate to drop or divest the dogs that are not profitable.**

Final analysis

Many people have questioned the basic assumptions of the BCG matrix, namely that markets are clearly defined; that market share is an appropriate indicator of cash generation; and that growth means that an infusion of cash is needed to extract a bigger pay-off at a later stage. Many critics make the important point that throwing money at a product or product group does not automatically make it grow or become more profitable. We have therefore concluded that the BCG matrix can be very helpful in forcing decisions when managing a portfolio of products, but it cannot be employed as the sole means of determining market strategy.

When constructing a matrix, it often makes more sense to use relative market shares, as markets are not always clearly defined. A single market can be comprised of many different elements and many substitute products. Markets can be concentrated, or widely divided among many small players. Remember too, that especially in immature markets, growth figures and market shares may not have reached a balance that justifies the rigorously positive or negative judgement of the BCG matrix.

References

Hambrick, D.C., MacMillan, I.C. and Day, D.L. (1982) 'Strategic attributes and performance in the BCG Matrix – A PIMS-based analysis of industrial product businesses'. *Academy of Management Journal* 25 (3): 510–31.

Henderson, B. (1969) 'The Product Portfolio'. *BCG Perspectives*: 66.

Henderson, B. (1973) 'The experience curve reviewed: IV. The growth share matrix or product portfolio'. *BCG Perspectives*: 135.

Blue ocean strategy

3

The big picture

Blue Ocean Strategy focuses attention on the creation of new markets at the product development stage. The concept is designed to encourage managers to focus on the creation of uncontested markets.

Most strategic models focus on achieving competitive advantages: the central question being how to be better than the competition. The Blue Ocean Strategy model does not focus on winning from competitors, but on making the competition irrelevant by creating 'blue ocean' opportunities. Blue oceans are uncontested marketplaces in which new demands of customers are satisfied (Kim and Mauborgne, 1997). 'Red oceans', in contrast, are competitive arenas in which competitors fight and consequently weaken each other.

Red ocean strategy	Blue ocean strategy
• Compete in an existing market place • Beat the competition • Exploit existing demand • Make the value / cost trade-off • Align the whole system of a firm's activities with its strategic choice of differentiation *or* low cost	• Create an uncontested marketplace • Make the competition irrelevant • Create and capture new demand • Beat the value / cost trade-off • Align the whole system of a firm's activities in pursuit of differentiation *and* low cost

Figure 3.1 Blue Ocean strategy

The Blue Ocean Strategy model encourages innovation and influences the focus of strategy development. Instead of using competitors as a benchmark, managers look beyond the limits of existing market boundaries to seek new opportunities to create new value for customers. Rather than trying to beat the competition directly, managers should take action to develop a business offering that opens up and captures a new market space (Kim and Mauborgne, 2005).

When to use it

Blue Ocean Strategy adds direction to the strategic management process. Development strategy often focuses solely on how to beat the competition. This will lead inevitably to a red ocean scenario in which competitors fight and consequently weaken each other. In order to direct the focus of strategy development towards the creation of blue oceans, the management team needs to answer four questions (Kim and Mauborgne, 1997):

- Which of the factors that our industry takes for granted should be eliminated?
- Which factors should be reduced well below the industry's standard?
- Which factors should be raised well above the industry's standard?
- Which factors should be created that the industry has never offered?

In this process, it is essential to focus on what customers value, rather than merely focusing on competitors or the core competencies of the firm. Instead, one should start from scratch. By answering these questions, it is possible to create entirely new concepts for product(s). As a result, a new so-called value curve can be created. This curve determines a new value proposition, which shows how the value of the new product differs from current products (Kim and Mauborgne, 1997).

Two types of blue ocean can be created using this process: either by launching a completely new industry; or by creating new opportunities from within the existing industry by expanding the strategic boundaries of the industry. Most blue oceans are created this way.

How to use it

Blue Ocean Strategy is not a well-structured plan that is easy to implement. On the contrary, it is a concept that can be used to focus strategic development (by answering the above questions). Nevertheless, there are six core principles at the heart of Blue Ocean Strategy that can be used as a guideline to tackle six key risks common to new product development strategy, namely: search risk, planning risk, scope risk, business model risks, organisational risk and management risk (Kim and Mauborgne, 2005). The six blue ocean principles can be interpreted as an 'implementation' guide for creating uncontested markets.

- The first principle – reconstruct market boundaries: identify commercially compelling blue oceans in which the *search risk* is minimised.
- The second principle – focus on the big picture, not the numbers: tackle the *planning risks* by focusing on the existing facts.
- The third principle – reach beyond existing demand: tackle the *scope risk* of aggregating the greatest demand for a new offering.
- The fourth principle – get the strategic sequence right: reduce the *business model risk* by focusing on how to build a robust model that ensures long-term profit.
- The fifth principle – overcome key organisational hurdles: reduce the *organisational risk* of executing a blue ocean strategy.
- The sixth principle – build execution into strategy: focus attention on the motivation and use of the competencies of employees to execute blue ocean strategy, thereby overcoming *management risk*.

Final analysis

The Blue Ocean Strategy model is a theoretical model that may be a revelation for many managers. However, the model primarily describes what to do (on an abstract level) instead of demonstrating how to do it. The model and related ideas are descriptive rather than prescriptive. Moreover, the cases mentioned by Kim and Mauborgne as examples of successful blue ocean innovations, are interpreted through a 'blue ocean lens', rather than being based on this model.

Although Kim and Mauborgne have made a valuable contribution to strategic management literature, not all firms should adopt this model. Blue Ocean Strategy may be a good strategy for many firms, but for others a fast-moving strategy, cost leadership, differentiation or focus strategy may be far more successful (Porter, 1979). Kim and Mauborgne provide the important insight that a firm can simultaneously pursue cost differentiation and low costs.

References

Kim, W.C. and Mauborgne, R. (1997) 'Value innovation: the strategic logic of high growth'. *Harvard Business Review* 75 (1) January / February: 102–12.

Kim, W.C. and Mauborgne, R. (2005) *Blue Ocean Strategy: How to create uncontested market space and make the competition irrelevant*. Cambridge, MA: Harvard Business School Press.

Porter, M. (1979) 'How competitive forces shape strategy'. *Harvard Business Review* 57 (2) March / April: 137–45.

4

Competitive analysis: Porter's five forces

The big picture

Porter's (1998) competitive analysis identifies five fundamental competitive forces that determine the relative attractiveness of an industry: new entrants, bargaining power of buyers, bargaining power of suppliers, substitute products or services and rivalry among existing competitors. Competitive analysis provides an insight into the relationships and dynamics of an industry, and allows a company to make strategic decisions regarding the best defendable and most economically attractive position.

When to use it

The model can be used to gain a better understanding of the industry context in which the business is operating. For example, a company may use it to analyse the attractiveness of a new industry by identifying whether new products, services or businesses are potentially profitable. The model can also be used to evaluate a firm's strategic position in the marketplace, as it takes account of a broad range of competitors beyond the obvious or immediate. This creates an understanding of the strengths of both the company's current competitive position and the desired position.

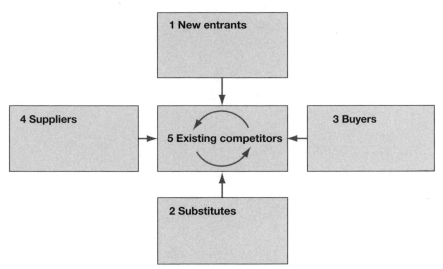

Figure 4.1 Porter's five forces

How to use it

The Porter model is an aid to evaluating the competitive arena from all perspectives based on five fundamental forces. By identifying the strength and direction of each force, it is possible to assess quickly the strength of the organisation's position, together with its ability to make a profit or maintain profitability in a specific industry.

For each of the five forces, consider how well your company can compete:

1. New entrants

Are there entry barriers for new contenders?

- The greater the importance of economies of scale, the higher the entry barrier.
- Competing with established brands and loyalty is harder (e.g. Coca-Cola).
- High up-front (risky) capital requirements make entry difficult.
- High switching costs for products are a great advantage for existing players.
- Is access to distribution channels difficult or legally restricted?
- Do existing companies have cost advantages that are independent of market scale (e.g. patents, licences, proprietary know-how, favourable access to raw materials, capital assets, experienced workers, subsidies)?
- A government-regulated industry could limit entry by requiring operating licences (e.g. UMTS wireless communication).
- Expecting a low level of retaliation by existing players makes entry easier for newcomers.
- The concept of 'entry deterring price': the bigger the margin, the more new entrants there will be.

2. Substitutes

How easily can your product or service be substituted with a different type of product or service?

For example, the bus is a substitute for the train. Porter argues that a substitute is particularly threatening if it represents a significant improvement in the price / performance trade-off.

3. Buyers' bargaining power

To what extent can buyers bargain?

- When buyers buy in large volumes, they are more likely to command better prices. For example, large grocery retailers pay lower wholesale prices than small stores.
- The larger the fraction of costs represented by the purchase price, the harder buyers will bargain.
- Undifferentiated products make it easier to play suppliers off against each other.
- Low switching costs increase buyer power.
- Low-profit buyers will be tough negotiators.
- The potential for 'DIY' production or backwards integration are strong bargaining levers. Partial in-house production or 'tapered integration' is not only a strong bargaining tool, it also provides a better understanding of a supplier's actual costs!
- The less the buyer's performance is affected by the product, the more price-sensitive the buyer will be.
- The more information a buyer has, the better his bargaining position is.

4. Suppliers' command of industry

What level of influence do suppliers have?

Suppliers can have a significant impact on an industry's profitability and margin distribution, depending on several levers. Competitive forces from suppliers mirror those of buyers:

- A few suppliers selling to relatively more buyers will be able to have a bigger say.
- The absence of substitutes increases supplier power, as buyers have little choice.
- Suppliers with alternative customers, industries and channels have more power.
- The supplier's product is indispensable or of great value to your company.

- Switching suppliers will incur high expenses or rapidly depreciate your company's assets.
- Suppliers may integrate forwards by producing for and selling to your customers.

5. Existing competitors

What advantages do competitors have?

Last, but not least, rivalry between existing competitors leads to tactics such as aggressive pricing and promotion, battles for customers or channels, and increased service levels. If there is an escalation of moves and countermoves (e.g. price wars), all industry rivals may end up losing. However, advertising battles may also be of benefit as it makes clear the differentiation between companies and brands. Although rivalry and its intensity change as the industry expands its marketing and technologies, the following are indicators of a competitive threat from existing industry rivals:

- many and/or equally strong competitors;
- slow industry growth, leading to a focus on dividing, rather than expanding the industry;
- high fixed-costs and asset-bases making rivals compete to turn stock and fill capacity;
- products are considered to be commodities and made available at low cost, which encourages buyers to switch supplier at no risk, and buy by price;
- diversity of competitors and their strategies, making it difficult to anticipate competitive moves;
- high stakes, for example, the challenge of building a customer base in cellular communication or sales on the Internet;
- high exit barriers for economic, strategic, emotional or legal reasons. Major exit barriers are specialised assets that are difficult to sell, fixed cost of exit (e.g. labour agreements, settlement costs) and the strategic importance of activities or brands for the corporation or its partners.

One of our clients, a national railway company, encountered many existing and potential competitive forces that could be described by Porter's five forces model.

The market was deteriorating and government subsidies had declined rapidly. New local railway companies had made timely entries into the market, focusing on the most profitable travel segments. Commercial customers could switch easily to road or water transportation to increase flexibility or lower costs, whichever was desired. The company was under pressure from the government to increase its return on investment for a future public offering, while simultaneously maintaining certain services. Advanced management of alternative transportation by means of regulated and private road transportation was starting to pose a serious threat to our client. Deregulation also invited foreign railway companies to explore the profitable opportunities in the client's domestic market. The company's personal travel customers were (and still are) represented by a powerful interest group. On the supplier side, fuel prices, transportation material and labour costs were increasing. Porter's five forces model has helped our client to identify and structure its competitive playing field as part of its strategy development process.

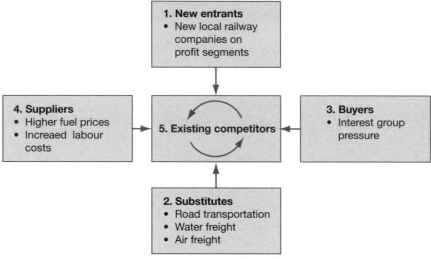

Figure 4.2 Example of Porter's five forces

Reprinted with the permission of The Free Press, a Division of Simon & Schuster Adult Publishing Group, from *CUSTOMER MARKETING METHOD: How to Implement and Profit from Customer Relationship Management* by Jay Curry with Adam Curry. Copyright © 2000 by The Customer Marketing Institute BV. All rights reserved.

Note: the illustration and description have been altered to provide a suitable example and do not therefore represent all the relevant facts.

Final analysis

Although it is arguably the most widely used and recognised model for strategic analysis, this powerful model has one major disadvantage, namely that it tends to emphasise external forces and the ways that a company can counter these forces. An organisation's intrinsic strengths and ability to develop its competencies independently of these forces are given much less consideration. The model can therefore be classified as reactive rather than pro-active, and is best used in combination with an inside–out approach. It is argued that Porter's five forces model combined with the Resource-Based View (RBV) could be more successful in developing a much more sound strategy.

Reference

Porter, M.E. (1980) *Competitive Strategy.* New York: Free Press.

Porter, M.E. (1990) *The Competitive Advantage of Nations.* New York: Free Press. (Republished with a new introduction, 1998).

5

Core competencies

The big picture

A core competence is something unique that a firm has, or can do, strategically well (Prahalad and Hamel, 1990). The concept of core competencies is based on Barney's idea that an organisation's inimitable and valuable tangible and intangible assets are key aspects of a firm's sustainable competitive advantage (Barney, 1991).

When to use it

The core competencies model is a strategic tool to determine the unique assets that can be used to create and offer value to customers. The process of defining core competencies encourages management to think about the strengths and capabilities that set the company apart from competitors. Whereas Porter's five forces model (see page 14) takes an outside–in approach and places the external environment at the starting point of the strategy process, the core competence model of Prahalad and Hamel (1990) does the opposite. It builds on the assumption that competitiveness derives ultimately from a company's ability to build core competencies that spawn unanticipated products at lower cost and more speedily than competitors can. In this way, the core competence model can be used to create sustainable competitive advantage.

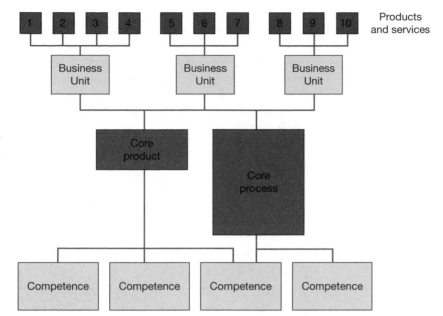

Figure 5.1 Core competencies

How to use it

The starting point for understanding core competencies is to realise that a business needs to have something that it can do well and that meets the following three conditions:

1 It provides consumer benefits.
2 It is not easy for competitors to imitate.
3 It can be *leveraged* widely to many products and markets.

A company that identifies, develops or acquires unique assets with which to build valuable products may create a long-lasting competitive advantage. In 1990, Prahalad and Hamel wrote an award-winning article on the core competence of a corporation for the *Harvard Business Review*. This theme was later developed and published as a book (1994) on how industries can compete for the future. The authors encourage managers to ask fundamental questions such as:

● What value will we deliver to our customers in, say, 10 years' time?
● What new 'competencies' (a combination of skills and technologies), will we need to develop or obtain to provide that value?
● What are the implications with regard to how we interact with our customers?

The fundamental question is where this uniqueness comes from, and how it can be sustained. Thinking about and trying to define a company's core competencies will stimulate management to rethink and – ideally – mobilise the organisation's intrinsic strengths. Foresight is a key ingredient in this process. The future will see the introduction of products and services that are not yet feasible. New industries and products will exist that are unimaginable today. Management needs to realise the impact of these uncertainties, and to consider what the competitive arena might look like in the future. Prahalad and Hamel (1990) claim that the process of thinking about core competencies helps to identify the extent to which an organisation has the capability to seize a part of that unknown future. In order to develop foresight, managers need to do two things:

1 Do not consider the company as a number of business units, but as a collection of core competencies.

2 Determine what the company's unique competencies are (or should be) by considering how the company functions; and its performance with regard to specific processes, products and services. For example, rather than being considered solely as an automobile manufacturer, Volvo cars should be thought of as a company with unique competencies in product design, human safety and protection, and vehicle testing.

Some tips for determining core competencies
- Throw away your existing notion of what your company is or could be.
- Explore and cross the frontiers of your business.
- Do not be afraid to talk about things you do not understand.
- Paradoxes are good – paradigms are bad.
- Pretend you are the customer.
- Think in terms of needs, not demands.

Once management has an idea ('foresight') of what core competencies the company has or should have, it must build the *strategic architecture*. This is not a business plan, but a framework that prepares the company to capture a (potentially) large share of future revenues in emerging opportunities. The strategic architecture addresses issues and timing for what is called a broad opportunity approach:

- Which competencies have to be developed?
- Which new customer groups must be understood?
- Which new channels should be pursued?
- What are the new development priorities?

Final analysis

In theory, the process of defining core competencies stimulates management to think about the strengths and capabilities that set the company apart from competitors. In practice, however, defining core competencies clearly is so difficult, that sometimes even Hamel and Prahalad seem to be unable to put their finger on it. In their zealous efforts to mention enough examples to bolster the universal application of core-competency thinking, they confuse core products and core competencies themselves.

Even with the benefit of hindsight, it is apparently difficult to identify core competencies, let alone come up with sharp definitions for the unknown future. Furthermore, it is frequently obvious that core competencies are not as unique and inimitable as management would like to think. Finally, if your core competencies are locked inside the heads of people who walk away from the organisation, you may want to reconsider what your core competencies really are.

Core competencies are:
- the collective learning within an organisation;
- the ability to integrate multiple skills and technologies;
- the capability to combine resources and knowledge to deliver superior products and services;
- what differentiates the organisation, and what makes it competitive;
- the very fabric of the corporation.

Checklist for identifying a core competency:
- Is it a significant source of competitive advantage?
- Does it uniquely identify the organisation?
- Is it widespread throughout the organisation?
- Is it difficult to copy?
- Is it difficult to put your finger on it, because it seems to be a combination of technologies, processes and 'the-way-things-are-done' in this organisation?

Examples of core competencies are:
- Sony – miniaturisation of electronic equipment.
- Honda – building high-performance engines and powered vehicles.
- Apple – making user-friendly computer interfaces and design.
- Canon – integrating precision mechanics, fine optics and micro-electronics.
- 3M – persistently innovating adhesives and substrates.

References

Barney, J.B. (1991) 'Firm resources and sustainable competitive advantage'. *Journal of Management* 17: 99–120.

Hamel, G. and Prahalad, C.K. (1994) *Competing for the Future: Breakthrough strategies for seizing control of your industry and creating the markets of tomorrow*. Boston, MA: Harvard Business School Press.

Prahalad, C.K. and Hamel, G. (1990) 'The core competence of the corporation'. *Harvard Business Review* 68 (3) May / June: 79–91.

Greiner's growth model

6

The big picture

Greiner's growth model helps to identify and understand the root cause of problems that a fast-growing organisation is likely to encounter, and makes it possible to anticipate them before they occur. It describes the phases that organisations pass through as they grow, regardless of the type of organisation. Each phase is characterised by a period of evolution in the beginning with steady growth and stability, and ends with a revolutionary period of organisational turmoil and change. The resolution of each revolutionary period determines whether an organisation will move forward to the next phase of evolutionary growth.

The Greiner growth model was based originally on five phases of growth, represented by five dimensions:

i)   an organisation's size;

ii) an organisation's age;

iii) an organisation's stage of revolution;

iv) an organisation's evolution; and

v)   the growth rate of its industry.

In 1998, however, Greiner added a sixth phase, namely 'growth through alliances'.

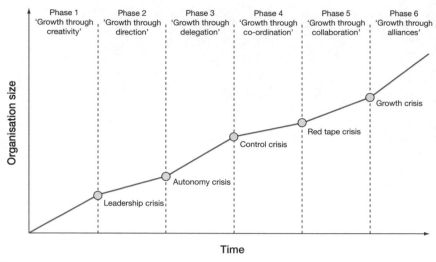

Figure 6.1 Greiner's growth phases

When to use it

Greiner's growth model should be used as a starting point for thinking about the growth of your organisation. It will help you to understand the specific problems that belong to the particular growth phase your organisation is in, and therefore provides you with the possibility to anticipate these problems in time. Finally, this model demonstrates that changes in management style, organisational structures and co-ordination mechanisms are appropriate and necessary at different phases in the development of a company.

How to use it

Based on the five dimensions named above, Greiner identified six phases of growth:

1 Phase 1: Creativity. In this phase, the emphasis is on creating both a product and a market. Characteristics of the period of creative evolution are:

● the founders are in charge; they are technically oriented and / or entrepreneurial, and are focused on making the product and selling it;

● communication is frequent and informal;

● hard work is rewarded by modest salaries and promise of ownerships benefits.

As the company grows, the organisation becomes more complex, and soon the founders are struggling with the burden of managing the company, instead of running it. Conflicts become more frequent and partners argue over new products and markets. Through lack of decisive direction, the company enters a *leadership crisis*. The first critical choice is to locate and install a strong business manager who can pull the organisation together.

2 **Phase 2: Direction.** Companies that enter the second phase have succeeded in installing a capable business manager. The characteristics of this phase are:

- functional organisation structure;
- accounting and capital management;
- incentives, budgets and work standards;
- more formal communication and hierarchy;
- directive top-down management.

The directive management style funnels energy efficiently into growth. However, as the organisation grows even more complex, top management is no longer able to oversee all operations, and lower-level management feel tied down, despite their greater knowledge of markets and products. The *autonomy crisis* is born. The solution adopted by most companies is to move towards more delegation.

3 **Phase 3: Delegation.** Delegation evolves from the successful application of a decentralised organisational structure. It exhibits the following characteristics:

- operational and market-level responsibility;
- profit centres and financial incentives;
- decision-making based on periodic reviews;
- top management acting by exception;
- rare and formal corporate communication, supplemented by 'field visits'.

Once again, the organisation embarks on a period of relative prosperity, until top executives feel a loss of control. Managers abroad and in the field are acting ever more independently, running their own campaigns. As Greiner effectively puts it, freedom breeds a parochial attitude. Soon, the organisation falls into a *crisis of control*. Top management's attempt to regain control usually drowns in the vast scope of operations and markets. The solution is in finding ways to co-ordinate rather than control.

4 **Phase 4: Co-ordination.** Those companies that survive the control crisis as a single entity will have found and implemented the techniques of phase 4:

- merging of local units into product groups;
- thorough review of formal planning;
- supervision of co-ordination by corporate staff;
- centralisation of support functions;
- corporate scrutiny of capital expenditure;

- accountability for return-on-investment at product group level;
- motivation through lower-level profit sharing.

As limited resources are used more efficiently and local management looks beyond its own needs, the organisation can grow once more. Product group managers have learned to justify and account for their decisions and are rewarded accordingly. Over time, however, the watchdog mentality begins to take its toll on middle and lower management. Eventually the rules and procedures become a goal rather than a means. The corporation is getting stuck in a *red tape crisis*. The organisation needs to increase its market agility, and people need more flexibility.

5 **Phase 5: Collaboration**, a new evolutionary path is characterised by:

- team action for problem-solving;
- cross-functional task teams;
- decentralisation of support staff to consult specific task teams;
- matrix-type organisational structure;
- simplification of control mechanisms;
- team behaviour education programmes;
- real-time information systems;
- team incentives.

This phase ends with an *internal growth crisis*, which means that the only way the organisation is able to grow further is by collaborating with complementary organisations.

6 **Phase 6: Alliances.** In this phase, organisations try to grow through extra-organisational solutions, such as mergers, creating holdings, and managing the network of companies around the corporation.

Greiner's growth model can be applied as follows:

1 Know where your organisation currently stands; in what phase it is.
2 Think about whether your organisation is at the beginning of a period of stable growth, or whether it is close to a *crisis*.
3 Realise the consequences of the coming transition not only for yourself, but also for your team. This helps to be prepared for the inevitable changes.
4 Plan and take preparatory actions to make the transition as smooth as possible.
5 Repeat these steps on regular basis, e.g. every 6 to 12 months.

Final analysis

Although the basic model was published in 1972, Larry Greiner's growth model is still very helpful in understanding growth-related problems, and the impact of possible solutions on an organisation. However, it is risky to classify the stages of organisational growth to the point where solutions are taken for granted. One must understand that this model should be used only to understand the state of the company, rather than to decide which solutions are best.

This model provides a simple outline of the broad challenges faced by a management team that is experiencing growth. The rate of growth, the effective resolution of revolutions and the performance of the company in each phase will still depend on the essentials of good management, such as leadership, a winning strategy, motivation of employees and a good understanding of your customers.

Reference

Greiner, L.E. (1998) 'Evolution and Revolution as Organisations Grow'. *Harvard Business Review* 76 (3) May / June: 55–68.

7

Kay's distinctive capabilities

The big picture

Kay's distinctive capabilities model is a strategy theory that adds to the understanding of the nature of (sustained) competitive advantage in business. In an efficient market, price always reflects the actual value of a product or service. Why then, are some companies able to command higher prices for seemingly similar products? How do these companies generate the higher added value? Why are some companies able to deliver more efficiently than others, or simply be the preferred supplier?

Resource-based theory sees the firm as a collection of assets or capabilities. In our modern economy, most of these assets and capabilities are intangible. The success of corporations is based on capabilities that are distinctive. Companies with distinctive capabilities have attributes that cannot be replicated by other companies, and therefore allow the company to generate above-average economic profits. Distinctive capabilities allow the company to create a competitive advantage. The concept of economic profitability is central to linking the competitive advantage of the firm to conventional measures of performance. Business strategy involves identifying a firm's capabilities by putting together a collection of complementary assets and capabilities, and maximising and defending the economic profitability generated by those capabilities.

1 Architecture

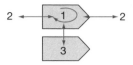

1 *Internal – between firm and employees and among employees*
2 *External – between firm and supplier / customers*
3 *Networks – between collaborating firms*

2 Reputation

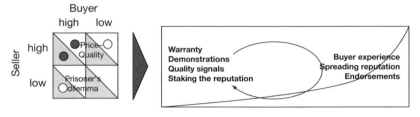

3 Innovation

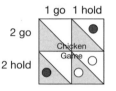

1 *Dealing with cost and uncertainty*
2 *Managing the process*
3 *Getting rewarded*

Figure 7.1 Kay's distinctive capabilities

When to use it

The model of Kay's distinctive capabilities can be used in the process of (re)defining a company's strategy, to broaden awareness of the sources of competitive advantage, and to find ways to sustain them.

Traditionally, resource-based theory focuses on establishing competitive advantage by commanding strategic assets. Kay complements this theory by identifying three relational capabilities as a source of competitive advantage, and by explaining why continuity and stability in these relationships are essential for a flexible and co-operative response to change.

How to use it

There is no set methodology for using this model. Kay uses many examples and game theory to illustrate the fundamental issues. The use of examples and training in game theory are key steps in narrowing the definition of competitive advantage based on relational capabilities.

Kay identifies three distinctive relational capabilities that allow companies to achieve competitive advantage: *architecture*, *reputation* and *innovation*. He argues that the successful creation and management of contracts and relationships within and around the enterprise create added value that can be a source of competitive advantage.

1 **Architecture** is a network of relational contracts within or surrounding the organisation, concerning employees (internal), and suppliers and customers (external). Architecture can add value with organisational knowledge and routines, flexible response to change, as well as an easy and open exchange of information. These abilities allow for:

- creation and coordinated use of organisational knowledge;
- establishment of a cooperative ethic; and
- implementation of organisational routines.

Organisational knowledge, as defined by Kay, is more than the sum of the expertise of those who work in the firm, and is unavailable to other firms. Such knowledge could be specific to a product, a service, or a process.

It is important to understand that relational structures are a product of social and commercial values. These values develop throughout the history of an organisation and cannot be easily created or changed. Distinctive capabilities related to architecture rest on relational contracting: there is a collective interest in co-ordinating efforts for the benefit of the organisation.

Organisational routines increase efficiency and improve co-ordination. However, there is an inherent danger with this approach that knowledge from outside the organisation may be dismissed, as 'not invented here'.

2 **Reputation** is the most powerful method of conveying information to consumers in a business relationship. When buyers search for and experience goods and services, the seller wants to signal quality, and to start a sequence of transactions on which to build up a relationship. How does the relationship start? Kay argues that the buyer and seller enter into a variation of the classical 'Prisoner's dilemma', familiar in game theory.[1] Selling high quality goods for a high price is fair for both buyer and seller. Overselling (selling low quality for a high price) leads to a bad experience for the buyer, but a fantastic profit for the seller. Underselling ruins the seller's potential profit margin (efficient market), but is a great deal for the buyer. Selling low quality for a low price generally leaves both parties feeling as if they have wasted their time. If either of the players plays the game only once, then obtaining a one-time great deal is the best strategy, otherwise a fair deal is the most beneficial for a long-term relationship.

If the seller has an established reputation it will help assure the buyer of high quality when unfamiliarity with the product or service means that an informed decision cannot be made. Reputation is built up over time through:

- the consumer's own experience;
- quality signals (e.g. price, promotion);
- demonstrations and free trials;

- self-imposed sanctions on product failure, such as a warranty or guarantee;
- word-of-mouth recommendation, promoting high ratings, brand leveraging etc.;
- association with the reputation and endorsements of influential people;
- staking the reputation once it is established.

A good reputation requires few resources to maintain it, as long as the underlying quality is not compromised.

3 **Innovation** rarely translates successfully into competitive advantage. This failure is rooted in three issues:

- the costs and uncertainty of the innovation process;
- innovation management;
- appropriate allocation of rewards.

The innovation process is costly and risky because the innovating company faces a dilemma. It is uncertain whether demand for the product will remain and whether there will be an increase in competition in the marketplace. There are two types of innovation, both are variants of the 'Prisoner's dilemma': the 'Chicken game'[2] and the 'Standards game'.

Chicken game: The name 'Chicken' has its origins in a game in which two drivers drive towards each other on a collision course: one must swerve, or both may die in the crash, but if one driver swerves but the other does not, he or she will be called a 'chicken'. The essence is that someone has to swerve, as there is not enough room for all. If we assume that an innovation will be successful, the outcome of two competitors' possible decisions would only be 'best' when one of them decides to hold back. If the innovation fails, the firm that did not hold back will be ruined. The chicken game is very common in the pharmaceutical industry.

Standards game: This occurs in a market where products require complementary products (e.g. hardware and software). It does not matter which product becomes the standard (e.g. VHS or Betamax). Everybody loses when there is no standard, and everybody wins when there is.

One possible strategy in both these games is *commitment*: boldly announcing that the firm will not back off. However, this strategy requires that the firm already has a reputation for commitment. Another strategy is simply being the first to market.

Final analysis

Using Kay's framework to identify distinctive capabilities allows management to gain better understanding of the successes and failures in the company's history. It may also help with understanding the values currently held, as opposed to those that are desirable in order to increase competitiveness.

The main problem with Kay's framework is that it is as abstract as the distinctive capabilities it attempts to describe; and as Kay puts it himself: if you can write it down, it can be copied.

Reference

Kay, J. (1993) *Foundations of Corporate Success: How business strategies add value*. Oxford: Oxford University Press.

Notes

1 For more information on the prisoner's dilemma, we refer to http://en.wikipedia.org/wiki/Prisoners_dilemma

2 For more information on the chicken game, we refer to http://en.wikipedia.org/wiki/Chicken_(game)

Market-driven organisation

8

The big picture

This model shows the multidisciplinary process of translating a corporate strategy into a marketing and sales policy and the client-related activities that are integral to the process. The marketing and sales plan of an organisation should derive from corporate strategy. The plan needs to be measurable in terms of specific activities

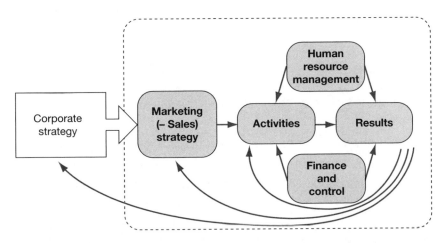

Figure 8.1 Market-driven organisation

and behaviour of all employees, whether they are focused on customers from within the organisation, or are more outward-facing. The label 'market-driven' implies that the customer is the central point of focus in the organisation, and that all activities and systems are designed from a customer's perspective. Using the market-driven organisation framework ensures that all processes in the organisation are aligned with corporate goals.

When to use it

The model is perfect for evaluating a company's marketing and sales effectiveness and efficiency. It can be applied to two specific situations, each with its own questions:

- Effectiveness of the operation.

  Specify or evaluate the marketing and sales policy by asking:
  - *Segmentation of the market:* Which customers should we focus on?
  - *Differentiation of the proposition:* How should we approach these customers?
  - *Target-setting:* What levels of sales, revenues or market share should we strive for?
- Efficiency of the operation.

  Organise or evaluate both the front and back office by considering:
  - *Lowering costs:* How can we improve the efficiency of the marketing and sales department?
  - *Building synergies:* What can we do to improve co-operation between departments, so that we focus more effectively on results?
  - *Balancing marketing/sales and operations:* How can we deliver tailor-made products in the front office without negatively affecting efficiency in the back office?

How to use it

In order to plan for appropriate marketing, sales and other support activities, it is necessary to decide upon:

- market segmentation: markets in which the company has to be active;
- customer focus: which customers are most relevant in each market; and
- company targets: which goals the company wants to achieve in each market segment.

The optimal marketing mix will combine clear knowledge of the specific needs of the chosen market segments with a deep understanding of customers' priorities and the criteria that influence their buying decisions.

A key performance indicator (KPI) is a metric used to help an organisation define and measure progress toward an organisational goal. Using three to five KPIs for each of the elements will ensure that marketing and sales activities are realised efficiently and effectively. The benefits package for sales employees should align with these KPIs, as rewards should not be based solely on sales or profits. The KPIs are then incorporated in the standard monthly or quarterly reports of the company. It is important to ensure that the results are evaluated frequently, and that the outcomes of this evaluation are fed back into the company. A closed Plan-Do-Check-Act circle must be implemented for this purpose (see p. 230).

Final analysis

The market-driven organisation model is important when analysing the marketing and sales policy and assessing the organisational setup of marketing and sales departments. The effects of using the market-driven organisation model can be strengthened by using other models described in this book, such as:

- Curry's Pyramid (see p. 111).
- Kotler's 4Ps of Marketing (see p. 136).
- Benchmarking (see p. 93).
- The branding pentagram (see p. 203).
- Ansoff's product market grid (see p. 3).
- The deming cycle: plan-do-check-act (see p. 230).

Reference

Kotler, P. (2000) *Marketing Management: The millennium edition* (10th edition). New York: Prentice-Hall.

9

Off-shoring / outsourcing

The big picture

This model can be used to decide whether organisational activities could and should be outsourced or off-shored. Outsourcing is the delegation of non-core operations to an external source that is specialised in the management of that operation. Off-shoring is comparable to outsourcing, but the business process – such as production, manufacturing or services – is moved to another country. This decision-making model helps to determine whether it is wise to off-shore or not.

When to use it

Companies usually choose to outsource or off-shore parts of their business for one or more of the following reasons: to reduce fixed costs; to increase focus on core competencies; or in order to use their labour, capital, technology and resources more effectively. The decision to move to another country is taken because there is a cost or skills advantage in doing so, or because there is a need for international focus.

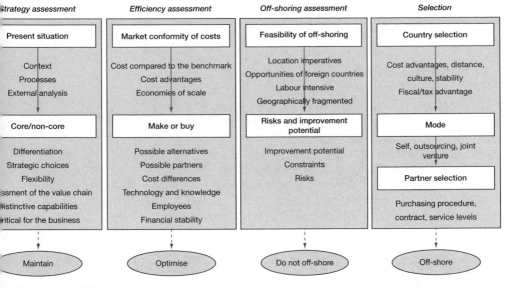

Strategy assessment	Efficiency assessment	Off-shoring assessment	Selection
Present situation	**Market conformity of costs**	**Feasibility of off-shoring**	**Country selection**
Context Processes External analysis	Cost compared to the benchmark Cost advantages Economies of scale	Location imperatives Opportunities of foreign countries Labour intensive Geographically fragmented	Cost advantages, distance, culture, stability Fiscal/tax advantage
Core/non-core	**Make or buy**	**Risks and improvement potential**	**Mode**
Differentiation Strategic choices Flexibility ssment of the value chain Distinctive capabilities critical for the business	Possible alternatives Possible partners Cost differences Technology and knowledge Employees Financial stability	Improvement potential Constraints Risks	Self, outsourcing, joint venture **Partner selection** Purchasing procedure, contract, service levels
Maintain	Optimise	Do not off-shore	Off-shore

Figure 9.1 Off-shoring

How to use it

The following steps are necessary in deciding which processes to off-shore, and to which country:

1 **Why choose off-shoring?** Examples of reasons to off-shore may include knowledge that competitors are moving off-shore to gain a cost advantage, or that profit margins are under pressure because of higher price competition.

2 **To which countries and with which partners?** In selecting an off-shore partner it is important to consider the type of experience, skills and culture that you need from your supplier in order to work together successfully. For example, the factors to consider in each potential country include: labour potential, expected quality of production, and the cost advantage. Develop several alternatives for further assessment before making a decision.

3 **What are the costs, profits and risks, and which processes are eligible for off-shoring?** Step three involves a thorough cost–benefit analysis for each of the different alternatives. Important components to consider include: wage levels, extra costs and charges, price levels and the effect on the internal *value chain* of the company. Analyse which parts of the organisation might be off-shored, and what the effects on the overall value chain would be.

4 **What happens next?** Finally, carry out a detailed feasibility analysis for each country, partner, process, and contract. At this point, there are still a number of uncertainties. Plans need to be elaborated upon further before any go / no-go decisions are taken. The same 4-stage model can be applied to

decisions concerning outsourcing, but excluding the international component.

Final analysis

The risk of using this model is in the temptation to skip certain steps in order to move quickly to the implementation stage. For example, by sourcing potential off-shore partners before thinking carefully about the strategic effects and consequences for existing personnel.

Off-shoring has been a controversial issue among economists. On the one hand, it is considered of benefit to both the countries of origin and destination, by providing jobs and lowering the costs of goods and services. On the other hand, job losses and wage erosion in developed countries will also result. Economists who are against off-shoring argue that highly educated workers with higher value jobs, such as accountants and software engineers, have been displaced by highly educated and cheaper workers from countries such as China and India. Furthermore, falling employment in the manufacturing industries has caused fear among workers. The controversy emanates mostly from the fear of uncertainty, as the effects of off-shoring have (not yet) been conclusively proven. This model rationalises the choices regarding off-shoring and outsourcing by helping decision-makers to reduce uncertainty.

Reference

Aron, R. and Singh, J. (2005) 'Getting off-shoring right'. *Harvard Business Review* 83 (12) December: 135–43.

Road-mapping

10

The big picture

Road-mapping concerns the creation of a common vision. It is a process by which experts forecast future developments in technology and in the marketplace, and identify the consequences of those developments for (individual) firms. The roadmap model provides a description of how the process of development might be structured.

The road-mapping process clarifies future goals (based mainly on experts' views of technological development), and the road to achieving those goals. Based on this analysis, it is possible to identify how an individual firm could contribute towards making this development happen, or how the firm can react to the development. This chapter uses a product–technology roadmap to explain the process.

A variety of roadmaps have been created in recent decades. When looking at technology-driven roadmaps, four different types and size can be identified:

- **Industry roadmaps** are those in which the expected development of an entire branch of industry is mapped out. The road-mapping process offers a way in which the risk to individual firms is minimised because several different parties decide on the priorities for future development of the technology, and what (research) should be contributed by each party. An industry roadmap can also be used to obtain finance (both private and public).

- **The corporate roadmap** is designed to help individual firms make strategic choices and may be based on the industry roadmap. This roadmap describes product–market combinations.

- The product–technology roadmap is one in which a market analysis, product assessment and a technology scan are combined to create an internal research and development (R&D) plan and rollout scenarios for introducing the product to market. The model described in this chapter is an example of a product–technology roadmap, which is created in combination with a technology roadmap.
- The competence–research roadmap focuses on the competence and research needed to create a particular (part of a) technology. This style of roadmap may either be compiled separately, or, as in the worked example, integrated as part of the whole.

When to use it

The product–technology roadmap can be used to focus more clearly on the future. It is useful for gaining professional insight into new market developments, particularly in technology-driven markets. New product development is essential for survival in these markets and is increasingly relevant due to the shortening of product life cycles. Road-mapping is therefore an essential strategy for firms that are continually searching for new products. Road-mapping aids the process of new product development by facilitating the structural identification of (new) markets, products and technologies.

Roadmaps generally consist of descriptions of:

- **Delivery**: the product descriptions and the research required.
- **Purpose**: market, product and technology analysis.
- **Timing**: the critical path and timing of delivery.
- **Resources**: the resources (money, people) and technology needed to create the products.

The advantages of road-mapping include the following points:

- Road-mapping provides the participating organisation with valuable strategic information.
- Long-range strategic planning will be based on gathering well-structured information, which will enable better decisions regarding future products and technologies.
- Internal and external data will be mapped, which will result in a well-structured vision of market factors, consumer needs, technological development, environmental factors and supplier changes.
- A better alignment between R&D spending and product development will result, because the opportunities for integrating new technologies into new products have been identified.

- Roadmaps may be the source of technology re-use options (same technology into new products).
- Results may reveal long-term strategic weaknesses and identify the gaps and uncertainties of products and technologies.
- Roadmaps are a powerful instrument for aligning the entire enterprise around a new development strategy and new product development. Project teams can quickly adapt to strategic changes.
- The potential for synergy is identified between suppliers and buyers, and between competitors.

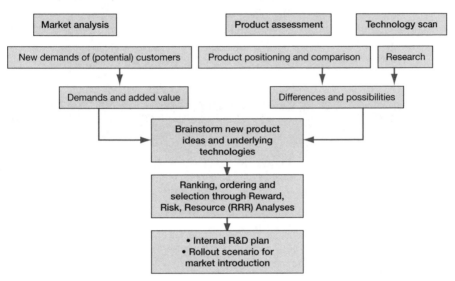

Figure 10.1 Road-mapping

How to use it

A technology–market roadmap is based on the results of

i) *market analysis,*

ii) *a technology scan,*

iii) *product assessment.*

Market analysis looks from the outside–in and is carried out to identify new and long-term demands of customers. The results provide an overview of the new demands and the added value created by the firm(s). A technology scan looks from the inside–out, and identifies the possible and likely new technologies. The product assessment also looks from the inside–out, and compares the product portfolio with other products available. The technology scan and the product assessment together provide an overview of the differences and possibilities for new products.

At the next stage the results of the roadmap are discussed during a *brainstorming session*. During this session, new product ideas are evaluated by considering the rewards – USPs (unique selling points) and ROI (return on invest-ment); the risks (technological and market readiness); and the resources (investment) required. Naturally, the products with the highest rewards and the lowest risk and resource requirements are the most valuable new products. From this analysis, an internal R&D plan can be created which is based on the research required to be able to produce the new product. In addition, it is possible to develop a rollout plan for market introduction.

Although the market analysis, product assessment and technology scan can be carried out by key persons within the organisation (presumably with the help of an external consulting firm), the most successful roadmaps are created by key persons from a range of different organisations and universities. One of the main success factors of roadmaps is the involvement of 'champions'. Champions are respected and well-known experts in a particular (technological) area. When an industry cham-pion lends their support to a roadmap, others will accept it more easily.

Other factors required for success are as follows:

- Roadmaps should be compiled by key individuals, who are known to be experts with specialist industry knowledge.
- Full management commitment is crucial if the roadmap is to have a positive impact on the organisation.
- Roadmaps should be updated on a regular basis to take account of on-going product, market and technological changes.
- An impartial person (such as a consultant) can perform interviews and facilitate the road-mapping process.
- Taking a uniform approach is crucial for effective communication, and can support linking between roadmaps.
- A roadmap should be used as a long-term approach to strategic development. If the strategic vision does not exceed a period of two years, it is not suitable for a roadmap.

Final analysis

Road-mapping is a method that facilitates the creation of a shared vision for the future; developing a shared view of the world is considered as important as the final roadmap. Therefore, road-mapping may not be successful for firms that have a vision of the world that differs from the dominant view (of the firms involved).

The main purpose of a roadmap is to inspire; by providing insights into ways to improve and renew. Although concrete activities and projects are described in a roadmap, the future is unknown and not always predictable. A roadmap is therefore only a visualisation of the future. Although it is based on technological and market facts, it should not be used as a document of prediction. Frequent updating of the roadmap is essential in order to incorporate current developments into the 'planned' vision of the future.

Reference

Farrukh, C., Phaal, R. and Probert, D. (2003) 'Technology road-mapping: linking technology resources into business planning'. *International Journal of Technology Management* 26 (1): 2–19.

11 Scenario planning

The big picture

Scenario planning asks questions about the future. It is a means of assessing strategy against a number of structurally quite different, but equally plausible, future models of the world. Scenarios provide a context in which managers can make decisions. By seeing a range of possible worlds, decision-makers will be better informed, and intentions based on this knowledge will be more likely to succeed.

Scenario exercises are based on the principles of transparency and diversity that try to make sense of the future development of key market forces.

- Transparency – refers to the process of making explicit assumptions about the relationships between key driving forces.
- Diversity – implies that there is no single 'best' scenario or 'high' or 'low' market projection. Diversity recognises that the future is uncertain and considers a number of different strategic routes (Ringland, 2002).

The contrasting objectives of scenario planning can be expressed as follows (van der Heijden, 2002):

i) a specific goal (one-off, problem-solving projects), *versus* a more general objective (longer-term projects that enable the survival of the organisation);

ii) projects undertaken to open up an organisation that is closed to new ways of thinking, *versus* projects to achieve closure on decisions and action in an organisation that is drifting.

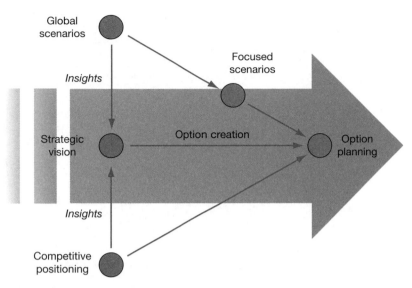

Figure 11.1 Scenario planning

These objectives lead to four types of scenario planning:

i) **Making sense** – a one-time exploratory exercise of scenario planning to gain an in-depth understanding of complex situations.

ii) **Developing strategy** – the use of scenarios to test the business proposition for the future in various, but relevant scenarios.

iii) **Anticipation** – the organisational ability to see, perceive and understand what is happening in the business environment, which requires the organisation to mobilise as many resources as possible to observe, perceive, experience, make sense, rationalise and decide. The anticipation purpose of scenarios highlights the importance of being a skilful observer of the external world through strategic conversations.

iv) **Adaptive organisational learning** – which goes one step further by introducing action in the process. This is comparable to the description of scenario learning of Fahey and Randall (1998), who showed that scenarios should be integrating into decision-making. This implies that the adaptive organisational learning framework moves from one-off strategy development to ongoing strategy planning and experience. See figure 11.2.

When to use it

Royal Dutch Shell uses scenarios for a wide range of purposes. In general, scenarios help the firm to understand the dynamics of the business environment, recognise new opportunities, assess strategic options, and take long-term decisions. Decision-makers can use scenarios to think about the uncertain aspects

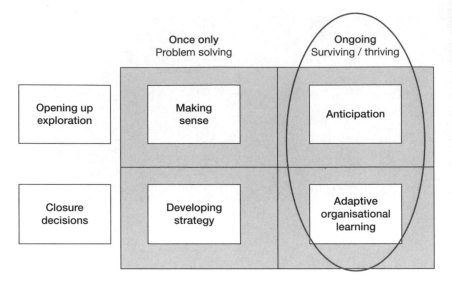

Figure 11.2 Categorisation of scenario objectives

of the future that worry them the most, or to discover the aspects about which they should be concerned. Royal Dutch Shell provides four reasons why scenario planning is an important tool for strategy development:

- **Confronting assumptions** – This relates very closely to the discipline of mental models. By exploring the assumptions that people hold individually and collectively about the future, it helps the firm to act more effectively at that moment.

- **Recognising degrees of uncertainty** – Scenario planning provides the organisation with a method for acknowledging and working with what they do not know.

- **Widening perspectives** – Scenarios address blind spots by challenging assumptions, expanding vision, and combining information from many different disciplines.

- **Addressing dilemmas and conflicts** – Scenarios can help clarify or resolve the conflicts and dilemmas confronting their users.

How to use it

Several methods of scenario planning have been put forward in management books (e.g. Schwartz 1991; van der Heijden 2002; Ringland 1998, 2002), but all scenario-planning processes start by identifying knowledge gaps and areas of uncertainty, and by setting up a scenario team comprised of employees and external facilitators. The process is structured during this phase. Next, key players are asked to explore the context (i.e. the business domain under study) through a series of interviews, with a view to challenging the team's current assumptions; this process is taken further during a series of workshops. Once the broad context of a scenario has been agreed, the driving forces are clustered and scenarios are developed. For each scenario, a coherent story is developed that highlights future implications. The relative impact of each scenario is explored in depth and its implications for the future considered carefully. This new understanding is then tested via various business stakeholders.

Van der Heijden (2002) adds *system thinking* as an additional step in the scenario planning process, in which the causal relationships in the stories are identified. By following these five steps, the scenario team develops a number of plausible futures for the organisation. The final step is to communicate the impact of the scenarios on the organisation: its strategic thinking, possible future strategies and corresponding actions. This implies that scenario planning is only valuable if various strategies or operational decisions are tested in different scenarios.

Final analysis

The effectiveness of using scenario planning lies in the ability of the scenario team to convince management to do what seems best. Changing the managerial worldview is a much more demanding task than actually building the scenario (Wack, 1985). Furthermore, the one-off use of a single scenario is not a powerful tool for strategy building or action. Learning and action require us to consider scenario planning as an ongoing cyclical process of exploration and exploitation.

References

Fahey, Liam and Randall, Robert M. (1998). *Learning from the future: Competitive foresight scenarios*, John Wiley & Sons, New York.

Heijden, K. van der (1996) *Scenarios: The art of strategic conversation*. New York: John Wiley & Sons.

Heijden, K. van der (2002) *The Sixth Sense: Accelerating organisational learning with scenarios*, New York: John Wiley & Sons.

Ringland, G. (1998) *Scenario Planning: Managing for the future,* New York: John Wiley & Sons.

Ringland, G. (2002) *Scenarios in Business*, New York: John Wiley & Sons.

Schwartz, P. (1991) *The Art of the Long View: Planning for the future in an uncertain world*. New York: Doubleday/Currency.

Wack, P. (1985) 'Scenario's: Shooting the Rapids'. *Harvard Business Review* 63 (6) November / December: 139–50.

12 Strategic dialogue

The big picture

The strategic dialogue is a generic seven-step model for formulating and progressing strategy. It is developed by Berenschot, based on 70 years of strategy consulting experience. Three main questions are considered in the context of the three phases and seven stages of the strategic process, from analysis through to implemention. At every step, other models can be used in conjunction with this model to achieve a suitable and satisfactory outcome. The three questions are:

1. 'What does your playing field look like?'

   The answer to this question reveals the strategic window for your organisation. It encompasses the dreams and visions of the organisation, and determines what type of (business) activities the organisation will perform now and in the future. Answering this question will determine what the organisation should be all about in the (near) future.

   ● This question is asked during Phase 1: the strategic stage (Step 1).

2. *'Which game(s) do you want to play?'*

   The answer to this question indicates the type of game(s) the organisation will play on the chosen playing field. For example, an organisation that defines its playing field by stating 'we are in the consulting industry', could answer this next question by stating what (consulting) products and services the organisation will offer and what (industrial and/or geographical) markets

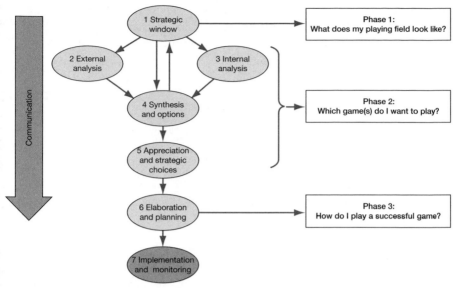

Figure 12.1 Strategic dialogue

the organisation will serve. A thorough analysis of the current games (product–market combinations) played on the existing playing field is required, to identify the critical success factors that have to be met by the organisation's products and services. With this analysis the match between external and internal possibilities can be appreciated, ensuring that demands of the (chosen) market(s) will be met with the (selected) products and services on offer. Answering this question will indicate which game(s) the organisation will be good at, and which game(s) the organisation will be asked to play on the playing field.

● This question is asked at each stage of Phase 2: during analysis, synthesis and determining strategic choice (Steps 2, 3, 4 and 5).

3 *'How do you play a successful game?'*

The answer to this question indicates the way the organisation intends to play the chosen game(s). It encompasses the mobilisation and alignment of all necessary resources in the organisation to ensure that not only the products and markets on offer but also the way they are offered meet the demands of the (chosen) market(s). This will be determined by matching external possibilities with internal potential, and results in mobilising and planning the organisation's own resources. This question determines the line-up and tactics that the organisation should use for the chosen game(s) to be played on the playing field. This question is asked at both stages of Phase 3: during elaboration and planning (Step 6), and implementation (Step 7).

Every organisation will benefit from progressing through these stages. The process may be undertaken very thoroughly, but in some cases a faster and more general approach is equally effective. The model is unique in that it involves a high level of employee participation, supported by thorough communication; it includes a broad and deep analysis; out-of-the-box creativity; and offers strategic choices.

The *strategic dialogue* presumes that strategy is the result of the formula:

$$\text{mobilisation} \times \text{formulation} \times \text{realisation}$$

Mobilisation = creativity, analysis, choosing, commitment, participation
Formulation = strategic plan, choices, consistency
Realisation = action plan, execution, milestones, monitoring

Based on this principle, it is assumed that the organisation's strategy will become a shared and internalised path towards increased wealth and productivity for the organisation.

When to use it

The strategic dialogue was developed originally as a methodology to overcome generic pitfalls that were frequently found during strategy formulation. These pitfalls involve three aspects of the strategy formulation process:

- the scope of the process;
- the execution of the process; and
- the choices made during the process.

These aspects, and a description of some of the pitfalls, are shown below:

Aspect	Pitfall	Description
Scope	'Me too'	Blindly following the competition
	'The grass is always greener'	The desire to enter new markets at any price
	'Collective truth'	Too much reasoning from a collective
	'We've always done it this way'	vision and too little analysis
		Rigidly holding on to what is known
Execution	'An elite activity'	Only involving top management
	'No time to discuss'	Taking too little time for the process
	'The controller as strategist'	Presenting budget adjustments as a new strategy
	'Paralysis by analysis'	Continuous analysis
	'Trying to keep everybody happy'	Strategy is a compromise
Choices	'Watch the bottom line'	Dominance of the financial considerations
		Being realistic in the short term, and
	'The hockey stick effect'	optimistic in the long term
		The top manager makes every decision
	'There is only one boss ...'	Not transforming choices into actions
	'Another good plan (for the file)'	

The strategic dialogue is a systematic approach to strategy formulation to be used in situations where both the formulation and implementation of a realistic and supported strategic plan is needed.

How to use it

The strategic dialogue consists of a process of seven steps that are executed partly in sequence and partly in parallel to one other. Each of the seven steps is supported by a strategic question (see above) and different submodels. The progression of analysis and implementation should be worked out by a team of multidisciplinary employees/managers. A description of the seven steps and their accompanying submodels follows. The submodels are not equally important in every situation. (To get a clearer view of which to use, and when, see the literature indicated at the end of this chapter.)

Step 1: Strategic window. Set up the strategy formulation process. This is the first exploration of mission, vision and ambition. Other models that can be used at this stage are:

- The value disciplines (see p. 77).
- Greiner's growth model (see p. 25).

Steps 2 and 3 cannot begin until Step 1 has completed.

Step 2: External analysis. Consider developments in the macro-economy, and in the micro-economy: markets, competitors and customers. Other models that can be used at this stage are:

- Competitive analysis: Porter's five forces (see p. 14).
- Curry's pyramid (see p. 111).
- Kotler's 4Ps of marketing (see p. 136).

Step 2 can take place in parallel with Step 3.

Step 3: Internal analysis. Consider technological and company-specific developments, in areas such as marketing, human resources, finance and control, IT, and production processes. Other models that can be used at this stage are:

- The value chain (see p. 70).
- The 7-S framework (see p. 83).
- The DuPont analysis (see p. 114).

Step 3 can take place in parallel with Step 2.

Step 4: Synthesis and options. Translate the internal and external analyses into strategic options (scenarios). Reciprocal checking of vision, mission and ambition happens at this stage. Other models that can be used in conjunction are:

- SWOT analysis (see p. 64)
- Ansoff's product / market grid (see p. 3)
- BCG matrix (see p. 8)
- Off-shoring / outsourcing (see p. 38)

Step 4 cannot begin until Steps 2 and 3 are complete.

Step 5: Appreciation and strategic choices. Assess risks and feasibility, resulting in a preferred strategy. Other models that can be used at this stage are:

- MABA analysis (see p. 151).
- Risk reward analysis (see p. 221).
- Scenario planning (see p. 46).

Step 5 cannot begin until Step 4 is complete.

Step 6: Elaboration and planning. Translate the preferred strategy into a coherent set of measures and goals. Other models that can be used at this stage are:

- Strategic HRM model (see p. 56)
- Henderson and Venkatraman's strategic alignment model (see p. 121)
- Milkovich's compensation model (see p. 155)

Step 6 cannot begin until Step 5 is complete.

Step 7: Implementation and monitoring. Implement the new strategy and monitor the progress and performance of set targets. Other models that can be used at this stage are:

- The balanced score card (BSC) (see p. 195).
- The EFQM excellence model (see p. 180).

Step 7 takes place only when all steps are complete and when the answers to the three associated questions have been assimilated.

Communication

During the course of these seven steps, participative communication and the involvement of employees are essential, to enhance the quality of the plan and make people feel involved. This is an important step towards a successful implementation process.

Final analysis

Formulating a successful strategy depends upon the quality of content and the method of implementation. However, of equal importance is the way in which the process is organised and the way the results are communicated to all parties. Efficient organisation and effective dialogue will greatly increase the success of the implementation phase. It is critical to get a number of factors right when first setting up the process, in order to optimise the chances of delivering successful results:

1 Determine who is to be involved, and which roles they are to assume during the strategy formulation process.

2 Decide how to organise enthusiasm and buy-in for the strategy with the rest of the organisation. A plan without any commitment from those supposed to execute it is unlikely to succeed.

3 Assess the quality of the team members' input with regard to both the analyses and the vision. Consider their willingness to think about the future in a systematic and fundamental way.

4 Decide which other models and instruments would be of value as part of the process.

5 Decide how to communicate with non-participants about and during the process. This becomes increasingly important once the results become visible.

6 Include processes to ensure that agreed procedures are adhered to, by all those involved, especially during the implementation phase.

References

Berenschot (2002) *Het strategieboek* I, Nieuwezijds, Amsterdam. [*The strategy book* I.]

Berenschot (2006) *Het strategieboek* II: *nieuwe speelvelden*, SDU, Den Haag. [*The strategy book* II: *new playing fields*.]

13

Strategic HRM model

The big picture

The model offers a structured approach towards developing a human resource strategy and a corresponding action plan. The premise of the model is that strategic human capital planning is a top-down process leading to tangible, measurable, and supported results.

When to use it

There are various questions for the HRM (human resource management) function to answer, preferably in a systematic way. For instance, how many people work for the organisation and how many will there be next year? Which categories of employees can be distinguished? What should their capabilities be? How can we make our new acquisition a success by impeccable integration? What are the consequences of our outsourcing strategy for human capital? When will the shortage on the labour market affect us? How can we strengthen our culture regarding leadership and collaboration? The strategic human resource management model offers a systematic approach for the development of a structured HR plan. The model is applicable to any type of organisation, even those without an HR function.

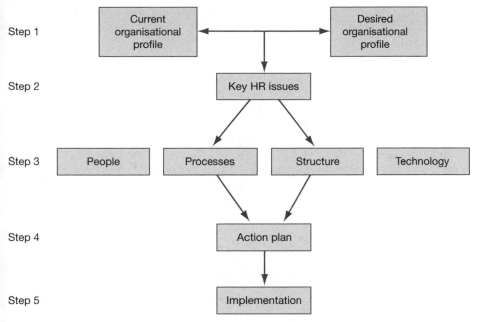

Figure 13.1 Strategic human resource management

How to use it

Strategic human resource management is not something that can be undertaken alongside another job function. This model describes an ideal approach, in which the people involved are committed and work together effectively. Furthermore, in an ideal situation, sufficient means are made available to execute the plan. It is generally more complicated in reality, but the systematic approach helps in staying on track, even in the real world.

The various steps of the model are:

- **Step 0**: Preparation.
- **Step 1**: Analysis of the current and future organisational profile.
- **Step 2**: Determining key issues for HRM.
- **Step 3**: Organisation of human resource management.
- **Step 4**: Making an action plan.
- **Step 5**: Implementation.

Step 0: Preparation

The approach starts with preparation. Attention must be paid to the involvement of management and the will and capacity of the organisation to change. Furthermore, a team has to be set up that is responsible for creating the strategic human capital plan. Additional analyses can be carried out regarding current performance to support the following steps with data and facts. Steps 1 to 3 can be regarded as the HR strategy:

Step 1: Analysis of the current and future organisational profile

In step 1, the current and desired profile of the organisation is determined by making use of organisational models; for instance, the EFQM excellence model (see p. 180) or the 7-S (see p. 83), are appropriate for this purpose. The following elements are recommended for inclusion in the profile analysis: environment; policy; structure; working processes; culture, governance, management; and human capital. The current and desired characteristics of each element are determined and compared; and those characteristics that are critical factors for success are identified. If skills or characteristics are missing from the set, a project to bring about change will be required.

Step 2: Determining key issues for HRM

The critical success factors, and most importantly, the differences between the present and desired organisational profile, are weighted and clustered into key issues for HRM. These issues connect the strategy of the organisation with the action plan for the HR department. These are often elements such as cultural change, human capital reduction, (out)sourcing and quality of leadership. It is wise to avoid the pitfall of including HR instruments such as recruitment or competency management at this early stage.

Step 3: Organisation of HRM

Once the key issues have been determined, HRM can be organised. The model makes a distinction between:

1 **Processes** – such as recruitment and selection, training, compensation and benefits;
2 **Organisation** – centralisation *versus* decentralisation, HR governance, management *versus* HR staff responsibility, outsourcing;
3 **Technology** – the required level of automation and the impact of a chosen service delivery model on IT;
4 **People** – the role of different actors in the execution of HRM: employees, management and HR professionals.

Strategy is determined by looking from these four perspectives; objectives for action are defined in line with the results.

Step 4: Making an action plan

The results of step 3 require action. Necessary actions that will turn step 3 into reality are recorded in an action plan. This plan not only keeps track of who will complete the different aspects and by when they need to be completed, but also looks at the commitment and willingness of management and HR professionals to prioritise the actions required.

Step 5: Implementation

Some additional details are worked out during implementation, further results are achieved, and the plan is evaluated and possibly fine-tuned. It is especially important to prevent strategic HRM from becoming an exclusive 'hobby' of the HR function.

Final analysis

This leading model has acquired a reputation for success in the Netherlands and Belgium. It has been taught at polytechnic universities with HR curricula since the early 1990s. In 2005, the model was modernised and the examples revised. When compared with many other strategic HRM models, the Dutch model is more concrete and better developed in practice.

This model has high validity because it is based on common sense. However, its potential is not always fully utilised in practice. The application and value of the model depend strongly on the HRM director responsible for implementation and their relationship with management. This aspect is often the factor that hinders good implementation. For example, a mismatch between the priorities of management and HRM can occur because entrepreneurship and personnel management do not always coincide. Another explanation might be that HR professionals are sometimes focused on HR instruments (such as training and performance management), they are disconnected from the primary process of the organisation, or they do not know how to measure the contribution of HRM. A third complication is a strong market trend towards isomorphism, fads and fashion. HR strategies are copied and adapted, rather than developed. These considerations could challenge the relationship between organisational strategy, HR strategy, and taking appropriate action.

The strength of the model is increased when the user adds hard data and measurable results to the steps, such as expected growth numbers, actual formation, age analysis, diversity, retention and labour market trends. It is therefore advisable to build the steps into the organisation's planning and control cycle.

Reference

Kouwenhoven, C.P.M., Hooft, P.L.R.M. van and Hoeksema, L.H. (2005) *De praktijk van strategisch personeelsmanagement.* Kluwer, Alphen aan den Rijn [*The practice of strategic HR management.*]

14 | Strategic human capital planning

The big picture

'Human capital' can be defined as the unique set of expertise, skills and knowledge that are contained within the workforce of an organisation. This model is used to analyse the most important elements of human capital planning, which lead to the development of an integrated action plan for managing present and future human capital. The model is both action- and practice-oriented, incorporating:

- analysis of the available human capital;
- analysis of the possible demographic developments of the current workforce;
- scenario development for anticipating changes in the organisation, market and labour market.

Using the human capital roadmap allows organisations to be flexible and scale their requirements to meet future challenges.

When to use it

When organisations require more control over their human capital as their primary source of competitive advantage, the human capital roadmap provides the different elements for analysis. Organisations aiming to optimise the allocation of human capital and increase flexibility may use the model to define HR scenarios for an uncertain future. Indeed, the human capital roadmap allows organisations to operate in a lean way in a stable (labour) market, while organisations in a dynamic environment are able to organise their workforce in such a way that it is prepared for changes that might occur in this dynamic environment.

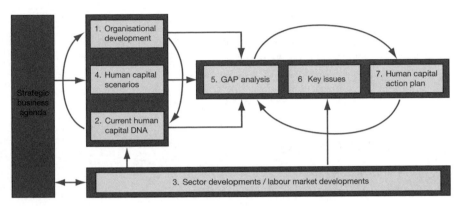

Figure 14.1 Strategic human capital planning

How to use it

The model comprises two main phases and various steps in each phase:

Phase 1: Analysis (the map):

1   Define current and future organisation profile

The current organisational profile is created by assessing the factors that affect human capital, namely: leadership skills, business strategy, organisational structure, company culture, work processes and systems. The future organisational profile can be created by additionally taking into account the strategic business agenda and market developments. Together, the current and future organisational profiles make up the organisational profile map.

2   Define current human capital capability and capacity

Defining the relative capacity of the current workforce to produce quantifiable results requires an understanding of the differences between jobs and the function of those jobs. This job differentiation is based on the strategic value of a job and its uniqueness. Differentiation based on jobs is definitely not the same as differentiation based on employees! This step results in the creation of a human capital DNA map.

3   *Analyse sector and labour market developments*

The labour market is an important determinant in human capital development. It allows an organisation to attract and retain human capital, or restricts it. The demands of human capital are achieved by analysing the relevant market or sector. Relevant parameters for human capital scenarios can be determined by means of this analysis.

4   *Develop human capital scenarios*

Input data for human capital scenarios are based on the results of steps 1, 2 and 3: analysis of organisational profile, labour market and sector developments. The implications of different scenarios on human capital are determined by taking into account the demographic changes of the current workforce.

Phase 2: Action (the road):

5   *Perform gap analysis*

Gap analysis enables an organisation to assess the difference between its present position and its desired position in the market. This gap is defined using all data gathered during Stage 1 concerning the capacity and capability of the workforce, and gives an insight into current and future human capital needs.

6   *Identify key issues*

Both the gap analysis and the analyses of the organisational profile, sector and labour market generate key issues for the organisation to address. These key issues may concern the transformation of business, the development of competencies and the culture of the organisation.

7   *Develop human capital action plan*

To transform key issues to actions, we use the levers of dynamic workforce management:
i)   labour market;
ii) organisation and processes;
iii) qualifications; and
iv) formation.

These levers form the starting point for a strategic agenda of activities concerning key HR issues such as governance, sourcing, mobility, leadership, compensation and information management.

Final analysis

Two observations can be made regarding the use of this approach for strategic human capital planning that will further enhance its value. First, the benefit of the model increases with the introduction of greater levels of differentiation between roles. Job differentiation allows the HR plan ultimately to be customised according to the needs of each category. Second, the gap analysis and the scenario building and analysis, can be facilitated with available commercial software. Note that the most valuable result of the model lies not in the analysis *per se*, but because it provides a creative and contingent way of thinking about human capital and aligning it with business. The first step in the model relies on the strategic HRM model that is explained on page 56.

15 SWOT analysis

The big picture

Any company undertaking strategic planning must at some point, assess its strengths and weaknesses. When combined with an inventory of opportunities and threats within or beyond the company's environment, the company is making a so-called SWOT analysis: establishing its current position in the light of its *strengths*, *weaknesses*, *opportunities* and *threats*.

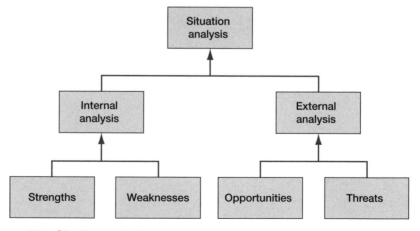

Figure 15.1 Situation analysis

When to use it

The SWOT analysis provides helpful information for matching resources and capabilities to the competitive environment in which the organisation operates. The
model can be used as an instrument for devising and selecting strategy, and is
equally applicable in any decision-making situation, provided the desired objective
has been clearly defined.

How to use it

The first step in carrying out a SWOT analysis is to identify the company's strengths,
weaknesses, opportunities and threats. A scan of the internal and external environment is therefore an important part of the process. Strengths and weaknesses are
internal factors. They are the skills and assets (or lack of them) that are intrinsic to
the company and which add to, or detract from, the value of the company, relative
to competitive forces. Opportunities and threats, however, are external factors: they
are not created by the company, but emerge due to the activity of competitors and
changes in the market dynamics.

- Strengths: What does the company do well? For example, does the
  company benefit from an experienced sales force, or easy access to raw
  materials? Do people buy the company's products (partly) because of our
  brand(s) or reputation? Note: a growing market or new markets are *not*
  classed as strengths; they are opportunities.
- Weaknesses: These are the things that a company lacks, or does not do
  well. Although weaknesses are often seen as the logical 'inverse' of the
  company's threats, the company's lack of strength in a particular discipline
  or market is not necessarily a relative weakness, provided that (potential)
  competitors also lack this particular strength.

	Strengths (S)	Weaknesses (W)
Opportunities (O)	SO strategies *Use strengths to take advantage of opportunities*	WO strategies *Take advantage of opportunities by overcoming weaknesses or making them relevant*
Threats (T)	ST strategies *Use strengths to avoid threats*	WT strategies *Minimise weaknesses and avoid threats*

Figure 15.2 SWOT analysis

Strengths and weaknesses can be measured with the help of an internal or external audit, for example, through benchmarking (see also Benchmarking model, p. 93). Opportunities and threats occur because of external macro-environmental forces such as demographic, economic, technological, political, legal, social and cultural dynamics, as well as external industry-specific environmental forces such as customers, competitors, distribution channels and suppliers.

- **Opportunities**: Could the company benefit from any technological developments or demographic changes taking place, or could the demand for your products or services increase as a result of successful partnerships? Could assets be used in other ways? For example, current products could be introduced to new markets, or R&D could be turned into cash by licensing concepts, technologies or selling patents. There are many perceived opportunities; whether they are real depends upon the extent and level of detail included in the market analysis.

- **Threats**: One company's opportunity may well be another company's threat. Changes in regulations, substitute technologies and other forces in the competitive field may pose serious threats; for example, resulting in lower sales, higher cost of operations, higher cost of capital, inability to make break-even, shrinking margins or profitability, and rates of return dropping significantly below market expectations.

Opportunities and threats can both be classified according to their potential impact and actual probability, as illustrated in figure 15.3.

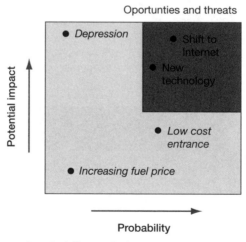

Figure 15.3 Impact and probability anaiysis

After the internal and external analysis, the results can be placed in a so-called *confrontation matrix*. In this matrix, the strengths, weaknesses, opportunities and threats can be listed and combined. Then points can be given to each of the combinations: the more important they are, the more points are awarded. This confrontation leads to an identification of the organisation's primary, and often urgent, strategic issues.

	O1	O2	O3	O4	O5	T1	T2	T3	T4	T5	TOTAL
Company Date:											
TOTAL											20
S1											
S2											
S3											
S4											
S5											
W1											
W2											
W3											
W4											
W5											

Figure 15.4 The confrontation matrix

The next step is to evaluate the actions the company has to take based on its SWOT analysis. Should the company focus on using its strengths to capitalise on opportunities, or acquire strengths in order to capture opportunities? Moreover, should the company try actively to minimise weaknesses and avoid threats?

'SO' and 'WT' strategies are straightforward. A company should do what it is good at when the opportunity arises, and avoid businesses for which it does not have the competencies. Less obvious and much more risky are 'WO' strategies. When a company decides to take on an opportunity despite not having the required strengths, it must:

● develop the required strengths; or

● buy or borrow the required strengths; or

● outmanoeuvre the competition.

In essence, companies that use 'ST' strategies will 'buy or bust' their way out of trouble. This happens when big players fend off smaller ones by means of expensive price wars, insurmountable marketing budgets, or multiple channel promotions. Some companies use *scenario planning* (see p. 46) to try to anticipate, and thus be prepared for, this type of future threat.

The steps in the commonly used three-phase SWOT analysis process are:

Phase 1: Detect strategic issues
1 Identify external issues relevant to the firm's strategic position in the industry and the general environment at large, with the understanding that opportunities and threats are factors that management cannot influence directly.
2 Identify internal issues relevant to the firm's strategic position.
3 Analyse and rank the external issues according to probability and impact.
4 List the key strategic issues and factors inside or outside the organisation that significantly affect the long-term competitive position in the SWOT matrix.

Phase 2: Determine the strategy
5 Identify the firm's strategic fit, given its internal capabilities and external environment.
6 Formulate alternative strategies to address key issues.
7 Place the alternative strategies in one of the four quadrants in the SWOT matrix:
  ● SO: internal *strengths* combined with external *opportunities* is the ideal mix, but requires an understanding of how the internal strengths can support weaknesses in other areas;
  ● WO: internal *weaknesses* combined with *opportunities* must be judged on investment effectiveness to determine whether the gain is worth the effort of buying or developing the internal capability;
  ● ST: internal *strengths* combined with external *threats* requires knowing the merit of adapting the organisation in order to change the threat into an opportunity;
  ● WT: internal *weaknesses* combined with *threats* creates a worst-case scenario. Radical changes such as divestment are required.
8 Develop additional strategies for any remaining 'blind spots' in the SWOT matrix.
9 Select an appropriate strategy.

Phase 3: Implement and monitor strategy
10 Develop an action plan to implement the SWOT strategy.
11 Assign responsibilities and budgets.
12 Monitor progress.
13 Start the review process from the beginning.

Final analysis

A SWOT analysis is a valuable self-assessment tool for management. The elements – *strengths*, *weaknesses*, *opportunities* and *threats* – appear deceptively simple but in fact, deciding what the strengths and weaknesses of a company are, as well as assessing the impact and probability of the opportunities and threats in the external environment is far more complex than it looks at first sight. Furthermore, beyond classification of the SWOT elements, the model offers no assistance with the tricky task of translating the findings into strategic alternatives. The inherent risk of making incorrect assumptions when assessing the SWOT elements often causes management to dither when it comes to choosing between various strategic alternatives, frequently resulting in unnecessary and/or undesirable delays.

References

Armstrong, J.S. (1982) 'The value of formal planning for strategic decisions'. *Strategic Management Journal* 3: 197–211.

Hill, T. and Westbrook, R. (1997) 'SWOT Analysis: It's time for a product recall'. *Long Range Planning* 30 (1): 46–52.

Menon, A., Bharadwaj, S.G., Adidam, P.T. and Edison, S.W. (1999) 'Antecedents and consequences of marketing strategy making. A model and a test'. *Journal of Marketing* 63 (2): 18–40.

16 The value chain

The big picture

According to Porter (1985), competitive advantage can only be understood by looking at the firm as a whole. Cost advantages and successful differentiation are found by considering the chain of activities a firm performs to deliver value to its customers.

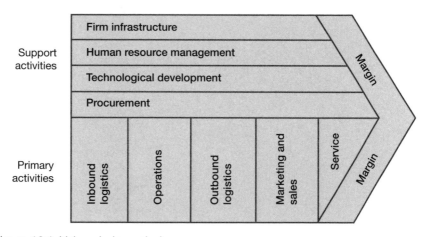

Figure 16.1 Value chain analysis

The value chain model divides the generic value-adding activities of an organisation into primary and secondary activities. An advantage or disadvantage can occur within any of the five primary or four secondary activities. Together, these activities constitute the value chain of any firm.

When to use it

The model can be used to examine the development of competitive advantage. By identifying the potential value to the company of separate activities, a firm can gain insight into how to maximise value creation while minimising costs, and hence create a competitive advantage.

The value chain is also useful for outsourcing and off-shoring decisions (see also p.38). A better understanding of the links between activities can lead to better make-or-buy decisions that can result in either a cost or a differentiation advantage.

How to use it

In order to analyse the competitive advantage (or lack of one), Porter suggests using the value chain to separate the company's activities in the value chain into detailed discrete activities. The relative performance of the company can be determined once the firm's activities have been broken down to a sufficient level of detail.

Porter has identified a set of generic activities. The primary activities include inbound logistics, operations, outbound logistics, marketing and sales, and services. The support activities include procurement, technology development, human resource management and the firm's infrastructure. Each activity should be analysed for its added value. Also the total combined value of all these activities when considered in relation to the costs of providing the product or service has to be analysed, since this will dictate the level (or lack) of profit margin.

- **Inbound logistics** – activities include receiving, storing, listing and grouping inputs to the product. It also includes functions such as materials handling, warehousing, inventory management, transportation scheduling and managing suppliers.
- **Operations** – include machining, packaging, assembly, maintenance of equipment, testing and operational management.
- **Outbound logistics** – refers to activities such as order processing, warehousing, scheduling transportation and distribution management.
- **Marketing and sales** – includes all activities that make or convince buyers to purchase the company's products. Included are: advertising, promotion, selling, pricing, channel selection and retail management.
- **Service** – is concerned with maintaining the product after sale, thus guaranteeing quality and/or adding value in other ways, such as installation, training, servicing, providing spare parts and upgrading. Service enhances the product value and allows for after-sale (commercial) interaction with the buyer.

- **Procurement** – is referred to by Porter as a secondary activity, although many purchasing gurus would argue that it is (at least partly) a primary activity. Included are activities such as purchasing raw materials, servicing, supplies, negotiating contracts with suppliers, securing building leases, and so on.
- **Technology development** – Porter refers to activities such as R&D, product and/or process improvements, (re)design and developing new services.
- **Human resource management** – includes recruitment and education, as well as compensation, employee retention and other means of capitalising on human resources.
- **Infrastructure** – such as general management, planning procedures, finance, accounting, public affairs and quality management, can make the difference between success and (despite the best intentions in the world) failure.

Final analysis

Since Porter introduced the value chain model in the mid-1980s, strategic planners and consultants have used it extensively to map out a company's strengths and shortcomings. When strategic alliances, and merger and acquisition (M&A) deals are analysed, the value chain is used frequently to gain a quick overview of a possible match. For example, if one company is strong in logistics, and the other in sales and service, together they would make an agile, highly commercial competitor.

There is one downside: it is difficult to measure or rate competitive strengths objectively. Especially when trying to map the entire value chain and apply quantitative measurements or ratings, many companies find themselves employing large numbers of strategic analysts, planners and consultants.

The term *value grid* has recently been introduced. This term highlights the fact that competition in the value chain has been shifting away from the strict view defined by the traditional value chain model (Pil and Holweg, 2006).

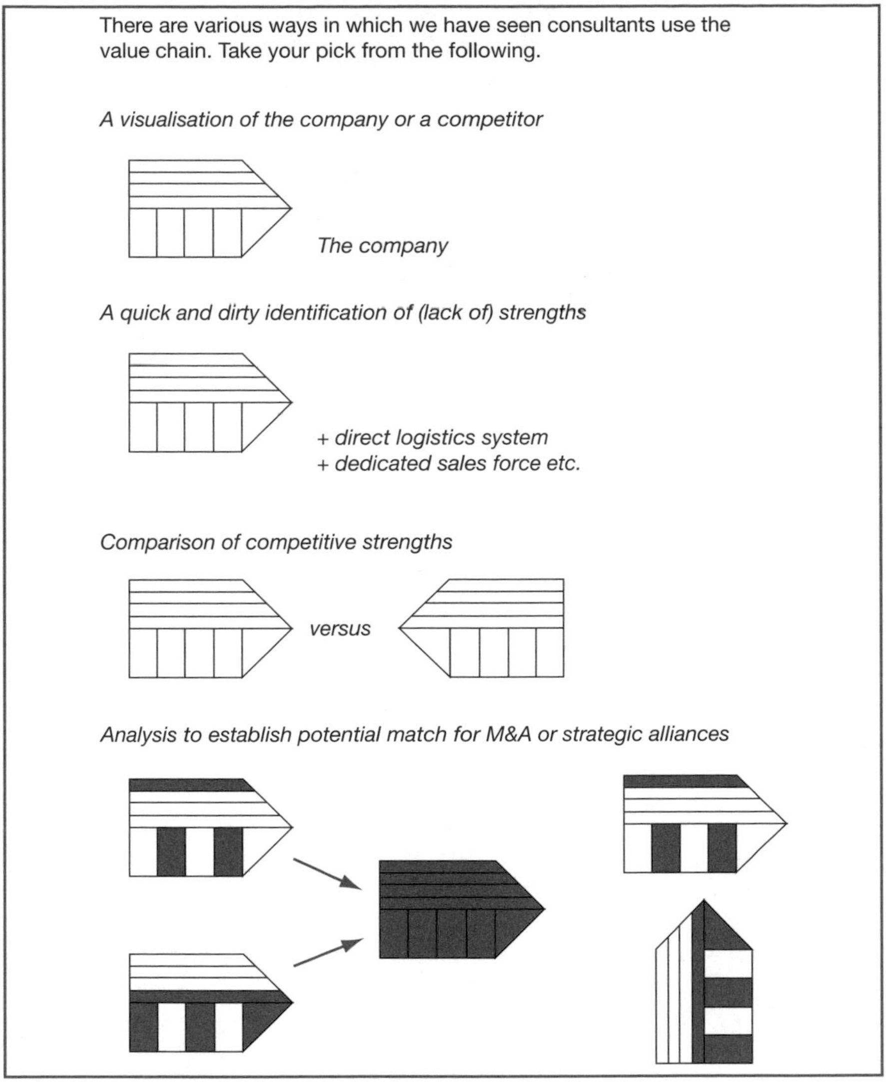

There are various ways in which we have seen consultants use the value chain. Take your pick from the following.

A visualisation of the company or a competitor

The company

A quick and dirty identification of (lack of) strengths

+ direct logistics system
+ dedicated sales force etc.

Comparison of competitive strengths

versus

Analysis to establish potential match for M&A or strategic alliances

Figure 16.2 The value chain: a versatile tool for consultants

References

Pil, F.K. and M. Holweg (2006) 'Evolving from value chain to value grid'. *MIT Sloan Management Review* 47 (4): 72–9.

Porter, M.E. (1985) *Competitive Advantage: Creating and sustaining superior performance*. New York: Free Press.

17 Value-based management

The big picture

Value-based management (VBM) is a tool for maximising the value of a corporation. VBM uses valuation techniques for performance management, business control and decision-making. The value of a company is determined according to its discounted future cash flows. Value is created when a company invests capital against returns that exceed the capital cost. All strategies and decisions are tested against potential value creation. There are several ways of using VBM. The simplest is the use of VBM for financial reporting. The earnings will be subjected to a capital charge (economic value added). VBM can also be used for capital budgeting and investment analysis. All investments are tested against the required capital charge. Properly executed, this approach aligns all activities and decision-making on the key drivers of value.

When to use it

Value-based management is used to set goals, evaluate performance, determine bonuses and communicate with investors, as well as for capital budgeting and valuations. Traditional accounting systems determine the value of organisations based on performance measurements such as earnings per share and return on equity. However, they take no account of the effectiveness with which resources are deployed and managed, i.e. the cost of the opportunity to invest capital. As a result, many companies that appear profitable on paper are, in fact, considerably less so.

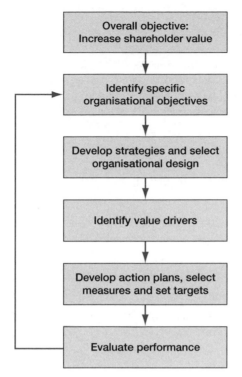

```
┌─────────────────────────────┐
│      Overall objective:     │
│  Increase shareholder value │
└─────────────────────────────┘
              │
              ▼
┌─────────────────────────────┐
│      Identify specific      │
│   organisational objectives │
└─────────────────────────────┘
              │
              ▼
┌─────────────────────────────┐
│  Develop strategies and select │
│    organisational design    │
└─────────────────────────────┘
              │
              ▼
┌─────────────────────────────┐
│     Identify value drivers  │
└─────────────────────────────┘
              │
              ▼
┌─────────────────────────────┐
│   Develop action plans, select │
│   measures and set targets  │
└─────────────────────────────┘
              │
              ▼
┌─────────────────────────────┐
│     Evaluate performance    │
└─────────────────────────────┘
```

Figure 17.1 Value-based management accounting framework

Attention must be paid to four areas for successful application:

1 Measurement;
2 Management;
3 Motivation;
4 Mindset.

Three steps have to be taken regarding measurement. First, establish rules to convert accounting profit to economic profit (i.e. adjust conventional earnings to eliminate accounting anomalies affecting economic results). Second, identify VBM centres within the organisation: these may be large or small, but must all be accountable for their own results. Finally, link these centres to harmonise decisions across the organisation. This allows VBM to be tracked, unit by unit, on a monthly basis.

Measuring value is one thing – acting on the results is another. Management and value must therefore become inextricably linked. Budgeting and planning techniques must be adjusted to incorporate the concept, and a link must be established between the operating and strategic levers.

By basing incentive compensation on an increase in value, managers can be motivated to think and act as if they were owners because they are paid like owners

– by increasing shareholder wealth, they simultaneously increase their own. Therefore, bonuses and other incentives must be linked to performance as opposed to budgets, allowing managers to focus on maximising wealth rather than merely meeting corporate expectations. Of course, a certain degree of risk must be involved, including penalties for underperformance. An additional advantage is that shifting from the constant negotiation of financial targets to a one-time setting of bonus parameters greatly simplifies the planning process.

How to use it

When using value-based management, the following issues have to be taken into account:

- Focus on better operational decisions instead of calculating the exact value. The true value of VBM is the interaction between the business issues and the value drivers.
- Avoid accounting complexity to the smallest detail.
- The absolute value is not important, but value creation is.
- Do not use VBM as a stand-alone tool, but integrate it in strategic planning and the planning and control cycle.
- Commitment and the active support of higher management is essential.

Final analysis

Despite being described as a measure of financial performance and, moreover, one which can be calculated theoretically, it is important to remember that VBM is not so much about generating a specific figure, as about capital growth in general. Implementing VBM can be complex. In particular, information about future cash flows is needed. Within VBM there could be great emphasis on shareholder value and a focus on short-term cash generation. In general, it is not advisable to go into detail too deeply or to use complex methods.

References

Ittner, C. D. and Larcker, D. F. (2001) 'Assessing empirical research in managerial accounting: A value-based management perspective'. *Journal of Accounting and Economics* 32: 349–410.

Rappaport, A. (1986) *Creating Shareholder Value: A guide for managers and investors.* New York: Simon & Schuster.

Stewart, G.B. (1990) *The Quest for Value.* New York: HarperCollins.

The value disciplines of Treacy and Wiersema

18

The big picture

The basic idea of this model is that no company can be all things to all people. The key issues upon which a company will fail or succeed in delivering unique value to its customers by fulfilling their needs, can be identified and discussed with the value disciplines model. Every good business should have a value proposition, an operating model and a value discipline.

Treacy and Wiersema (1995) claim that there are three generic value disciplines that enable an organisation to deliver value to its customers:

- **Operational excellence** – in pursuit of optimal running costs;
- **Product leadership** – to offer the best product (technically, and using the latest technology); and above all, to be the first to do so;
- **Customer intimacy** – to offer the best total solution, by being most dependable and responsive to the customers' needs.

Leaders in operational excellence offer relatively high-quality products at relatively low prices. However, these organisations do not offer the newest products or services. Instead, they observe the market's direction and execute the activities recognised as the critical success factors, exceedingly well. Their focus is on efficiency, streamlining processes, supply chain integration, low inventories, no frills and the dynamics of managing volume. Standardisation of (modular parts of) products and processes is the key.

Product leaders are inventors and brand marketers. These organisations experiment constantly with new products, services or experiences. Their markets are either unknown or highly dynamic. Margins can be sky-high, simply because of the high risks involved. The focus must therefore be on research and development, design and short time-to-market in order to score a few big hits to make up for their unquestionably countless failures. Technological innovation and product life cycle management are the keys.

Leaders in 'customer intimacy' will do anything to satisfy their (small set of) customers, as long as they believe the customer is worth it. These organisations do not believe in one-off transactions. They invest time and money in long-term relationships with a few customers. They want to know everything about their customers and work closely with them. The focus is on exceeding expectations, customer retention, lifetime value, reliability and 'always being nice'. Customer relationship management (CRM) is the key.

Treacy and Wiersema argue that market leaders are successful because they do not pursue all the value disciplines simultaneously. Although combinations of the three value disciplines are not impossible, they can give rise to conflict, confusion and (other) inefficiencies. Treacy and Wiersema therefore claim that it is imperative to choose between the values. In addition, they claim that the value discipline, if chosen deliberately and acted upon vigorously, can produce significant value for the organisation.

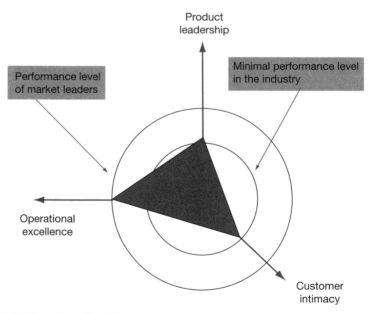

Figure 18.1 The value disciplines

When to use it

Organisations constantly question the needs of their customers, and the true value of what they offer. The value disciplines model helps to answer these questions. The use of the value disciplines model often provides new insights, especially when an organisation reflects on its *raison d'être* and how it (wants to) serve its (desired) customers.

How to use it

Opting for a specific value proposition depends upon matching the possibilities of the organisation with the requirements necessary to fulfil the customer's needs. Three rounds of discussion are usually necessary to gain full understanding of the situation. In each round, management will reflect on the current situation, consider ideas and options, assess these options, and ultimately choose a specific value proposition with which to compete.

In the first round, senior management agree on answers to the following questions:

- Which type of value means the most to our current customers?
- How many customers focus on each type of value?
- What is the industry standard? Are there any competitors doing a better job in this regard?
- Why are we better or worse than our competitors?

The second round requires senior management to determine what the three value disciplines would mean for their business, including any major changes that might be called for. This results in several options for consideration.

In the third round, each of the options is fleshed out. Often internal high-performers are involved in this final round, not only to relieve the strain on executive agendas, but also to ensure their support, by giving them (a feeling of) influence over the company's future activities. Finally, every option has to be detailed with regard to how the organisation can be aligned with the chosen (new) value discipline. This means describing the organisation's operating models, business processes, structure, culture, management systems and information technology, as well as the corresponding value drivers that apply when choosing that value discipline. In addition, (rough) estimates of financial feasibility, potential revenues, key success factors and the potential pitfalls have to be determined. After the third round, senior management will make the decision regarding which option is right for the organisation.

Final analysis

The value disciplines model of Treacy and Wiersema is highly regarded and is accepted worldwide. Too often, however, the model is misused, for instance when consultants and managers force an organisation to choose and excel with only a single value proposition. In this way, the model leads to forced decision-making. Such a one-dimensional choice will focus too short-sightedly on a single value proposition. True market leaders do not just excel in one (predetermined) value discipline, but also compete on all value disciplines, or even initiate new value disciplines such as sustainability. In addition, market leaders also try to jack up the industry standards.

One could raise the question of whether companies have a choice. For instance, any business-to-business service provider is likely to end up with operational excellence. So is any wholesaler. High-tech companies are likely to be product leaders; otherwise, they would not be in business. Also, changing a multi-billion, globally operating company away from focusing on efficiency when the stock market plunges, seems an unlikely course of action. The three value disciplines do not capture all possible strategic options. For instance, corporate strategic decisions, such as 'build or buy' and corporate *versus* product branding are not covered by the model. We therefore recommend using the model in combination with other strategic models.

Furthermore, the value disciplines model focuses on value for the customer, and inherently emphasises the natural tendency of organisations to move along with changing customer needs and market developments, trying to do everything to avoid losing a customer. Over-focusing on customer needs will result ultimately in the organisation paying less attention to its own competencies and possibilities. Hence, the model should not be used too rigorously or stand-alone.

Reference

Treacy, M. and Wiersema, F. (1995) *The Discipline of Market Leaders: Choose your customers, narrow your focus, dominate your market.* London: HarperCollins.

[PART TWO]

Tactical models

se models help to organise a company's processes, resources
nd people. They address important 'how to' questions when
analysing and designing excellent organisations.

The 7-S framework

19

The big picture

The 7-S framework is a diagnostic model used for effective holistic organisation. It was developed originally to encourage broader thinking about how to organise a company effectively. Strategy implementation needs to give comprehensive consideration to how a strategy can work, in conjunction with seven key elements: strategy, structure, systems, skills, staff, style and shared values. The premise of the model is that these seven elements have to be aligned, because they mutually reinforce each other.

The seven interdependent organisational elements may be classified as either 'hard' or 'soft'. Hard (rational, tangible) elements are strategy, structure and systems. Soft (emotional) elements are shared values, style, staff and skills. The seven 'S's' that make up the 7-S framework are as follows:

- **Strategy** – refers to the organisation's objectives and the deliberate choices that are made in order to achieve them, such as prioritising certain products and markets or the allocation of resources.

- **Structure** – refers to organisational structure, hierarchy and co-ordination, including the division of labour and the integration of tasks and activities.

- **Systems** – are the primary and secondary processes that the organisation employs to get things done, such as manufacturing systems, supply planning, and order-taking processes.

- Shared values – are those values that underlie the company's very reason for existence. They are therefore placed at the centre of the framework. Shared values include the core beliefs and expectations that employees have of their company.
- Style – refers to the unwritten yet tangible evidence of how management really sets priorities and spends its time. Symbolic behaviour and the way management relate to their workers are the indicators of the organisation's style.
- Staff – comprises the people in the organisation, in particular their collective presence.
- Skills – are the distinctive capabilities of the workforce and the organisation as a whole, and are independent of individuals.

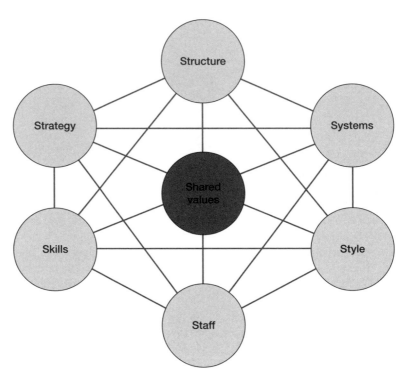

Figure 19.1 The 7-S framework

When to use it

The 7-S framework is an appropriate checklist for defining and analysing the most important elements of an organisation. The framework enforces the user to work with a high level of discipline, and at the same time allows for both 'soft' and 'hard' perspectives on the organisation. The model can be used to analyse the present organisation or a future situation, and it may help to identify gaps and inconsistencies between them. It can also be used to assess the viability of a strategic plan from the perspective of an organisation's capability to succeed with the proposed strategy. In this case, the 7-S framework is like a compass, indicating whether all organisational elements are pointing in the same direction.

How to use it

The 7-S framework can best be used as a matrix or table for assessing the impact of the proposed strategy of the organisation. Construct a matrix in which conflicts and possible solutions or combinations of the seven S's are listed. Then decide either how to adjust the strategy; or change the organisation to adapt the strategy. If this method is followed with a high level of discipline, the 7-S framework makes a strategy more 'wholesome' than most strategies have ever been.

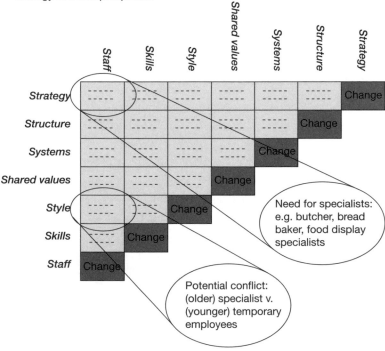

Sammy's supermarket chain. Sammy's is moving away from its traditional middle-of-the-road retail model towards an upscale, fresh, full-service, convenience-oriented grocery and fresh market. An initial decision to hire specialists may have consequences reaching far beyond the scope of the strategy at it was prosposed.

Figure 19.2 7-S matrix

Note that the founders of the 7-S framework intended to use it in a much more sophisticated way: it was postulated that a firm's success depends on the successful management of vectors of contention (opposite poles) of the 7-S elements or dimensions. The smartest companies use conflict to their advantage.

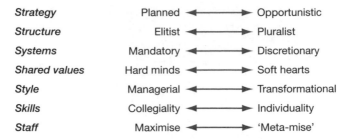

Strategy	Planned	←——→	Opportunistic
Structure	Elitist	←——→	Pluralist
Systems	Mandatory	←——→	Discretionary
Shared values	Hard minds	←——→	Soft hearts
Style	Managerial	←——→	Transformational
Skills	Collegiality	←——→	Individuality
Staff	Maximise	←——→	'Meta-mise'

Figure 19.3 7-S vectors of contention

Final analysis

The 7-S framework is a clear and robust diagnostic model. However, the 'soft' elements of the 7-S framework present a challenge to use because it is hard to define them in a measurable way. Consequently, the 7-S framework is often used in a stripped-down manner: listing issues against a checklist. The integral use of the framework, which consists of analysing the relationships between the seven S's, or analysing organisational conflicts within the seven S's, is often omitted. Used in this way, it does not provide improvement suggestions. After all, the development of a new organisational capability requires more than an understanding of why current capabilities are insufficient. However, there are plenty of additional models that operate on the level of the individual S's, that may unlock unforeseen potential.

References

Pascale, R.T. (1990) *Managing on the Edge: How successful companies use conflict to stay ahead*. New York: Simon & Schuster.

Pascale, R.T. and Athos, A. (1981) *The Art of Japanese Management: Applications for American executives*. New York: Simon & Schuster.

Activity-based costing 20

The big picture

Activity-based costing is a cost accounting model. It is used to allocate all costs, based on time spent on activities relating to products and services provided for customers. Traditional cost accounting models allocate indirect costs (overhead) based on volume. As a result, the costs of high-volume products tend to be over-rated, whereas the costs of low-volume products are underrated. Contrary to traditional cost accounting methods, activity-based costing (ABC) calculates the 'true' costs of products, customers or services by attributing indirect costs based, not on volume, but on required or performed activities.

Instead of using broad arbitrary percentages to allocate costs, ABC seeks to identify cause-and-effect relationships to assign costs objectively. Once the costs of the activities have been identified, the cost of each activity is attributed to each product, to the extent that the product uses the activity. In this way, ABC often identifies areas of high overhead costs per unit, and is able to direct attention towards finding ways to reduce the costs, or to charging more for costly products.

There is an underlying assumption when using the ABC model that costs are generated not by the products or customers themselves, but by the activities required to make or serve them. As different products require different activities, each of which uses a different level of resources, the allocation of costs should be weighted accordingly.

When making business decisions, knowledge of true costs can help to:

- establish economic break-even points;
- identify 'profit-makers' and 'losers' (i.e. assess 'customer value');
- highlight opportunities for improvement;
- compare investment alternatives.

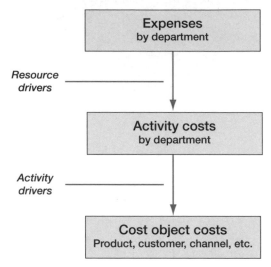

Figure 20.1 Activity-based costing

When to use it

Activity-based costing can be useful if the overhead is high and the products/customers are highly varied regarding complexity and handling costs. Activity-based costing turns indirect costs into direct costs. A more accurate cost management system than traditional cost accounting, ABC identifies opportunities for improving the effectiveness and efficiency of business processes by determining the 'true' cost of a product or service.

Other models that are similar to ABC are total cost of ownership (TCO) and life cycle costs. TCO is a calculation that reflects the total cost of the investment including one-time purchases, recurring costs and operating costs. The TCO concept is widely used in information technology (IT) implementations where the benefits are hard to quantify and the focus is on minimising the project costs. A life cycle cost analysis calculates the cost of a system or product during its entire life span.

How to use it

There are five steps involved in performing a simple ABC analysis:

1 Define the cost objects, indirect activities and resources used for the indirect activities;
2 Determine the costs per indirect activity;
3 Identify the cost drivers for each resource;
4 Calculate the total indirect product costs for the cost object type;
5 Divide the total costs by quantity for indirect cost per individual cost object.

Cost objects are products, customers, services or anything else that is the object of the cost-accounting endeavour. Activities could be anything a company does to operate its business: receiving, loading, packing, handling, calling, explaining, selling, buying, promoting, calculating/computing, writing orders, reading orders, etc. Indirect activities are not directly attributable to cost objects. Resources are machines, computers, people or any other capacity or asset that can be (partly) allocated to an activity.

Final analysis

ABC enables segmentation based on true profitability and helps to determine customer value more accurately. As such, it is the first step toward activity-based management (ABM). ABC does not assess efficiency or the productivity of activities, even though this may be extremely important for improvement. In addition, ABC assumes that it is possible to identify unique cost objects, activities and resources. At the end of the day, the outcome of an ABC analysis is only as accurate as its input.

Reference

Kaplan, R.S. and Cooper, R. (1998) *Cost and Effect: Using integrated cost systems to drive profitability and performance.* Cambridge, MA: Harvard Business School Press.

21

Beer and Nohria
E and O theories

The big picture

Beer and Nohria have employed two different approaches to organisational change in the world today according to their observations, research and experience. They called them *Theory E* and *Theory O* of change:

- **Theory E.** The purpose of theory E is the creation of economic value, often expressed as shareholder value. Its focus is on formal structure and systems. It is driven from the top by the extensive aid of consultants and financial incentives. Change is planned and programmatic.

- **Theory O.** The purpose of theory O is the development of an organisation's human ability to implement strategy, and to learn about the effectiveness of the changes made from the actions taken. Its focus is on the development of a high-commitment culture. Its means consist of high involvement, where consultants and incentives are relied on far less to drive change. Change is emergent, rather than planned and programmatic.

Both approaches must be implemented simultaneously to create sustainable change in an organisation. As with all managerial actions, these approaches are guided by different assumptions made by the corporate leaders regarding the purpose and means of change. In effect, both approaches to organisational change represent theories used by senior executives, and the consultants and academics who advise them.

Dimensions of change	Theory E	Theory O	Theories E and O combined
Goals	Maximise shareholder value.	Develop organisational capabilities.	Explicitly embrace the paradox between economic value and organisational capability.
Leadership	Manage change from the top down.	Encourage participation from the bottom up.	Set direction from the top and engage the people below.
Focus	Emphasise structure and systems.	Build up corporate culture: employees' behaviour and attitudes.	Focus simultaneously on the hard (structures and systems) and the soft (corporate culture).
Process	Plan and establish programmes.	Experiment and evolve.	Plan for spontaneity.
Reward System	Motivate by financial incentives.	Motivate by commitment – use pay as fair exchange.	Use incentives to reinforce change but not to drive it.
Use of consultants	Consultants analyse problems and shape solutions.	Consultants support management in shaping their own solutions.	Consultants are expert resources who empower employees.

Figure 21.1 Theories E and O

When to use it

The difference between the two theories is explained in Figure 21.1, by comparing six different dimensions of change. In addition, a combination of both approaches is proposed which shows, as the authors argue, how to create the best of both worlds.

How to use it

The theory can be used by companies that want to determine a strategy for change. Instead of using only one theory or sequencing both theories, a company should implement both theory E and theory O at the same time. The simultaneous use of both theories can be the source of sustainable competitive advantage. The company should explicitly confront the tension between E and O goals and embrace the paradox between the two theories.

The company should be led by a leader at the top who clearly sets and organises company changes. At the same time, this leader should listen and look for input from the lower levels of the company by shifting power from the company's headquarters to the point where the company does business.

The company should focus simultaneously on 'hard' and 'soft' changes. Hard changes such as corporate structure and systems should be carried out, while making 'soft' changes to the dynamic of the corporate workplace and its culture. The goal should be to make the company financially sound and a great place to work.

The company should look for spontaneity. Rather than following a strict pattern of reorganisation or a policy of experimentation, the company should seek to learn. Managers should be encouraged to learn at all costs. However, those who do not or cannot learn should be replaced. The idea should be for the company to use what it has learned to remove dead weight.

The company should use a variety of incentives to encourage good work within the corporate structure. Rather than paying managers only when they meet financial goals, the company should also pay managers when they meet performance-related goals. Employees should also be rewarded for meeting performance-related goals. Rather than relying on incentives that concentrate only on a single issue, the company should tailor its incentives towards encouraging managers and employees to become the best they can be.

Finally, consultants should encourage managers to not just think and act blindly according to a set of procedures. The presence of consultants will often make managers renounce any sense of leadership; instead, consultants should help managers to become better leaders. Managers should be encouraged to use consultants as a tool and nothing more.

Final analysis

The basic question this model tries to answer is, 'Should the focus (in change) be on economic maximisation and efficiency (theory E) or on institutional culture and stability (theory O)?' Traditionally, organisations tend to focus more on one aspect than the other. However, a theory E approach can fail, and so can a theory O approach, and conversely, either may succeed. Trying to combine them might be successful, but it requires great skill and will to achieve satisfactory results. Companies should not shrink from this challenge.

Reference

Beer, M. and Nohria, N. (2000) *Breaking the Code of Change*. Cambridge, MA: Harvard Business School Press.

Benchmarking

22

The big picture

Benchmarking is the systematic comparison of organisational processes and performances based on predefined indicators. The objective of benchmarking is to find the gap between the best practices and the present performance of the organisation in order to create new standards and / or improve processes.

There are four basic types of benchmarking:

1 **The internal benchmark** – a comparison of performance and practices between parts of an organisation, e.g. between business units.

2 **The competitive benchmark** – a comparison of the indicators and performances of an organisation and its direct competitors.

3 **The functional benchmark** – a comparison of the indicators and performances of an organisation and a number of organisations within the broader range of the industry.

4 **The generic benchmark** – a comparison of the indicators and performances of an organisation with organisations from unrelated industries to find overall best practices.

All types of benchmark can be helpful: they give an organisation insight into its strengths and weaknesses; they are objective; they uncover problems and indicate possible improvements; and they point out norms, new guidelines and fresh ideas to improve an organisation's performance.

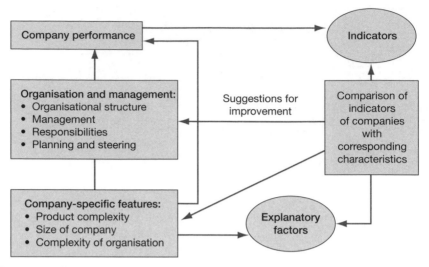

Figure 22.1 Benchmarketing

Different methods for benchmarking vary to the extent that they include situational characteristics and / or explanatory factors to account for differences between organisations. Moreover, some benchmarking methods include prospective trends and developments of best practices, or other practical issues that may arise in an industry.

When to use it

The use of benchmarking depends on the goal. Bearing in mind the difference between intention and action, we can define the objective of benchmarking as the provision of an answer to any one of the following questions:

- How good are we at what we do?
- Are we as good as others at what we do?
- How can we get better at what we do?

The scope of a benchmarking project is determined by the impact it may have on the organisation; the degree to which the results can be communicated freely, in order to increase the success rate of corresponding improvement projects; and on the level of effort required to achieve results that are valuable in practice.

How to use it

Ideally, the organisations (or peers) that are being used in benchmarking, should perform better than, or at least equally as well as the target organisation (or peers). In general, peers are identified via industry experts and publications. However, differences in products, processes, structure, or the type of leadership and management style, make it difficult to make direct comparisons between organisations.

It is possible to overcome this difficulty in a practical way. Research indicates that it is possible to compare organisations in cross-section for some indicators, based on explanatory factors. Reliable delivery of a product, for instance, depends on the complexity of the product. Therefore, a group of firms that have a similar level of product complexity will have similar indicators and will be a suitable peer group for benchmarking reliable delivery performance. See the figure below.

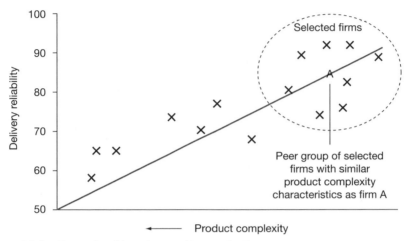

Figure 22.2a Example of benchmarteking: selecting a peer group

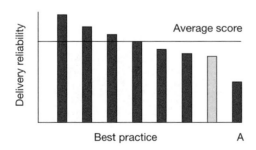

Figure 22.2b Example of benchmarketing: finding best practice

Assumptions made about the performance of the target firm can be made more accurate by benchmarking the indicator (for example, 'delivery reliability') according to a number of explanatory factors.

Benchmarking entails the following (sometimes overlapping) steps:

1 Determine the scope of the project.

2 Choose the benchmark partner(s).

3 Determine measure(s), units, indicators and the data collection method.

4 Collect the data.

5 Analyse discrepancies – get to the facts behind the numbers.

6 Present the analysis and discuss implications in terms of (new) goals.

7 Generate an action plan and/or procedures.

8 Monitor progress by continuously performing a benchmark.

Final analysis

Benchmarking is not straightforward. Too often, semi-committed managers or consultants perform benchmarking without the use of predetermined measurements or the proper tools for detailed analysis and presentation. Undoubtedly, many benchmarking projects end in dismay; an exercise often justifiably portrayed as being as futile as comparing apples and pears. Even when performed in a structured way, the 'we are different from them' syndrome prevents benchmarking from leading to changes for the better. Furthermore, competitive sensitivity can stifle the free flow of information, even inside an organisation.

By applying explanatory factors, benchmarking can provide not only comparative data that may prompt management to improve performance (indeed, it highlights improvement opportunities), but also indicate original, but proven solutions to apparently difficult problems. We therefore argue that it is precisely the differences between the firms in the peer group that should be encouraged, rather than trying to exclude organisations because of so-called 'non-comparable' products or processes.

Reference

Watson, G.H. (1993) *Strategic Bench-marking: How to rate your company's performance against the world's best.* New York: John Wiley & Sons.

Business process redesign

23

The big picture

Hammer and Champy (1993) define business process redesign (BPR) as the fundamental reconsideration and radical redesign of organisational processes, in order to achieve drastic improvement of current performance in cost, quality, service and speed. Value creation for the customer is the leading factor for process redesign, in which information technology often plays an important role.

1 Determine scope and goal	2 Redesign process structure	3 Install management	4 Implement and integrate
Indicator for need:	**Key elements:**	**Key elements:**	**Key elements:**
• Conflicts	• Focus on output	• Define management	• Install management
• Meetings	requirements	tools	• Manage change
• Non-structured	• Critical success	• Performance	management
communication	factors	measurement	
• Strategic dialogue	• Efficiency	• Learning	
		• Compensation	

Figure 23.1 Business process redesign

When to use it

BPR is useful in cases where there are:

- Numerous conflicts in (parts of) the organisation;
- High frequency of meetings;
- Excessive amounts of non-structured communication (such as memos, e-mails, and announcements).

Successful BPR projects executed by Berenschot consultants have yielded such remarkable results as:
- **70 per cent reduction in order delivery time;**
- **60 per cent reduction in average inventory level;**
- **25 per cent increase in revenues;**
- **50 per cent reduction in indirect labour;**
- **98 per cent delivery reliability, up from 70 per cent.**

How to use it

There are four important rules to bear in mind with any BPR project:

1 Determine strategy before redesigning.
2 Redesign each primary process (i.e. a set of transformations of input elements into products with specific properties) first and subsequently optimise the secondary processes (i.e. processes that support the proper working of the primary processes).
3 Optimise the use of information technology.
4 Organisational structure and governance models must be compatible with the primary process.

Furthermore, there is a general condition for success with BPR, namely that management and employees must both participate. Often, the decision to redesign entails a 'back to square one' approach. In an effort to allow discussion of any new views on how to design the organisation, the existing organisational structure and processes are considered as being 'non-existent', or irrelevant in the redesign.

Once the need for the redesign is established, the second step in the BPR process is redesigning (part of) the organisation in accordance with strategic requirements. The following questions have to be asked:

- What is the focus of our efforts (think of products, services and target customers)?
- What are the critical success factors?
- How can we achieve maximum efficiency based on the required output levels?

The third step is determining the required management of the newly designed organisation. Typical questions here are:

- How can we ensure that processes will function as intended?
- How can we measure performance?
- How can we adjust for improvements if necessary?
- How can we compensate or reward?

The final step comprises the implementation of the new organisational structure, the installation of management and procedures, and the integration of the organisation's work methods into its environment.

Final analysis

BPR is a difficult concept to put into practice. Lack of adequate project management, limited management support, and 'the delegation' of BPR projects to the IT department are generally fatal, and they are the three main reasons for BPR failure in practice. A further problem with BPR is that, although it makes sense on the 'hard' functional side, the 'soft' people side can be harder than foreseen initially (e.g. getting people to work in a new structure and with new rules). Many BPR projects stall during the design phase.

Neither redesigning organisational structures and processes, nor implementing new technologies as part of a BPR project will automatically remedy all the flaws in an organisation, let alone provide a permanent, sustainable solution. That is the very reason why employees, management and an organisation's culture are called the 'key enablers' of BPR.

Reference

Hammer, M. and Champy, J. (1993) Reengineering the Corporation: A manifesto for business revolution. New York: Harper Business.

24

Competing values of organisational effectiveness

The big picture

The competing values framework is a model for judging the effectiveness of organisations (Quinn and Rohrbaugh, 1983), but it can also be used to assess and define supervision and management development programmes. The study of Quinn and Rohrbaugh (1983) was an attempt to gain a better understanding of organisational effectiveness criteria, which resulted in a multi-dimensional scaling or spatial model with three dimensions:

- internal *versus* external focus of the organisation;
- flexibility *versus* stability of the organisation; and
- process *versus* goals orientation (the means to achieving the end).

When to use it

In an organisational context, the framework can be used in four ways:

- to develop supervision and management development programmes;
- to understand various organisational functions and processes;
- to examine organisational gaps; and
- to diagnose an organisation's culture.

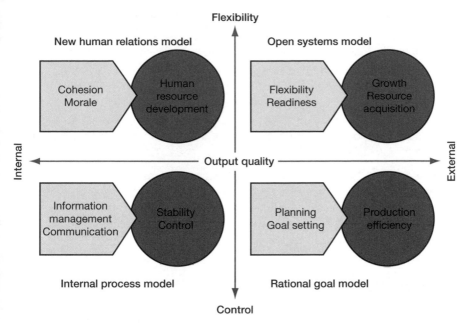

Figure 24.1 Competing values

How to use it

The dimensions of the model reflect well-known organisational dilemmas. The first dimension: internal *versus* external organisational focus, represents a basic organisational dilemma in which, at one end of the scale, the organisation is viewed as a socio-technical entity, and at the other as a logically designed tool for accomplishing business goals.

Flexibility *versus* stability is another basic organisational dilemma. Order and control do not mix well with innovation and change. Many social theorists have (successfully) argued for authority, structure and co-ordination, while others have found evidence for individual initiative and organisational adaptability.

Finally, a study of organisational effectiveness cannot be complete without observation of the tendency of means, methods, procedures and rules to become functionally autonomous, i.e. become goals in themselves.

The integration of these dimensions results in four basic models of organisational effectiveness:

1   Internal process model – based on hierarchy, with an emphasis on measurement, documentation and information management. These processes bring stability and control. Hierarchies seem to function best when the task in hand is well understood and when time is not an important factor.

2   Open systems model – based on an organic system, with an emphasis on adaptability, readiness, growth, resource acquisition and external support.

These processes bring innovation and creativity. People are not controlled but inspired.

3 Rational goal model – based on profit, with an emphasis on rational action. It assumes that planning and goal-setting results in productivity and efficiency. Tasks are clarified, objectives are set, and action is taken.

4 Human relations model – based on cohesion and morale, with an emphasis on human resource and training. People are seen not as isolated individuals, but as co-operating members of a common social system with a common stake in what happens.

While the models seem to be four entirely different perspectives or domains, they can be viewed as closely related and interwoven. They are four sub-domains of a larger construct: organisational and managerial effectiveness. The four models in the framework represent the unseen values for which people, programmes, policies and organisations live and die.

Final analysis

The debate surrounding the model that describes organisations and the issues they face is ongoing. In an effort to derive a framework for organisational analysis, Quinn and Rohrbaugh approached a large number of organisational researchers and experts to determine the key dimensions of organisational issues. The fact that the three dimensions of the model so closely describe three major areas of debate and research indicates that the authors have been quite successful in their effort to provide a framework for organisational effectiveness.

In anticipation of criticism, Quinn and Rohrbaugh agree that the spatial model is a type of oxymoron: a combination of seemingly contradictory and simple concepts. However, the theoretical paradoxes are not necessarily empirical opposites. They argue that an organisation might be cohesive and productive, or stable as well as flexible. Does its apparent simplicity limit the scope of the model? Quinn and Rohrbaugh would seem to argue the contrary, as they state that the process of creating the model is, in itself, productive. Quinn and Rohrbaugh present a number of alternative methods for comparing and describing their model; for instance, using Parson's functional prerequisites model, in which core values, co-ordination mechanisms, and organisational structures are presented.

References

O'Neill, R.M and Quinn, R.E. (1993) 'Editor's Note: Applications of the competing values framework'. *Human Resource Management* 32 (1): 1–7.

Quinn, R.E. (1988) *Beyond Rational Management: Mastering the paradoxes and competing demands of high performance*. San Francisco, CA: Jossey-Bass.

Quinn, R.E. and Rohrbaugh, J. (1983) 'A spatial model of effectiveness criteria: Towards a competing values approach to organizational analysis'. *Management Science* 29: 363–77.

25 Core quadrants

The big picture

Every person has certain core qualities that truly describe the 'self'. A core quality pervades every aspect of the individual's life, such as words, feelings, deeds and values. Stripped of all the conscious and unconscious external protective and regulatory barriers of everyday life, your core quality describes 'the real you'. What is your *core quality*? The core quadrants model of Ofman (2001) can help you to determine, describe and diagnose your core quality.

When to use it

The core quadrants can be used to find out what your strengths and weaknesses are, as well your pitfalls, challenges and allergies. Once you are aware of these, you can more easily recognise these characteristics in others as well. Furthermore, it gives you a better understanding of your reactions to others. When you have a better understanding of your own core competencies, you can gain greater insight into the rational problems of others and increased self-awareness.

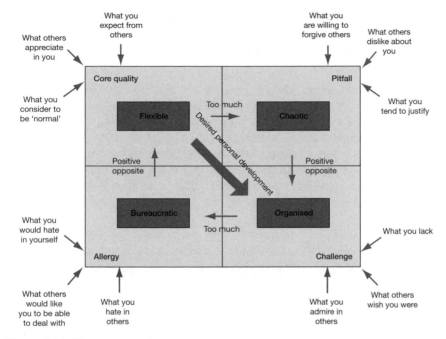

Figure 25.1 The core quadrants

How to use it

Although it is difficult to put a finger on exactly what your core quality is, it is easier when you look at it from different perspectives:

- What is your major *pitfall*? (Too much of your core quality.)
- What is your biggest *challenge*? (The opposite of your pitfall.)
- What is your *allergy* in terms of core qualities in others? (The opposite of your core quality – and too much of a challenge.)

The core quadrant shows the different, yet interdependent, perspectives of your core quality. An understanding of, and active consideration for these core qualities, pitfalls, challenges and allergies strongly increases efficiency and effectiveness of human interaction.

The power of this model lies in the fact that it offers four perspectives on a 'core quality'. Nevertheless, there are subtle differences. The same core quality may have slightly different pitfalls, challenges and allergies. It is therefore important to specify the quadrants in more detail for each individual.

To this end, Ofman suggests that three additional perspectives be added to each of the four elements, which can then be combined to form a personalised 'super quadrant':

- something that *you* would say, feel, like, condone, wish, miss or hate *about yourself*;

- something that *you* would say, feel, like, condone, wish, miss or hate *about others*;
- something that *others* would say, feel, like, condone, wish, miss or hate *about you*.

The super quadrant is uncomfortably revealing: inconsistencies between the three 'super quadrant' perspectives are a relatively sure indicator that you are not who and / or how you want to be. You are in fact, trying to hide your true feelings, avoid your pitfalls and curb your dislike of your allergy. In other words, you are 'acting'.

Incongruity in a core quadrant can also be an indicator that you might be describing the symptoms or effects of a pitfall. For example, the core quality 'enthusiasm' could lead to the pitfall fanaticism, leading to negative feedback, causing disappointment, fuelling retreat and eventually egotism. Yet, egotism itself is not the pitfall.

The core quadrants can be used to prepare for meetings where people with opposing core qualities interact. Instead of a confrontation, both parties can muster (more) respect and try to learn from each other.

Final analysis

Core quadrants have proved to be very helpful in increasing mutual understanding and respect among people with opposing core qualities. There is, however, an inherent danger in 'classifying' oneself or someone else incorrectly. It is important to involve others in the perspectives.

Ultimately, the continual effort of remaining aware of one's core quality, though difficult, is perhaps the closest approximation of being true to oneself and succeeding in life.

Reference

Ofman, D.D. (2001) *Inspiration and Quality in Organizations*. 12th edition. Antwerp: Kosmos-Z&K.

Covey's seven habits of highly effective people

26

The big picture

Wildly popular throughout the 1990s and into the twenty-first century, Stephen Covey (1989) has changed the face of many an ambitious manager's bedside table. Covey claims that highly effective people have *seven habits* that make them very successful in life and business:

1 Be proactive.
2 Begin with the end in mind.
3 Put first things first.
4 Think win–win.
5 First understand, and then be understood.
6 Synergise.
7 'Sharpen the saw.'

In addition, Covey argues that highly effective managers do exactly what they feel is both right and important, and they do it consciously.

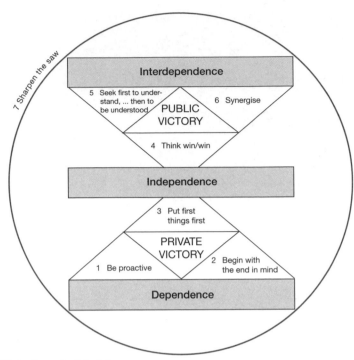

Figure 26.1 Covey's 7 habits

When to use it

The seven habits model is a theory that tries to give an insight into why successful people are successful in both business and in personal life. It is therefore highly applicable for leaders and managers. The model provides a self-help programme, based on an inside-out approach. According to Covey, our personal paradigms affect our interactions with others, which in turn affect how others interact with us. Improving interactions thus starts with a thorough understanding of our own paradigms and motives. To become successful, one should examine how effectively one acts and interacts.

How to use it

According to Covey, one first has to break loose from being dependent on others. People may become independent by adopting the first three habits:

Be proactive. From now on, *you* take responsibility for your own behaviour. You do not blame circumstances, conditions, or – perhaps most importantly – your conditioning for your behaviour. You actively choose your response to any situation and any person. You must be prepared to respond in a way that makes you feel proud. If that requires extra hard work or makes you feel uncomfortable, so be it.

Begin with the end in mind. When, and whatever you undertake, you must visualise the result or future that you want to achieve. You must have a clear vision of where you want to go, or you will not go there at all. You must know exactly what you want to accomplish, or you choose not to accomplish it at all. You live your life and make decisions according to your deeply held beliefs, principles or 'fundamental truths'.

Put first things first. By taking full control and remaining disciplined, you can focus on the most important, but not necessarily the most urgent activities. Covey's list of such important activities includes building relationships, writing a personal mission statement, making a long-range plan, doing your workout, and preparing for that presentation next week. Do all those things now that otherwise would be squeezed in at the last minute, delayed or even dismissed. They will help you eliminate those urgent activities that recently topped your over-loaded to-do list, but really were not as important. Now that you have reached the point of being independent, and you are using your time to *pursue* your most important goals in life *effectively*, you must increase your effectiveness with others around you.

Think win–win. You must believe in 'abundance': there is plenty for everyone. One person's success does not necessarily require someone else's failure. You seek solutions to problems that allow all parties involved (including yourself) to benefit.

Understand first, before trying to be understood. By this means you can make people around you feel like winners. You might actually learn something from them in the process, now that you have finally decided to *shut up* and *listen*. In fact, you must listen with the firm intention of understanding the other person fully and deeply on an intellectual, analytical and emotional level. Diagnose before you prescribe, says Covey.

Synergise. Finally, you need to open your mind to fresh, creative ideas. You become an agent for innovation, a trailblazer and a pathfinder. You are convinced that the whole is greater than the sum of its parts. You value differences between people and try to build upon those differences (see references, and further reading on Belbin's team roles, p. 199). You think of creative ways to resolve conflict.

Sharpen the saw. You have now reached a stage of interdependence. You are effective and admired by family, friends and co-workers. Nevertheless, you should never allow yourself to rest on your laurels. You must constantly try to improve yourself, and retain a relentless eagerness to learn and explore.

Final analysis

The question is, what drives people to do the things they do, and how can they become happy doing them? Covey appeals to business managers and all other professionals who take themselves seriously, by bringing it all back to one commonly understood concept: effectiveness. What happened to that world trip you dreamed of 20 years ago? Effectiveness, and having the time to do all those important things that make us love life and others love us, is the ultimate dream of the overworked manager.

References

Covey, S.R. (1989) *The Seven Habits of Highly Effective People*. New York: Simon & Schuster.

Covey, S.R. (2004) *The 8th Habit: From effectiveness to greatness*. New York: Free Press.

Curry's pyramid: customer marketing and relationship management

27

The big picture

If you can successfully identify your most valuable customers, acquire them, keep them and increase their purchases, you will generate significantly more value than with a one-size-fits-all approach. The customer pyramid paradigm provides a company with a mechanism for segmenting its customer base and, in so doing, visualising and analysing customer behaviour, loyalty and value within each of those customer segments. Jay and Adam Curry (2000) revitalised the concept of the customer pyramid.

When to use it

Customer relationship management (CRM) seems to be the latest 'hot' business topic, but it is much more than a technology fad. In fact, the CRM debate has been going on for more than three decades. Curry's pyramid provides a guide to the organisation via the implementation of CRM. It forces an organisation to segment customers in terms of revenue generation, which indicates how important a customer is. Customers are treated differently in each segment of the pyramid. Marketing and sales resources are allocated differently in the various customer segments. In addition, Curry's pyramid provides an insight into cross-selling and up-selling opportunities.

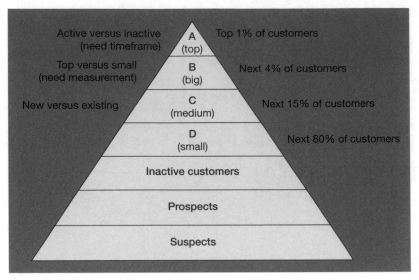

Figure 27.1 Curry's pyramid

How to use it

Customers can be segmented in the *customer pyramid* based on company-specific factors. These factors usually include, but are not limited to, turnover and profitability per customer. The segmentation reflects how an organisation considers and treats a (future) customer, segments of customers or the entire potential customer base. The *80/20 rule* is often used. This popular rule says that 20 per cent of the customers account for 80 per cent of the profit, and that the other 80 per cent only contribute the remaining 20 per cent. In practice, the percentages are different; the key idea behind the rule is that not all customers are profitable – some even cost you money!

Once a company knows who its most valuable (potential) customers are, it has to undertake the following steps:

1 Gather as much relevant information about (potential) customers as possible, in particular the big and top customers.

2 Analyse this information and if necessary, redesign the information requirements.

3 Set goals for how you want your customer to perceive you, as provider of their products, services and/or experiences.

4 Choose media, systems and content for communicating and interacting with customers.

5 Develop rules of engagement and 'packages' for each customer segment.

6 Embed a customer-driven culture in the company.

7 Develop your customer management systems as you learn.

Final analysis

There is a plethora of models and tools available to support managers and business analysts in customer marketing and relationship management. One of the inherent dangers is the tendency to focus on getting CRM software installed (which is readily available) as opposed to taking the time to consider the scope of potential customers.

The success of an organisation in targeting, acquiring and retaining customers is obviously influenced by many more factors than customer relationship management alone. Pricing and the intrinsic value proposition of the product or service are just two examples of factors that are swept all too easily under the corporate marketing header. More generic problem areas also exist, such as the lack of a coherent marketing strategy, or cultural endorsement of a customer-centred approach.

Reference

Curry, J. and Curry, A. (2000) *The Customer Marketing Method: How to implement and profit from customer relationship management*, New York: Free Press.

28 The DuPont analysis

The big picture

The DuPont analysis can be used to illustrate how different factors impact on important financial performance indicators, such as, the return on capital employed (ROCE), the return on assets (ROA), or the return on equity (ROE). While these ratios can be calculated by using a simple formula, the model provides more insight into the underlying elements that make up the ratios. It is similar to sensitivity analysis, in the sense that the model makes it possible to predict the effect of variability in one or more input variables. The tool is well-known in purchasing management, as it shows the tremendous impact effective purchasing can have on profitability.

When to use it

The model can be used in several ways. First, it can be used as the basis for bench-marking (see p. 93), i.e. comparing different companies in an industry to answer the question of why certain companies realise superior returns compared to their peers. Second, it can be used to predict the effect of possible management actions.

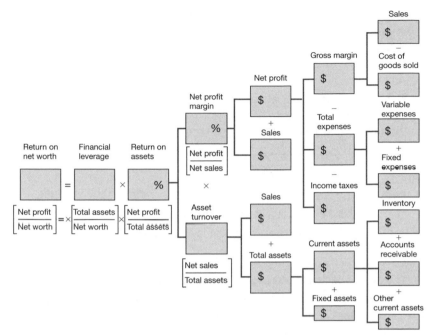

Figure 28.1 DuPont analysis

The DuPont analysis will show big differences between industries. If one looks at the ROE, a high score can be caused either by 'operational efficiency' or by 'capital efficiency'. High turnover industries (e.g. retailers) tend to face low profit margins, high asset turnover and a moderate equity multiplier. Other industries, such as fashion, depend on high profit margins. In the financial sector, the ROE is determined mainly by high leverage: gaining large profits with relatively low assets. It is essential to choose peers carefully when analysing how to improve the profitability of a specific company.

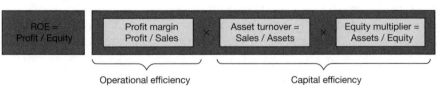

Figure 28.2 Return on equity = operational and capital efficiency

How to use it

The following steps have to be performed in a DuPont Analysis:

1 Insert basic information into the model. In particular, identify the information on sales, interest-free liabilities, total costs, equity, current assets and non-current assets.

2 Calculate the other parameters using the formulas in the figure. This provides you with a basic view of current profitability.

3 Determine which possible improvements can be made, and how much impact they will have on costs, sales and assets. The effect of a measurement (potential improvements) can be calculated and used as input in the model, whereas the model shows the effect on the ROCE, ROA and ROE.

4 Compare different potential performance-improving actions with respect to their required investments (time, money and organisational pressure) and their impact on profitability.

Do's

- Analyse peers to identify how they realise a certain ROCE, ROA and/or ROE. This indicates the areas that need to be improved.
- Analyse which parameters are essential to improve profitability.

Don'ts

- This is not a decision-making tool. The comparison of the impact of an improvement action is a first step. Often a detailed analysis to evaluate the possible outcome of potential improvement actions is also required.
- Do not overlook non-financial issues that are not addressed by this approach.

Final analysis

The DuPont analysis helps to determine the factors that most influence profitability. However, identifying these factors is only part of the story. The next step is to find appropriate actions that will improve profitability. Managing this improvement project in the real world is a challenging task. Root cause analysis / Pareto analysis (see p. 224) may help to determine which actions are appropriate. The balanced score card (including key performance indicators) can also be used to measure a company's progress regarding critical parameters (see p. 195). However, the DuPont analysis focuses only on financial parameters, and excludes other important factors such as employee motivation, whereas these non-financial factors are often very important.

References

Bodie, Z., Kane A. and Marcus, A.J. (2004) *Essentials of Investments*, 5th edition: 458–9. New York: Irwin/McGraw-Hill.

Groppelli, A.A. and Nikbakht, E. (2000) *Finance*, 4th edition: 444. New York: Barron's Educational Series.

Ross, S.A., Westerfield, R. and Jaffe, J. (1999) *Corporate Finance,* 5th edition. Maidenhead: McGraw-Hill.

Factory gate pricing

29

The big picture

Factory gate pricing (FGP) is a modern replenishment method aimed at removing unnecessary transportation costs and improving the efficiency of the supply chain. It involves retailers asking their suppliers to provide products at 'factory gate prices', i.e. product costs exclude the cost of delivery to the retailer. The retailer then takes over responsibility for, and control of, product replenishment, and collects the products from the suppliers when needed. In this approach to replenishment, the retailer no longer pays a premium for transportation by the supplier (or a third party logistics service provider), as goods are bought 'at the factory gate'.

FGP offers two potentials for cost-saving in the supply chain. First, the retailer has access to a complete range of products from various suppliers, for which the costs of transportation and inventory are offset against the advantages of co-ordinated delivery. The retailer is able to plan the logistics of each collection and delivery in advance thereby optimising the cost and use of transportation when collecting goods from various suppliers. Second, the combination of primary and secondary distribution trips on one route (i.e., backhauling), leads to lower costs. Primary distribution refers to the collection of goods from the suppliers, whereas secondary distribution refers to the distribution of goods to the various outlets of the retailer.

Uneconomical vehicle movements are avoided by collecting products from several different sources on the same journey, and ensuring that every vehicle is full when it sets out on its delivery route.

Figure 29.1 Factory gate pricing

When to use it

FGP is especially appropriate when the number of suppliers in the supply chain is far greater than the number of retailers. It is the ratio of the number of dispatching points (supplier locations) and the number of delivery points (retailer locations) that matters. The synergy between ease of supply and speed of delivery is an important type of advantage. The closer together the suppliers are located, the greater the efficiency of the process and the greater the advantage to the retailer.

An important consideration in the FGP process is the intrinsic value of the shipments, which depends on both the volume and the value per volume. High volumes create full truckloads, and transportation costs are then pretty well fixed, no matter who is responsible for transportation. However, a high frequency of small-volume deliveries can easily result in less than full truckloads, and it then becomes reasonable to optimise trips and loading, especially if the value per volume is high. If the value per volume is low, there is no need to trade off the transportation costs against the inventory holding costs. Whereas, when value per volume is high, it is possible to offset the transportation costs against the holding costs.

Other prerequisites for the introduction of FGP are the logistical capabilities of retailers and the willingness of these retailers to share the benefits fairly with the various suppliers. In addition, lack of trust may obstruct the successful adoption of FGP. However, these barriers would challenge any collaborative replenishment method.

The benefits of FGP are:
- **Efficient transportation** – is about improving transport efficiency by understanding the true costs. For example, suppliers who are highly skilled and cost-efficient at providing transport solutions will continue to provide this service to the retailer. However, FGP provides suppliers who do not see transport as their core competency or who do not have a highly efficient operation with the opportunity to transfer the responsibility to the retailer or logistics provider.
- **Improved availability** – Increased retailer / supplier collaboration has a positive effect on the entire supply chain. FGP aims to ensure that more products are available on the shelf for consumers.
- **Lower prices for consumers** – lowering transport costs leads to lower prices that will benefit the consumer.
- **Environmental** – larger vehicle loads mean fewer journeys, which, when coupled with increasingly sophisticated route planning systems, results in the reduction of harmful emissions.

How to use it

Companies that are potentially interested in adopting factory gate pricing should ask:

i) whether a reduction of delivery frequency is possible, and

ii) whether transferring the responsibility for transportation leads to cost advantages or service improvements,

as these are the considerations that largely determine the possible advantages of FGP. A number of other conditions are also important. These include:

i) the transport flexibility of the retailer (i.e. flexibility of contracts with logistical service providers, or the presence of a fully equipped transport fleet), and

ii) the characteristics of the products (e.g. freshness, size and weight), which determine the possibility of combining different products in one vehicle.

Furthermore, one should also take the existence of delivery time windows into account, as well as the degree of transparency of the supplier's pricing methods.

With FGP, suppliers are no longer responsible for the transportation of their products. However, the suppliers' docking capacity must be increased, as picking and loading in the suppliers' distribution centres will change dramatically. On the other hand, administrative activities will be reduced due to the reduction in transportation activities and responsibilities.

Retailers generally face a necessary increase in transportation and loading capacity, and an increase in administrative activities. Indeed, the retailers' purchasing strategies must account for the separation of products and related transportation services. In general, suppliers have to lower their prices.

Final analysis

A retailer's incentive to participate in FGP is the increased purchasing power and various economy-of-scale advantages. Suppliers, on the other hand, are generally not content with these developments and are reluctant to participate in FGP, arguing that the associated increased (price) transparency weakens their negotiating position. The absence of a fair mechanism for reallocating synergetic advantage impedes the introduction of FGP, as it prevents the creation of trust.

Alternatives to FGP are VMI (vendor managed inventory, see p. 188), CPFR (collaborative planning, forecasting and replenishment) and CRP (continuous replenishment planning). CRP is a relatively simple strategy in which consecutive supply chain members (i.e. a supplier and a retailer) exchange information on real demand, true stock levels and deliveries. The supply chain members replenish with the aid of point-of-sale data instead of triggering replenishment, based on simple inventory models and traditional economic order quantities. In this approach, supply chain members collaborate in the co-ordination stage, where information replaces inventory. CRP leads to frequent deliveries of small quantities based on actual usage (i.e. a demand-pull is created). The similarities between VMI and FGP are that both concepts shift major supply chain decisions and responsibility for stock levels to one supply chain member in order to reduce costs and improve customer value.

Reference

Assen, M.F. van, Hezewijk, A.P. van and Velde, S.L. van de (2005) *Reconfigurations of Chain and Networks*. Amsterdam: Elsevier Business Publishers.

Henderson and Venkatraman's strategic alignment model

30

The big picture

Henderson and Venkatraman's strategic alignment model maps the relationships between the firm's strategy and IT, and between operations and the IT infrastructure. It helps to assess the alignment of the IT strategy with the business strategy. The model distinguishes two dimensions:

- **The strategic fit** – the degree to which the internal organisational infrastructure and processes are in harmony with the external strategy.
- **The functional integration** – the degree to which the IT-related technological planning and business planning are aligned.

The model uses the term 'strategic fit' for the degree of technological fit between the four strategic quadrants based on the two dimensions (as shown in Figure 30.1); and it clarifies two things:

1. An effective support of the business strategy by IT.
2. An IT infrastructure that suits the operational processes that result from the strategic choices.

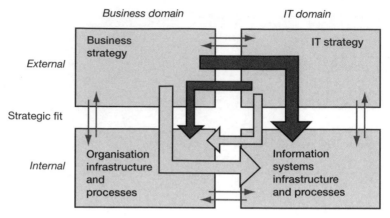

Figure 30.1 The strategic alignment model
One time permission to reproduce granted by Ivey Management Services in October 2008.

When to use it

The model underlines the fact that the IT strategy can never be considered or modified without being aligned to the business strategy. This is something that cannot be emphasised too strongly. The model functions as a tool to complete this necessary alignment.

The model should be used as a framework to map the relationships between business strategy and IT strategy, and between operations and IT infrastructure, in situations where IT is very important for realising the chosen business strategy. The model provides insight in three ways:

1 It identifies the link between the business strategy and the IT strategy.
2 It recognises the (strategic) value of the IT strategy and the automation system as providing support for, and possibly steering, the business strategy.
3 It optimises the potential for use of IT within the company.

How to use it

Henderson and Venkatraman's vision entails four dominant strategic perspectives that are aligned as illustrated by the various arrows in Figure 30.1:

Strategic development (the counter-clockwise arrow from top-left)

In this traditional view of strategic management, there is a hierarchical relationship between a company's business strategy and information systems infrastructure and processes. The (board of) management defines the strategy, which is subsequently translated into an IT infrastructure. Business strategy is considered to be the driver of both organisational infrastructure (structure follows strategy) and the logic of the IT infrastructure.

Technological potential (the clockwise arrow from top-left)

The business strategy is the starting point for the IT strategy and infrastructure. The management view of technology, as defined within the business strategy, will drive the choices in IT strategy. The IT strategy is then translated into an appropriate IT infrastructure. The technological potential differs from the strategic perspective (above) because it demands that the IT strategy is formulated in line with the business strategy. The IT strategy should also support the specification of the (internal) IT infrastructure and processes. The infrastructure, when implemented, must be consistent with the (external) IT strategy.

Competitive potential (the counter-clockwise arrow from top-right)

The competitive potential differs in perspective from the previous strategic perspectives, because it assumes that the business strategy is changeable in line with IT capabilities. Exploiting the IT capabilities could influence the development of new products or services, new ways of steering and managing relationships, and new elements of the business strategy. The (board of) management only supports the business strategy in this perspective, in the sense that it envisages how emerging IT capabilities and new ways of governing will influence the business strategy. The IT manager should translate the developments and trends in the IT environment into opportunities and threats for the (board of) management.

Service level (the clockwise arrow from top-right)

From the service level perspective, the business strategy is indirect and only barely visible. The organisational infrastructure is based on the IT infrastructure, which is the sole result of the IT strategy. There is a danger that an organisation built in this way will require huge investment in IT processes, acquisitions and licences. Management should therefore be involved in resource allocation.

Final analysis

The model assumes that both business strategy and IT strategy are the responsibility of top management. In reality, IT projects go wrong because top management considers them from the perspective of the IT strategy alone. In effect, they have 'delegated' the IT strategy to 'experts'. The model does identify the need for alignment, but it does not offer solutions for this frequent conflict.

References

Henderson, J.C. and Venkatraman, N. (1991) 'Understanding strategic alignment'. *Business Quarterly* 55 (3): 72.

Henderson, J.C. and Venkatraman, N. (1993) 'Strategic alignment: leveraging information technology for transforming organisations'. *IBM Systems Journal* 32 (1): 4–16.

Hofstede's cultural dimensions

31

The big picture

Hofstede's cultural dimensions can be used to develop an effective strategy to co-operate with people from various countries. By studying survey data about the values of employees at IBM in over 50 countries, Hofstede concluded that there were big differences in these cultural values. In many countries, the challenges and problems around these cultural values seemed the same, but the interpretations and subsequent solutions sought differed strongly per country. His model is an aid to becoming more effective when interacting with people from other countries. The types of (different) values that were identified in the study represent the four dimensions of culture:

1 Power distance;
2 Individualism / collectivism;
3 Masculinity / femininity;
4 Uncertainty avoidance.

However, based on the differences between Western and Eastern countries, a fifth dimension was added, namely:

5 Long-term orientation.

Knowing the differences between national cultures makes it possible to understand specific behaviour. Becoming aware of and recognising these differences is the first step to becoming more effective when interacting in multi-cultural environments.

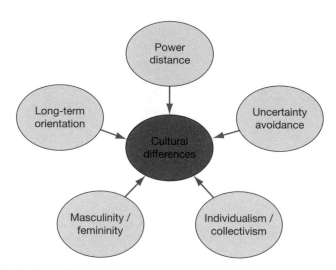

Figure 31.1 Hofstede's dimensions of culture

When to use it

The chances are that most of us have business dealings with people from different cultural backgrounds on a daily basis. Internationalisation leads to more international clients, partners and suppliers, and may also result in hiring employees from all around the world. This trend increases the risk of cultural misunderstandings and failures. Hofstede's cultural dimensions model and the scores of nationalities involved on these dimensions, may help to prevent these frictions and to get off to a good start with potential clients or partners.

How to use it

Hofstede's cultural dimensions model is not a guideline for interaction between people; it just helps to understand certain behaviour.

Power distance index (PDI) is the extent to which the less powerful members of organisations and institutions accept and expect power to be distributed unequally among individuals. If an Austrian and a Malaysian marketing manager, working on the same hierarchical level within an organisation are compared, the difference in PDI becomes visible. The Malaysian manager (high PDI) has hardly any responsibility or power compared to the Austrian (low PDI). In a Malaysian organisation, power is much more centralised.

Individualism (IDV) (and collectivism, on the other side of the continuum), describes the relationship between the individual and the collective that prevails in a given nation. Individualism pertains to societies in which the ties between individuals are loose; everyone is expected to look after themselves and their immediate family. Collectivism pertains to those in which people are integrated into strong, cohesive in-groups. Those in-groups continue to protect these people throughout their lifetime in exchange for unquestioning loyalty. In US companies, for instance, people are more self-interested and less interested in the well-being of the whole team compared to Asian companies.

Masculinity (MAS) is the opposite of femininity. These constructs refer to the differences between the sexes. In masculine cultures, assertiveness is the predominant characteristic *as opposed to personal goals and nurturing*. In Japan, ambition, competitiveness, accumulation of wealth and material possessions are valued, whereas in Sweden relationships and quality of life are much more important.

Uncertainty avoidance index (UAI) indicates to what extent a culture programmes its members to feel threatened by ambiguous situations. Uncertainty-avoiding cultures try to minimise the possibility of such situations by strict laws and rules, and safety and security measures. In addition, these cultures are characterised by long-term employment. Others have a low UAI and are therefore more likely and relatively willing to take risks.

Long-term orientation (LTO) *versus* short-term orientation. Values associated with long-term orientation are thrift and perseverance; values associated with short-term orientation are respect for tradition, fulfilling social obligations and saving one's 'face'. Asian countries, such as China, Vietnam and Japan score relatively high on the LTO index, while Western countries such as Australia, Germany and Norway score relatively low.

Do's
- **Realise that the actions and reactions of people from other countries may be completely different from what you are used to.**

Don'ts
- **Be aware that the possible differences are no guarantee for effective interaction, as no two individuals are alike.**

Final analysis

Hofstede's cultural dimensions model has been useful in creating awareness of the various cultural differences that become apparent when a firm starts to operate internationally. However, over the past few decades distances have decreased, cultures have mingled, and differences are often less visible. In addition, one could question the ratings of some countries, depending on whether all cultural groups within that country are represented or not. In either case, ratings on dimensions may vary among the inhabitants of that specific country. Finally, no two individuals are alike, and one must therefore realise that misunderstandings can still happen.

References

Hofstede, G. (2001) *Culture's Consequences*: *Comparing values, behaviours, institutions, and organisations across nations*. Thousand Oaks, CA: Sage Publications.

Hofstede, G. (1991). *Cultures and Organisations: Software of the mind*. London: McGraw-Hill.

House of purchasing and supply

32

The big picture

The house of purchasing and supply is a framework developed by A.T. Kearney. It can be used to plan, evaluate and monitor the leadership practices in procurement by following the example of successful firms. The framework is the outcome of the study 'Leadership practices in procurement' conducted by A.T. Kearney in 1996. Seventy-seven high-performing firms from various industries in North America and Europe participated. The framework consists of three basic levels: *direction-setting processes*; *core procurement processes*; and *supporting/enabling processes*; and eight dimensions, so-called 'rooms' that comprise more than a hundred detailed items that differentiate leaders from laggards:[1]

Direction-setting processes:

- Procurement strategy. Capitalise on supply market opportunities as an integral part of the business strategy to drive value creation through innovation, cost leadership and marketing and revenue realisation.
- Organisational alignment. Embed procurement skills and knowledge in the organisation's key business processes.

Core procurement processes:

- Sourcing. Apply advanced techniques to leverage the full value potential across the entire expenditure base, thus helping the firm to understand its own core competencies.
- Supplier relationship management. Effectively manage the tension between the value creation potential and the risks of each relationship.
- Operating process management. Automate operating processes by the aggressive and innovative use of e-business technologies.

Supporting processes:

- Performance management. Link procurement figures to corporate results and strategic objectives by making transparent the contribution that procurement makes towards results.
- Knowledge and information management. Continuously capture and share knowledge across processes, geographies, business units and external relationships.
- Human resource management. Create ambassadors of procurement excellence through training, incentives and the aggressive rotation of high-potential professionals throughout the organisation.

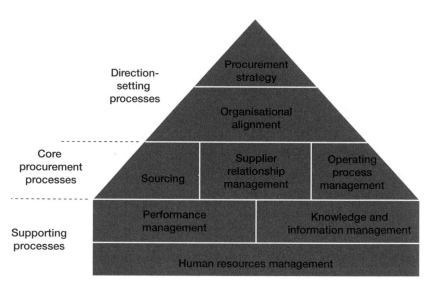

Figure 32.1 The house of purchasing and supply

When to use it

The house of purchasing and supply is an appropriate framework for analysing and modifying any organisational procurement function to make it more effective. The framework helps to identify opportunities for improvement, with benchmark data regarding the procurement function, and consequently stimulates professionalism.

How to use it

The 'Assessment of Excellence in Procurement' study questionnaire is freely available on-line.[2] Respondents receive a tailored feedback report containing their results compared to other organisations, and even world-class leaders. Consequently, this assessment can accelerate professionalism by quickly identifying strengths and opportunities, and charting the course of action to prepare for the future. As such, many organisations use the assessment periodically to monitor their progress.

Final analysis

The house of purchasing and supply is one of many frameworks used to describe the scope of the procurement function, and to determine its level of professionalism. Due to the available benchmark data, the framework can be used repeatedly, especially by large international organisations.

The study that forms the basis of the framework began with 50 respondents, and grew into a study with over 600. As such, the framework has become a means of communication between many organisations. However, the benchmark is time-consuming, and the limited number of publications or other information about the information is a serious drawback.

Reference

A.T. Kearney (2000). 'The new procurement mandate: growing within tomorrow's supply webs'. White paper, downloadable at
http://www.atkps.com/news/mandate.pdf (accessed on 6 April 2008).

Notes

1 A.T. Kearney (2000). 'The new procurement mandate: growing within tomorrow's supply webs'. White paper, downloadable at:
   http://www.atkps.com/news/mandate.pdf
2 http://www.atkearney.com/main.taf?p=1,3,6,28

33 The innovation circle

The big picture

The innovation circle is a model for efficiently analysing and successively managing the life cycle of a new innovation. Innovation – that is, the creation of new products, processes and services – is an essential process for creating a (long-term) competitive advantage. However, innovation processes are often complex and not easy to manage. This model has identified which phases in the life cycle of an innovation are the most important, and in greatest need of management focus and attention.

The creation of new products, processes and services is a key challenge for management. The innovation circle identifies three main phases that are necessary to manage the life cycle of an innovation successfully: *creation*, *implementation* and *capitalisation*.

1 The creation phase. The 'seeds' of new products, processes and services are discovered and organised in the creation phase. This phase comprises three steps: *receive incentives*, *idea creation* and the *function creation process* (FCP):

- Receive incentives – in this step, the external incentives that initiate the innovation process are distinguished and interpreted. Examples of external incentives are: diminishing growth, weakening of the brand, the decline of customer satisfaction and the development of new technologies (or other areas of knowledge).

- Generate ideas – in this step, the generation of new ideas is the key. The external stimuli (the incentives received) provide the initiative to create new (product) ideas. Idea creation can be stimulated by a creative climate in which variety and exploration stand central, and where chaos and energy are the main drivers. For example, brainstorming sessions in which out-of-the-box thinking is stimulated can result in the creation of (many) new ideas. The best new ideas will be selected and go through to the next phase. During this process the focus should be on the needs of customers. Creation of (new) value for customers is the ultimate goal. The customer value can be recognised by identifying the rewards (ROI), risks (technological and market) and resources (investment).

- Function creation process (FCP) – in this step, the ideas are transformed into manageable functions. In addition, the risks are identified and can therefore be controlled. If the functions are clear, it is time to move on to the next phase.

2 The implementation phase. In this phase, the new product, process or service is further developed. The market introduction is prepared and executed. This phase is divided into two steps: the *product creation process* (PCP) and the *market introduction*.

- Product creation process (PCP) – during the PCP the new product and / or service is developed from the specifications created during the FCP phase. In this step, the product is tested, for example by developing a prototype and running demos.

- Market introduction – in this step, all aspects of the market introduction are managed. This also implies the preparation of the following phase (ORP).

3 The capitalisation phase. In the last phase, the commercialisation of the new product, process and / or service is managed. This phase addresses the issue of how to create value (money) for the firm from the innovation(s) created. It is divided into three steps, in which operational excellence is key: the *order realisation process* (ORP), *the service realisation process* (SRP) and *utilisation*.

- Order realisation process (ORP) – in this step, the management of the continuous, repeating stream of product deliveries is executed. This is concerned with the management of the logistics and production of the new product. Integration with the existing logistics and the production of current products is crucial in generating synergy and scale advantages.

- Service realisation process (SRP) – in this step, the management of providing (additional) services is undertaken. New services have to be integrated into the current service process.

- Utilisation – the last step of the innovation circle concerns the management of the new product's revenues. This implies the continued preservation of the product's margin. Reductions in production costs and small adjustments to the product are ways in which the margin of a product can be preserved. This phase ends when the life cycle of the product has ended.

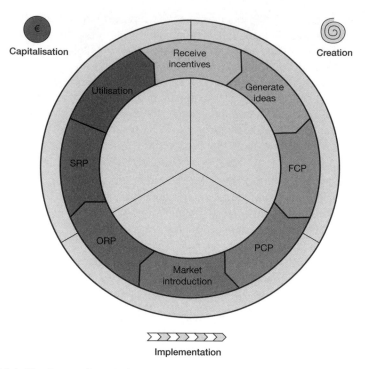

Figure 33.1 The innovation circle

When to use it

The innovation circle can be used to manage the life cycles of a variety of innovations without overlooking relevant aspects of the innovation process. As the innovation process is divided into successive phases, management attention can be more easily directed to the right subject during the life cycle of the innovation.

How to use it

The three phases of the innovation circle – creation, implementation and capitalisation – should be managed differently. In the creation phase, the search for new ideas is dominant. In this phase, management is directed towards managing creativity, but not in the same way as programme and project management, as search processes are not directed at a clear goal. (Clear goals are prerequisites in programme and project management). Rather, this phase can be managed by starting parallel research to explore different solutions. This iterative process ends when, with a degree of certainty, the most appropriate solution to the problem is found.

The implementation phase can be managed more tightly. The goal of this phase is clear from the outset, and includes the different functions of the product, process and / or service. The necessary resources (mainly time and money) are therefore reasonably well-known and manageable. This phase can be managed well by project management.

In the capitalisation phase, the new product, process and / or service is integrated into the ongoing operation, for which operational excellence programmes are appropriate.

Final analysis

The innovation circle is an analytical tool for managing an innovation process that provides a structure for overseeing its inherent complexity. Various analytical tools for new product management have been developed during the past few decades. The best-known tool is probably the stage gate model (Cooper, 1986). The stage gate model and the innovation circle are comparable, in that they both provide an approach to managing the different stages of an innovation process. However, the innovation circle differs from the stage gate model in two ways. First, the innovation circle directs more attention to the capitalisation phase. As such, management is not only focused on creating new products, but also on the creation of new products that are commercially interesting, and which can be integrated within the present operational infrastructure. Second, the innovation circle differs because of its shape. It represents a continuous process, implying that innovation should not stop at the end of a product life cycle. The end of a product could be a powerful incentive for new product ideas.

Reference

Cooper, R.C. (1986) *Winning at New Products*. Reading, MA: Addison-Wesley.

34 Kotler's 4Ps of marketing

The big picture

Commonly known as the 'Four Ps', the marketing mix is a description of the strategic position of a product in the marketplace. The premise of the model is that marketing decisions generally fall into the following four controllable categories:

- Product (characteristics);
- Price;
- Place (distribution);
- Promotion.

When grouped into these four categories, marketing decisions can be justified and chosen deliberately, taking into account the intended effects. This concept has been popularised by Kotler and Dubois (1994), and Kotler and Keller (2000).

When to use it

The marketing mix is a tactical toolkit that an organisation can use as an integral part of its marketing strategy to realise its corporate strategy. As an organisation can adjust the 'four Ps' categories on a regular basis, it is able to keep pace with the changing needs of customers in a specific market segment, and of other stakeholders in the marketing environment.

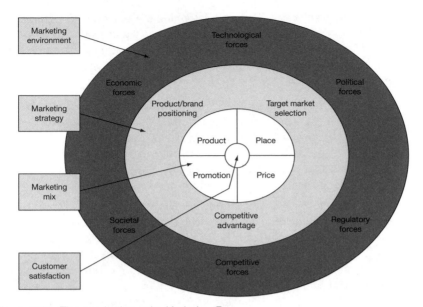

Figure 34.1 The marketing mix: Kotler's 4Ps

KOTLER, PHILLIP; KELLER, KEVIN LANE, *MARKETING MANAGEMENT: ALALYSIS, PLANNING, IMPLEMEN-TATION AND CONTROL*, 12th edition, © 2006, p.27. Reprinted by kind permission of Pearson Education

How to use it

There are three basic steps:

1 Step 1: Research. In order to develop a marketing mix that precisely matches the needs of the customers in the target market, an organisation first has to gather information.

Product decisions	Price decisions	Distribution (place) decisions	Promotion decisions
Brand name	Pricing strategy	Distribution	Promotional strategy
Functionality styling	(skim and	channels	(push or pull)
Quality	penetration)	Market coverage	Advertising
Safety	Suggested retail	(inclusive, selective	Personal selling and
Packaging	price	or exclusive	sales force
Repairs and support	Volume discounts	distribution)	Sales promotions
Warranty	and wholesale	Specific channel	Public relations and
Accessories and	pricing	members	publicity
services	Cash and early	Inventory	Marketing
	payment discounts	management	Communications
	Seasonal pricing	Warehousing	budget
	Bundling	Distribution centres	
	Price flexibility	Order processing	
	Price discrimination	Transportation	
		Reverse logistics	

2 Step 2: Analyse the variables and determine the optimum mix. Optimal marketing has to be determined, which will allow the organisation to strike a balance between satisfying its customers and maximising the organisation's profitability. This means making decisions regarding the issues in each of the categories illustrated in the table overleaf.

- *Product* – Do you actually produce what your customers want? Possible decisions and activities regarding the product include: new product development; modification of existing products; and elimination of products that are no longer attractive or that are unprofitable. There is also a variety of activities closely linked to the product that can be considered, such as branding, packaging, guarantees and the handling of complaints.

- *Place* (distribution) – Are your products available in the right quantities, in the right place, at the right time? Can you achieve this while keeping inventory, transport and storage costs as low as possible? Analyse and compare the various distribution possibilities, after which the most appropriate option can be selected. Again, there are a number of activities related to this category, such as: selecting and motivating intermediaries; controlling inventory and managing transport; and organising storage as efficiently as possible.

- *Promotion* – How can you best inform/educate groups of customers about your organisation and its products? Different types of promotional activities may be necessary, depending on whether the organisation wishes to launch a new product, to increase awareness with regard to special features of an existing one, or to retain interest in a product that has been available in the same form for a long time. Therefore, decisions must be taken as to the most effective way of delivering the desired message to the target group.

- *Price* – How much are your customers willing to pay? The value obtained in an exchange is critical to consumers, in addition to which price is often used as a competitive tool, not only in price wars, but also for image enhancement. Pricing decisions are thus highly sensitive.

Step 3: Check. Monitoring and control on an ongoing basis are essential to ascertain the effectiveness of the chosen mix and how well it is being executed.

Final analysis

One of the problems with the 'Four Ps' is that they have a tendency to keep increasing in number, prompting the question 'Where does marketing stop?' Of all the candidates, the 'people' factor is undoubtedly the most widely accepted fifth 'P'. After all, people manipulate the marketing mix as marketers; they make products/services available to the marketplace as intermediaries; they create the need for marketing as consumers / buyers; they play an important role when it comes to service levels, recruitment, training, retention, and so on.

It is tempting to view the marketing mix variables as controllable, but remember that there are limits: price changes may be restricted by economic conditions or government regulations; changes in design and promotion are expensive and cannot be effected overnight; people are expensive to hire and train. Do not forget to keep an eye on what is happening in the outside world, as some events may have a greater impact than you think.

Ultimately, successful marketing is a matter of gut feeling and acting on hunches. While the marketing mix is a useful instrument when it comes to analysing and ordering, the multitude of marketing decisions has to be considered.

References

Kotler, P. and Dubois, B. (1994) *Marketing Management: Analysis, planning, implementations, and control*. Upper Saddle River, NJ: Prentice-Hall.

Kotler, P. and Keller, K.L. (2000) *A Framework for Marketing Management,* 3rd edition. Upper Saddle River, NJ: Prentice-Hall.

35

Kotter's eight phases of change

The big picture

Kotter's eight phases of change is a systematic approach to achieving successful, sustainable change by breaking down the change process into eight phases. It is based on a study of more than 100 companies that have been through a change process. Kotter (1990, 1995) found out that the most common mistakes made during change processes are: allowing too much complacency; failing to create a substantial coalition; under-estimating the need for a clear vision; failing to communicate the vision clearly; permitting roadblocks; failing to create short-term wins; declaring victory too soon; and not anchoring changes in the corporate culture. Kotter claims that these errors can be avoided by understanding why organisations change, and the numerous steps required to realise the change.

When to use it

In today's dynamic business world, the ability to *lead* change has become an important requirement for creating and maintaining success in all organisations. Kotter makes a clear distinction between leading change and managing it. He states that management consists of a set of processes that keeps a complex system of people and technology running smoothly. Leadership, on the other hand, defines the future, aligns people with that vision, and inspires them to pursue it. The eight phases of change approach provides a systematic tool for leading that process, enabling people to bring about lasting changes within their organisations, and avoiding (possibly) fatal mistakes.

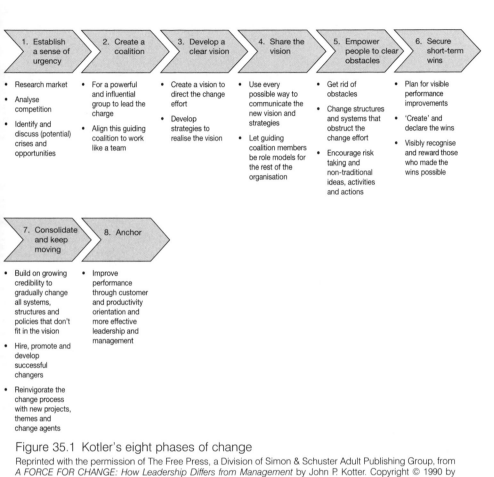

Figure 35.1 Kotler's eight phases of change

Reprinted with the permission of The Free Press, a Division of Simon & Schuster Adult Publishing Group, from *A FORCE FOR CHANGE: How Leadership Differs from Management* by John P. Kotter. Copyright © 1990 by John P. Kotter, Inc. All rights reserved.

How to use it

Kotter stresses the importance of going through all eight phases as described below in detail. However, if running multiple change projects, it is likely that an organisation will find itself in more than one phase of the model at any given time. The phases are:

1 **Create a sense of urgency**. In dealing with complacency, it is important to eliminate false signs of security. Management has to ensure that the relevant people feel a sense of urgency due to a crisis or a potential crisis, and that they are convinced that doing business as usual is no longer an acceptable option.

2 **Put together a guiding team.** A strong guiding coalition is needed in order to create change in an organisation. The members of this group need to recognise the value of the envisaged change, and must share trust and commitment. Furthermore, they should possess the credibility, skills, connections, reputations and formal authority to provide change leadership.

3 **Create vision and strategy.** Vision is a central component in leading change. It is the bridge between current and future states, providing a sense of direction and aligning efforts. The best visions are sensible, clear, simple, elevating and situation-specific.

4 **Communicate the changed vision.** Communicating the vision to everyone involved is crucial if everyone is to understand and commit to the change. Communicating the vision inadequately and with inconsistent messages are both major pitfalls that hinder successful change.

5 **Empower people.** The guiding coalition should remove any barriers to action that may be entrenched in the organisational processes and structures, or exist in the perception of employees. This allows everyone to participate in the change effort.

6 **Generate short-term wins.** Change may take time and significant effort. Therefore, people should be encouraged and endorsed by creating short-term wins. These wins should be unambiguous, visible to many, and closely related to the change effort.

7 **Consolidate and enable more change.** Build momentum by consolidating the accomplished gains, using them as stepping-stones to greater wins, and enabling people to generate new activities related to the vision driving the effort.

8 **Anchor new approaches in culture.** Having made effective changes, leaders must now make the changes permanent and prevent things from reverting to the way they were. Kotter states that the real key to lasting change lies in changing the corporate culture itself, through consistency of successful action over a sufficient period.

Final analysis

Kotter does not shy away from the complexity of organisational change by offering a simplistic approach. He recognises that there are many ways of making mistakes in change efforts. In fact, even successful change efforts are messy and full of surprises. However, anyone attempting to make a change effort in an organisational setting should consider Kotter's model precisely in order to prevent making the 'common mistakes', and be able to face challenges specific to the particular change effort in hand.

References

Kotter, J.P. (1990) *Force for Change: How leadership differs from management*. New York: Free Press.

Kotter, J.P. (1996) *Leading Change*. Cambridge, MA: Harvard Business School Press.

Kotter, J.P. (2002) *The Heart of Change: Real-life stories of how people change their organisations*. Cambridge, MA: Harvard Business School Press.

36 Kraljic's purchasing model

The big picture

Kraljic's (1983) purchasing model is used to determine an adequate purchasing strategy per product (or service) that optimises the trade-off between costs and risks. Appropriate guidelines can be derived from it to manage the relationships with various suppliers, by categorising supply items in a two-by-two matrix. Kraljic developed this model as an internal tool for BASF. However, the model became well-known after it was published in the *Harvard Business Review* in 1983. The general idea of Kraljic's purchasing model is to 'minimise supply vulnerability and make the most of potential buying power'.

The model categorises products on the basis of two dimensions: *financial impact* and *supply risk*. This results in four quadrants, each of which requires a distinct purchasing strategy:

- **Strategic items** – have a high supply risk and a high financial impact. In general, these items are scarce, high-value materials, such as rare metals and high-value components. Depending on the relative power position of the parties involved, the purchasing strategy for strategic items is aimed at partnership or collaboration.

- **Leverage items** – are items with low supply risk, but high financial impact. An abundant supply is available; however, the items are very important to the organisation. Electric motors and heating oil are examples of leverage items. Leverage items require a purchasing strategy based on competitive bidding or tendering.

- Bottleneck items – have a low impact on the profit of the organisation, but these items do have a high supply risk. Mostly, this supply risk is due to production-based scarcity, and global, predominantly new suppliers with new technologies. Examples of bottleneck items are electronic parts and outside services. The purchasing policy for bottleneck items aims at securing continuity of supply. Furthermore, alternative products and suppliers must be developed in order to reduce dependence on suppliers.

- Non-critical items – items that have low supply risk and low financial impact are labelled non-critical items. An abundant supply is available, and the items are needed simply for functional efficiency. Examples of non-critical items are all types of commodities, such as steel rods, coal and office supplies. As the handling of non-critical items often takes more money than the value of the product itself, these products require a purchasing strategy aimed at reducing administrative and logistical complexity.

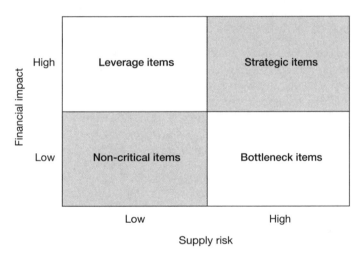

Figure 36.1 The four quadrants of Kraljic's purchasing model

When to use it

Kraljic's model is used to determine distinct purchasing strategies per product (or service) that enable an organisation to develop different strategies for each of the suppliers, so that each supplier will receive the appropriate amount of attention. The model is an effective tool for supporting the discussion, visualisation and illustration of the possibilities of differentiated purchasing and supplier strategies. The model enables an organisation to make its purchasing function more effective and efficient due to the structured and systematic approach the model offers.

How to use it

In order to fill in the two-by-two matrix and subsequently determine the adequate strategy, all products (and services) must first be segmented. A good rule of thumb for grouping products logically is to evaluate whether products can reasonably be purchased from one or more supplier(s).

Second, the financial impact and the supply risk are determined for each of the product segments:

- The financial impact – concerns the impact on the profit of a given supply item, measured against criteria such as: purchasing volume; the percentage of the total purchase cost; product quality; and business growth. The higher the volume or amount of money involved, the higher the financial impact.

- The supply risk – relates to the complexity of supply, assessed according to criteria such as: availability; number of suppliers; competitive demand; make-or-buy opportunities; storage risks; and substitution possibilities. Sourcing a product from just one supplier without an alternative source of supply generally indicates a high supply risk.

Finally, the lines that divide the quadrants must be determined, because what exactly distinguishes high from low, for both supply risk and financial impact, is more or less arbitrary. This will result in a mapping of the segments in the matrix and a recommendation of the purchasing strategy to follow.

Note, however, that the appropriate purchasing strategy is not merely determined rationally by classifying the products, but also by the strategic choices of the organisation. Emotional and relational aspects are also important when choosing or maintaining suppliers.

Final analysis

Kraljic's model provided the first comprehensive portfolio management approach for purchasing and supply management. Kraljic's basic ideas and concepts have become the dominant approach in the profession. The Kraljic matrix has become the standard in the field of purchasing portfolio models. Its terminology has been generally accepted, and it has become the standard for both scientists and practitioners.

References

Kraljic, P. (1983) 'Purchasing must become supply management'. *Harvard Business Review* 61 (5) September / October: 109–17.

Weele, A.J. van (2002) *Purchasing and Supply Chain Management: Analysis, planning and practice*. London: Thomson Learning.

Lean thinking / just-in-time

37

The big picture

Lean thinking is also known as lean manufacturing, or the Toyota philosophy. Lean focuses on the removal of *muda* (waste and inefficiencies), which is defined as anything that is not necessary to produce the product or service. In lean thinking, inventories are considered to be the root of all evil. High inventories cover up all the real problems of an organisation and prevent it from becoming more flexible and efficient. If the inventories are reduced on a structural base, the real problems will become apparent, and then they can be solved accordingly.

Lean, and in particular its operations strategy just-in-time (JIT), is a Japanese management philosophy developed by Taiichi Ohno for the Toyota manufacturing plants. Lean thinking forces any firm to continuously identify and remove sources of waste according to the *seven zeros*:

1 Zero defects;
2 Zero (excess) lot sizes;
3 Zero setups;
4 Zero breakdowns;
5 Zero (excess) handling;
6 Zero lead-time;
7 Zero surging.

According to the seven zeros, lean thinking advocates flow production, with the emphasis on JIT delivery.

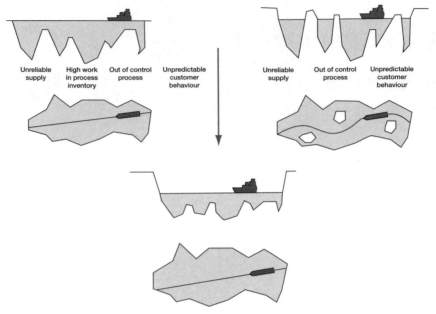

Figure 37.1 Lean thinking

When to use it

While lean thinking has shown itself to be very effective in high-volume repetitive operations, it can be applied to any organisation as long as management adheres to the assumptions underlying lean:

- People value the visual effect of flow.
- Waste is the main restriction to profitability.
- Many small improvements in rapid succession are more beneficial than any analytical study.
- Process interaction effects will be resolved through value-stream refinement.

How to use it

There are five essential steps in lean:

1 Identify the drivers to create value – (identify value and explore customer requirements). The evaluation of value drivers must be made from the perspective of internal and external customers. Value is expressed in terms of how well a product or service meets the customer's needs, at a specific price, at a specific time.

2 Identify the value stream – (the sequence of activities that add value to a product or service). Activities that contribute to value are identified with the aid of value stream mapping, in which all activities are evaluated according to whether they add value to the product or service. Finally, non-value-added activities are eliminated where possible.

3 Make the activities flow – (ensure flow-type production: make products and services flow through the processes). Additional improvement efforts are directed towards making the activities in the value stream flow. Flow is the uninterrupted movement of a product or service through the system to the customer. Major inhibitors of flow are work in queue, batch processing and transportation. These buffers slow down the time from product or service initiation to delivery. Buffers also tie up money that can be used more effectively elsewhere in the organisation, and cover up the effects of system failures and other types of waste.

4 Let the customer pull products or services through the process – (pull production control). Synchronise production with actual customer demand. Products must be pulled out of the system based on actual customer demand. The value stream must be made responsive to providing the product or service only when the customer needs it – not before and not after.

5 Optimise the system continuously – search for perfection by continuously improving processes with the help of Kaizen-events (see p. 213), the elimination of waste, and good housekeeping.

Final analysis

Implementing lean seems so easy! However, in order to implement lean successfully, various issues and elements must be considered (in the following order):

- What results do we really want from JIT? Is it worthwhile in view of the costs and obstacles of implementation? Conduct a quick scan of costs and benefits, including a possible project plan.

- The sequence of JIT implementation is of critical importance. Lowering inventories before creating flexibility in production can lead to lousy delivery performance. In general, implementation has been most successful when it starts at the very end of the production process, and then gradually works upstream. However, the 'best' order of implementation depends on the individual situation. Increasing inventory levels temporarily should be considered in order to ensure delivery performance during the implementation.

- Definitely do not start by forcing suppliers to adopt JIT until implementation is well under way or completed.

- Does the product design qualify for JIT production or delivery? Are alterations necessary?

- Next, redesign the production process to enable JIT. More often than not, significant improvements and efficiencies can be created during this stage.
- Adjust information systems to meet the demands of the primary process.
- Seek improvements with suppliers and customers. This should yield the final, significant results of JIT.

The principle objective of lean is to reduce waste (especially excess inventories). Nevertheless, inventories cannot be eliminated altogether, as all supply systems require a work-in-process inventory to realise any output at all. The more variability (e.g. different types of order, different types of technologies) in the system, the more buffers are required to hedge for variability. Hence, for a lean production system to operate successfully, it is important not only to have a pull-controlled production system, small batch sizes and reduced setup times, but also to have stable and reliable demand and a corresponding operation. In dynamic business environments, other approaches such as the theory of constraints (see p. 184) or quick response manufacturing (see p. 170) are more appropriate.

- **Do not expect to be able to just scrap waste.**
- **Do not believe that control is about output and process indicators.**
- **Do not underestimate the power of the Gemba house (see p. 213).**
- **Do not underestimate the cultural and managerial aspects of lean. These aspects are just as important, or possibly even more important, than the techniques and tools of lean production. There are many examples of lean projects that have failed due to a misunderstanding of the impact of lean on the organisation.**

Reference

Ohno, T. (1988) *Toyota Production System: Beyond large-scale production*. New York: Productivity Press.

MABA analysis

38

The big picture

A MABA analysis compares the relative market attractiveness (MA) of a business activity or product–market combination with business attractiveness (BA), as determined by the ability to operate in a specific product–market combination. The MABA matrix is a useful tool for making decisions related to the business portfolio. Market attractiveness is determined by external indicators such as: profit margins; the size of the market; market growth (expectations); concentration; stability; and competitiveness. Porter's five forces analysis (see p. 14) and the BCG matrix (see p. 8) are appropriate models for assessing these indicators.

When to use it

The MABA analysis is used in particular to analyse and indicate new business opportunities. Business attractiveness is determined largely by company-related indicators, such as the extent to which the product–market combination, market segment or business activity is a logical match with the company's current products, services, activities or competencies. The position of a company in the value chain or network of suppliers and customers is also of importance. Is the company able to benefit from economies of scale or other synergetic effects by taking on a particular alternative product–market combination?

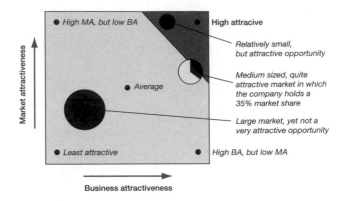

Note: By using a bubble instead of a dot, one may indicate the (relative) size of a market.
Additionally or alternatively, a slice of the pie could indicate the market share of the company.

Figure 38.1 The MABA analysis

How to use it

The first step in a MABA analysis is to decide which indicators are deemed important in determining the two dimensions of attractiveness, and how relatively important they are (weighting). It is obvious that an independently derived set of indicators and weights will lead to results that are more objective. The second step is to define the product–market combinations, the opportunities and the segments or activities that will be subject to the MABA analysis. Although these need not be mutually exclusive, one important factor to take into account is the extent to which one opportunity affects the attractiveness of another.

Managers and consultants find it very useful to put the most attractive business opportunities in either the top-left or the top-right corner of the matrix. Some analysts create a matrix with quadrants or even more blocks within the matrix. Another way of emphasising the most attractive opportunities or weeding out the better from the worse, is the application of curved or diagonal lines that serve as separators or thresholds. Sometimes points in the MABA matrix are replaced with 'bubbles' indicating the market size in units or money, and a pie segment to indicate a company's actual market share.

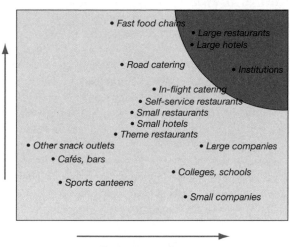

Market attractiveness
- Product match
- Current position in channel
- Buyers' concentration
- Homogeneity

Within the figure:
- Fast food chains
- Large restaurants
- Large hotels
- Road catering
- Institutions
- In-flight catering
- Self-service restaurants
- Small restaurants
- Small hotels
- Theme restaurants
- Other snack outlets
- Large companies
- Cafés, bars
- Colleges, schools
- Sports canteens
- Small companies

Business attractiveness
- Growth
- Size
- Profitability / margins
- Outlet concentration
- Competition

Figure 38.2 Example MABA analysis for food-producing company

A major food-producing company wanted to enter the second stage of development of its professional foods division. With so many new opportunities and a relatively immature organisation for this market, a MABA analysis was conducted.

The actual MABA analysis was carried out in a number of stages. Three important parts are:

- average annual growth percentage *versus* relative activity in the product–market–channel combination with bubbles indicating market size;
- individual product-level analysis of penetration of products in channels *versus* the relative importance of a product in the channels, based on average turnover per outlet relative to all products;
- the company's relative growth in all the relevant markets *versus* the average annual growth of these markets (in correspondence with BCG's growth-share matrix) with pie-sliced bubbles.

The MABA analysis helped our client to identify three major opportunities, while the process of identifying product–market combinations led in itself to a new organisational structure.

Note: As in most cases, reality proved far more complex than can be captured in a single MABA analysis. The underlying analyses for assessing the market and business attractiveness were more extensive than described in this brief case.

Final analysis

The MABA analysis is a very powerful model for helping companies to prioritise new opportunities. Especially in situations where funds or management time are scarce, the model is a great help in decision-making. Remember that it is a model for strategic analysis similar to the BCG matrix.

The MABA analysis is much less powerful when discussing existing businesses. The managers and consultants involved will usually challenge assumptions and indicator ratings in such detail that the model loses its most profound quality: to simplify a complex situation.

The weakness of any MABA analysis lies in choosing and weighting indicators. Different indicators and weights can lead to very different results. There is also a risk of creating a false sense of objectivity when the indicators are quantified, i.e. quantification only improves accuracy on a subjectively chosen scale.

The MABA analysis is limited to two (or three) artificially combined dimensions. Many, and more extensive, MABA analyses have to be performed using different indicators to compensate for this weakness.

Reference

Kotler, P. (2000) *Marketing Management*. The millennium edition, 10th edition. New York: Prentice-Hall.

Milkovich's compensation model

The big picture

The compensation model is a conceptual framework for the design, implementation and assessment of a remuneration strategy in organisations. It was originally designed by Milkovich and Newman (2007) in order to examine strategic choices in managing all aspects of compensation. The model describes three dimensions:

1 Policies – that outline the foundation of the system;
2 Techniques – that link the policies and the pay objectives;
3 Objectives – of the pay system.

When to use it

The compensation model provides a framework for examining current pay systems. It also plays a central role in creating and implementing an organisation's remuneration strategy.

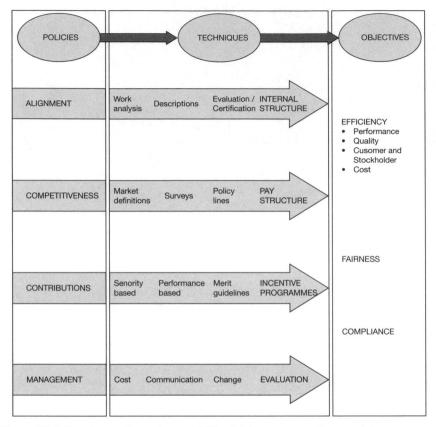

Figure 39.1 The three dimensions of Milkovich's compensation model
Compensation by Milkovich, G.T. and Newman, J.M. (New York: McGraw-Hill, 2007) © The McGraw-Hill Companies, Inc

How to use it

1 Objectives – are the central force of the system. Compensation systems are designed to achieve certain goals. The right-hand side of the model (see figure 39.1) shows the basic objectives of pay systems: efficiency, fairness and compliance. *Efficiency* can be described as controlling labour costs while improving performance and quality, in order to satisfy customers and stakeholders. *Fairness* refers to treating employees fairly by recognising the contributions and needs of employees. *Compliance* is about conforming to compensation laws and regulations.

2 Policies – serve as guidelines for managing compensation in ways that accomplish the system's objectives. Employers must pay attention to all of the policy decisions shown in the column on the left of the model. The concept of *internal alignment* refers to pay relationships within the organisation and the logic behind these relationships. The extent to which

the organisation is willing to compensate in comparison with its market *(external competitiveness)* is of great importance. *Employee contribution* is concerned with individual differences in pay, based on output, competencies, length of service or seniority. The last important policy in the model concerns *managing* the pay system. Even the best pay system in the world would be useless without explicit agreements about who is responsible for application, maintenance and decision-making.

3 **Techniques** – make up the pay system. Pay techniques vary from job analysis to surveys and merit guidelines, and reflect the method of tying the system's objectives to compensation policies. For example, benchmarking is a method used for mapping external competitiveness. Internal alignment can be determined by job-evaluation and job-matching. When using the pay model, it should be clear throughout the process whether the model contributes towards achieving organisational goals. In addition, as there is rarely a single approach to using the model, a constant re-evaluation of the current approach to the model is needed.

Final analysis

When designing, examining or implementing pay systems, it is essential to consider the organisational culture and organisational phase. This is foremost in determining which instruments to apply, as well as how sophisticated the application should be.

Reference

Milkovich, G.T. and Newman, J.M. (2007) *Compensation*. New York: McGraw-Hill.

40

Mintzberg's configurations

The big picture

The organisational configurations framework of Mintzberg describes six organisational configurations. These organisational configurations help with understanding what drives decisions and activities in an organisation. The essence is that a limited number of configurations can help to explain much of what is observed in many organisations. The basic configurations help in discerning organisations and their (typical) core problems. The use of the basic configurations can help to prevent the choice and design of 'wrong' organisational structures and the ineffective co-ordination of activities.

When to use it

Mintzberg's configurations approach can be used to explore the organisational structures and processes associated with each strategy of an organisation. Management is able to determine not only which category their organisation falls into, but also what changes are required to make the organisation internally consistent, and to solve current co-ordination problems.

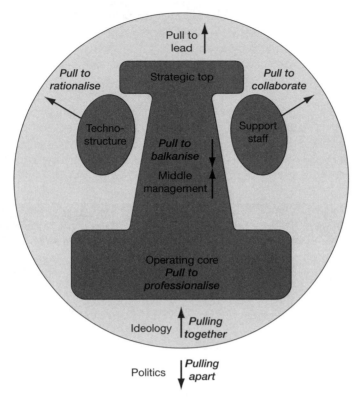

Figure 40.1 Six elementary building blocks of organisations

MINTZBERG, HENRY; *STRUCTURE IN FIVES DESIGNING EFFECTIVE ORGANIZATION*, 2nd Edition, © 1992, p.154. Reprinted by kind permission of Pearson Education, Inc, Upper Saddle River, NJ.

How to use it

When using Mintzberg's (1990) configurations model to analyse and redesign (parts of) an organisation, one must start by identifying an organisation's basic building blocks. According to Mintzberg, all organisations consist of six elementary building blocks:

1 the operating core;
2 the strategic top management;
3 the middle management;
4 the techno-structure;
5 the support staff; and
6 the ideology part.

Typically, the first three building blocks are connected by a single chain of formal authority. In the figure, these parts are therefore illustrated as a single piece. The techno-structure and support staff on both sides influence the core indirectly, while the ideology represents the norms and values (the 'strong culture') that surround, yet penetrate the very fabric of the organisation. These six organisational building blocks are internal determinants of how an organisation evolves. In addition, there are many external forces, such as shareholders, suppliers and customers, all of which have an impact on the organisation.

After the identification and configuration of the organisational building blocks, a company has to analyse and design appropriate co-ordination mechanisms. Labour, governance and control can be distributed differently between the building blocks of the organisation. Hence, the use of different co-ordination mechanisms determines the final structure of an organisation. Moreover, when organisations lack appropriate co-ordination, they are likely to become politicised because various parts of the organisation will fight to fill the power vacuum. Mintzberg distinguishes six co-ordinating mechanisms, as shown in figure 40.2:

Configuration	Prime co-ordinating mechanism	Key part of organisation	Type of decentralisation
Entrepreneurial organisation	Direct supervision	Strategic top	Vertical and horizontal centralisation
Machine organisation	Standardisation of work	Techno-structure	Limited horizontal decentralisation
Professional organisation	Standardisation of skills	Operating core	Horizontal decentralisation
Diversified organisation	Standardisation of output	Middle management	Limited vertical decentralisation
Innovative organisation	Mutual adjustment	Support staff	Selected decentralisation
Missionary organisation	Standardisation of norms and values	Ideology	Decentralisation
Political organisation	None	None	Any

Figure 40.2 Mintzberg's configurations

Next, Mintzberg claims that the essence of organisational design is the manipulation of design parameters such as: job specialisation; behaviour specialisation; training; indoctrination; unit grouping; unit size; planning and control systems; and liaison devices (e.g. positions, task force committees, integration managers and matrix structure). The most important parameter in Mintzberg's organisation configurations model, however, is the way in which power is distributed throughout the organisation. The distribution of power refers to the types of decentralisation, and varies for each organisational configuration as shown in the table.

Finally, the choice of the design parameters is also determined by contextual factors that are mostly beyond management's control (e.g. age, size, technical system and elements in the environment such as various stakeholders).

Final analysis

Due to the robust nature of Mintzberg's basic configurations, there is the risk of using the configurations as blueprints. It is, however, extremely difficult for organisations to match or even compare to these configurations because of the relatively limited number of criteria for defining the organisational configurations, but also because there are many hybrids or combinations of multiple configurations in practice. In our opinion, it is irrelevant whether an organisation can be exactly classified as innovative or entrepreneurial. The essence of Mintzberg's model is that it helps one to understand the relationship between the nature of an organisation and its co-ordination mechanisms. As Mintzberg says, there is no single right way to manage an organisation: what is good for General Motors is often completely wrong for Joe's Body Shop.

References

Mintzberg, H. (1983, 1990) *Structures in Five*: *designing effective organisations*. New York: Prentice Hall.

Mintzberg, H. (1989) *Mintzberg on Management*. New York: Free Press.

41

Monczka's purchasing model

The big picture

Monczka's purchasing model (also known as the Michigan State University (MSU) purchasing model) is a procurement model used to assess the maturity (i.e. the level of professionalism) of an organisation's procurement function, and to suggest improvement programmes to enhance development, in the form of a roadmap. Monczka launched the Global Procurement and Supply Chain Benchmarking Initiative (GPSCBI) in 1993. A total of 150 multi-national companies shared the process knowledge and quantitative data of their supply chain operations. Analysis of the most successful processes has resulted in the MSU purchasing model, which is a roadmap for purchasing excellence.

The model contains eight strategic purchasing processes and six strategic enablers. The strategic purchasing processes aim to improve performance due to more effective supplier management. The enabling processes aim to create conditions and means for the strategic processes to be executed professionally. Learning modules are available for each of the processes.

The eight strategic purchasing processes are:

- insourcing / outsourcing;
- developing commodity / article group strategies;
- establishing and leveraging a world-class supply base;
- developing and managing supplier relationships;
- integrating the supplier into a new product / process development process;
- integrating the supplier into the order realisation process;
- supplier development and quality management; and
- strategic cost management.

The six strategic enabling processes are:

- establishing globally integrated and aligned purchasing and supply chain strategies and plans;
- developing organisation and teaming strategies;
- deploying globalisation;
- developing purchasing and supply chain measurements;
- developing and implementing enabling ICT systems; and
- human resource management.

When to use it

Organisations use the model for measuring the maturity of the procurement function. The model, however, functions not merely as a yardstick, but also as a roadmap. It allows organisations to determine both the present and the desired situation. Moreover, the model's benchmarks stimulate the exchange of best practices within the organisation and between organisations.

How to use it

The model comprises self-assessments to measure the organisation's maturity level. Assessment criteria are developed for each of the 14 processes to rank maturity on a ten-point scale. The lower levels correspond to operational criteria, while the higher levels correspond to tactical and strategic criteria. The self-assessment follows a strict stepped approach, in that an organisation must comply with all the criteria at a certain level before the criteria of the next level become relevant. Accordingly, an organisation can develop and perform projects tailored to improve and professionalise the procurement function, based on the outcome of the maturity assessment, which will take it to the next maturity level. Note, however, that the measured maturity level is not a report mark. It is up to the organisation to decide which maturity level is desirable and appropriate. For some organisations, this

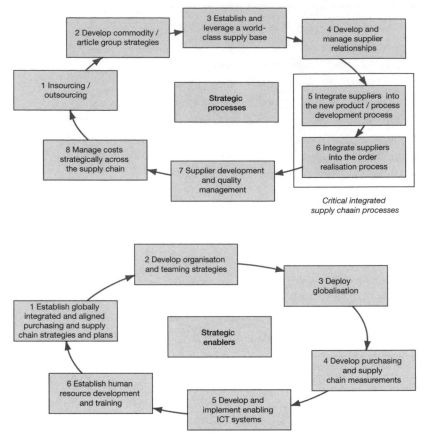

Figure 41.1 Monczka's purchasing model

might be an eight, whereas a five may be sufficient for others. The decision will depend on the type of organisation and the type of industry in which the organisation operates.

Both the strategic and enabling processes must be followed to produce durable results. When only the strategic processes are addressed, the organisation will lack unity or information infrastructure. Dealing with the enabling processes alone will result in investments that have insufficient or no return.

Final analysis

The MSU purchasing model offers a much broader perspective of procurement than many other well-known purchasing models. The use of the model leads to the integration of the organisation's activities and its suppliers. However, it is debatable whether all the model's processes should be gone through for each category or segment, and whether the processes should be carried through in the given sequence. Nevertheless, the model facilitates a professional approach to procurement.

Reference

Trent, R.J. and Monczka, R.M. (1998) 'Purchasing and supply management: Trends and changes throughout the 1990s'. *Journal of Supply Chain Management* 34 (2): 2–11.

42 Overhead value analysis

The big picture

Overhead value analysis (OVA) is a technique used to find opportunities to reduce overhead costs. The model focuses on the reduction and optimisation of indirect activities and services in organisations. An OVA makes improvement opportunities explicit, and compares the costs of indirect activities with the output of the primary processes, for which it uses Porter's value chain model (p. 70).

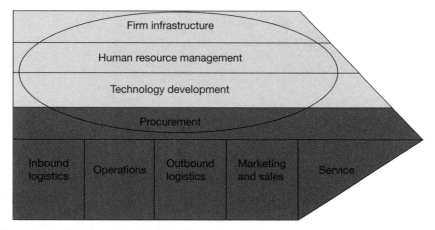

Figure 42.1 Overhead depicted in the value chain

When to use it

An OVA can be used to reorganise and eliminate excess overhead activities. In practice, however, management uses it as both a preventive measure and a last resort. The intended result is not necessarily limited to lowering costs; many organisations simply want to increase awareness of the service demands of the (internal) customer. It is clear that an overhead value analysis has a significant impact on the indirect activities of the people involved.

> Deteriorating financial results and a lack of organisational versatility were the early signs that the client, a manufacturer of military and advanced remote control technology, needed to reassess its indirect organisational functions. An OVA team set out to identify overhead activities and made an initial orderly list of all activities and costs. Next, it was decided to engage in a full OVA project to restructure the organisation and drastically reduce the number of indirect functions. The result was a transformation from a functional organisation to a market-driven business unit structure: departments delivered value to their internal customers, and many tasks that had formerly been divided into primary and secondary functions were decentralised. The change process enjoyed wide support in the organisation, as all parties involved felt that they were participating in their own 're-invention'.

How to use it

There are six basic steps for an overhead value analysis:

1   The first step is to *create a foundation* including a definition of the required output, the required activities and an assessment of the end product.

2   The second step is to make an *orderly listing of activities and costs*. This step includes estimating the costs of input / resources, the costs of activities and the allocation of the cost to products, generally with the help of *activity-based costing* (ABC; see p. 87).

3   In step three, a *customer evaluation* of the service and output is required. Relevant aspects are: necessity (i.e. critical, desired or nice-to-have), quality, quantity and cost. Customers are asked for both an assessment of the current output and an indication of the improvements that need to be made. Both interviews and questionnaires are used in the customer evaluation.

4   In step four, the OVA team must *identify cost-saving opportunities* based on the possible improvements identified. This forces the organisation to make a statement with regard to priorities for output and required activities.

5 Step five is to *prioritise opportunities* with the aid of the four elements used earlier in the customer evaluation:

- Necessity: is value added?
- Is quality of output sufficient?
- Is quantity of output sufficient?
- Can it be done at reasonable cost?

The identification and prioritisation of opportunities overlaps with the question of whether or not to eliminate, change, automate, integrate and / or outsource certain activities. This is very much a pragmatic process executed by management in conjunction with experts and managers of the overhead departments.

6 Finally, as a project in itself, the final step is to *implement* the set of changes discussed and decided upon in the previous five steps.

The success factors of an OVA project are:
- The organisational objectives are known.
- The organisational structure is in place.
- The scope of OVA is determined.
- No other projects are interfered with, or otherwise disrupt the OVA.
- There is sufficient support throughout the organisation.

Final analysis

The results of an OVA analysis are often represented as statistics, whereas most of the data gathering is, in fact, qualitative. Since the required data are obtained from employees whose jobs may be put up for debate, it may be helpful to use a benchmark to verify the data provided. Other potential pitfalls of OVA are:

- insufficient data and information;
- insufficient support for results and arguments;
- insufficient support for implementation.

Both management and analysts should make the process as easy as possible for the *people (employees) involved.* Getting everybody involved to the point where plans are regarded as being self-made is a major contribution to the potential success of OVA. OVA is often used in combination with *activity-based costing* (see p. 87).

References

Davis, M.E. and Falcon, W. D. (1964) *Value Analysis, Value Engineering: The implications for managers.* New York: American Management Association.

Mowen, M.M. and Hanson, D.R. (2006) *Management Accounting: The cornerstone for management decisions.* Mason, OH: Thomson South-Western.

43

Quick response manufacturing

The big picture

Quick response manufacturing (QRM), was developed by Rayan Suri (1998). QRM means responding to customers' needs by rapidly designing and manufacturing products tailored to those needs. QRM focuses on continuously reducing the lead-times of all activities in a company, resulting in improved quality, lower cost and quick response.

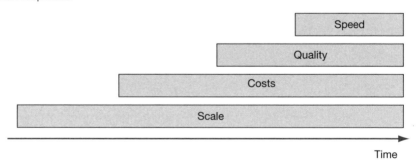

Figure 43.1 Quick response manufacturing

When to use it

QRM has its roots in a strategy called *time-based competition* (TBC), which was proposed by George Stalk and Thomas Hout (1990). The basis of TBC is the use of *speed* to gain a competitive advantage: a company using a TBC strategy delivers products or services faster than its competitors can. The TBC strategy can be applied to any business, including banking, insurance and hospitals. QRM is the application of TBC to manufacturing firms. By focusing on manufacturing companies, QRM sharpens the principles of TBC and adds a number of new dimensions.

How to use it

QRM is a practical strategy. It embodies the concept of pursuing lead-time reduction, together with detailed management principles, manufacturing methods, analysis techniques and tools, and a systematic methodology to achieve the desired reduction in lead-times. It is based on the idea that workers and managers need to understand some of the basic dynamics of manufacturing systems. Specifically, they need to know how capacity planning, resource utilisation, and lot-sizing policies interact with each other, and how they affect lead-time.

Firms have to incorporate QRM policies in all areas. This involves rethinking how the company operates in each area, not just the obvious areas such as manufacturing and supply management, but also areas such as shipping, equipment purchase, employee hiring, accounting and performance appraisal. All of these policies need to be brought into line with the QRM ideal. Moreover, the QRM programme has to be implemented in both shop floor and office operations. We have found that office operations constitute a significant portion of the total lead-time for products, yet they are often overlooked as an opportunity for lead-time reduction.

Final analysis

The difference between QRM and lean (see p. 147) is that the latter aims to reduce non value-adding types of waste (through continuous improvement programmes), whereas QRM focuses on continuously reducing lead-times through quality improvement, increasing process dependability and the elimination of waste. Lead-time reduction cannot be carried out as a tactical project. QRM has to be an organisational strategy led by top management. In order to significantly impact lead-times, firms must change their traditional ways of operating and redesign organisational structures. Such changes cannot be made without the total commitment of top management. Therefore, the first step in a QRM programme must be to educate senior managers about QRM strategy, and get them to buy into the roadmap for implementation.

A key aspect of the QRM approach is to *reduce lead-times*. Some popular manufacturing management approaches appear as a collection of disjointed ideas; managers and employees have to remember a list of assertions such as the 'five Ss' of the 5-S of Kaizen method (see p. 213). In contrast, the entire set of principles in QRM strategy are derived from one theme, yet these principles are powerful enough to span the entire organisation, from the shop floor to the office, from order entry to accounting, from purchasing to sales. Such an approach is more palatable to managers than a disparate collection of ideas, because it enables them to broadcast a consistent message to the entire organisation.

References

Stalk, G. Jr. and Hout, T. M. (1990) *Competing Against Time; How time-based competition is reshaping global markets*. Boston, MA: Harvard Business Press.

Suri, R. (1998) *Quick Response Manufacturing*. New York: Productivity Press.

Senge
The fifth discipline

44

The big picture

The fifth discipline is a model developed by Senge (1990) that describes the five disciplines necessary to create a learning organisation: personal mastery; mental models; shared vision; team learning; and systems thinking. Systems thinking is the discipline that integrates all five disciplines. A 'discipline' is a series of principles and practices that we study, master and integrate into our lives. The five disciplines must be considered at three different levels:

- **Practices** – what you do.
- **Principles** – guiding ideas and insights.
- **Essences** – the state of being those with high levels of mastery in the discipline.

Each discipline provides a vital dimension that organisations have to learn.

When to use it

The fifth discipline is a model that can be used to create a learning organisation. That is, an organisation where people continually expand their capacity to create the results they truly desire, and where new and expansive patterns of thinking are nurtured; where collective aspiration is set free, and where people are continually learning to see the whole together.

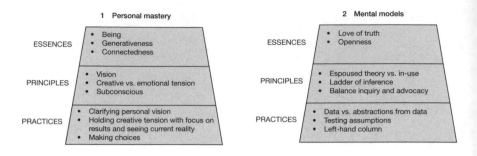

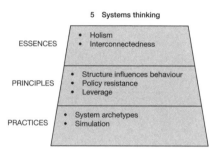

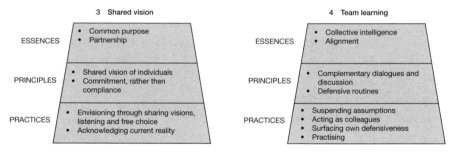

Figure 44.1 Senge's five disciplines

How to use it

The five disciplines necessary to create a learning organisation are:

1 Systems thinking. Systems thinking is the cornerstone of the learning organisation. This is the discipline that integrates the others into a learning organisation, and fuses all disciplines into a coherent body of theory and practice.

2 Personal mastery. Organisations learn only through individuals who learn. Individual learning does not guarantee organisational learning. Nevertheless, without it there is no organisational learning. Personal mastery is the discipline of 'continually clarifying and deepening our personal vision, focusing our energies, developing patience, and seeing reality objectively'.

3 Mental models. These are 'deeply ingrained assumptions, generalisations, or even pictures and images that influence how we understand the world and how we take action'. The discipline of mental models starts with turning the mirror inward, learning to unearth our internal pictures of the world, bringing them to the surface and holding them up to rigorous scrutiny. It also includes the ability to carry on 'learning-full' conversations that balance inquiry and advocacy, where people expose their own thinking effectively, and throw that thinking open to the influence of others.

4 Building shared vision. Senge claims that the capacity to develop and share a clear picture of the future situation is important for leaders to inspire employees to learn. Such a vision has the power to be elevating and may encourage experimentation and innovation. It can also foster a sense of the long term, which is fundamental to the 'fifth discipline'.

5 Team learning. Team learning is viewed as 'the process of aligning and developing the capacities of a team to create the results its members truly desire' (Senge 1990: 236). It builds on personal mastery and shared vision – but these are not enough. People need to be able to act together. When teams learn together, Senge suggests, not only can there be good results for the organisation, but members will learn more quickly than they would otherwise.

Final analysis

Senge has written his book *The Fifth Discipline* to both inspire managers and leaders, and to identify which interventions can be made to turn an organisation into a 'learning organisation', and how this can be done. Senge is especially concerned with localness and openness in an organisation.

The question is whether Senge's vision of the learning organisation and the corresponding disciplines has contributed to more informed and committed action with regard to organisational life. Although there are some problems with Senge's conceptualisation, it makes people prosper. The emphasis on building a shared vision, team working, personal mastery and the development of more sophisticated mental models, and the way he runs the notion of dialogue through these, does have the potential to realise more pleasant and creative workplaces. The use of systems thinking to integrate other dimensions of *The Fifth Discipline* also allows us to have a more holistic understanding of organisational life.

References

Flood, R.L. (1998) 'Fifth Discipline: review and discussion'. *Systemic Practice and Action Research*, 11 (3): 259–73.

Senge, P.M. (1990) *The Fifth Discipline: The art and practice of the learning organisation*. New York: Currency.

Senge, P.M. (1999) *The Dance of Change: The challenges of sustaining momentum in learning organisations*. New York: Currency/Doubleday.

Six sigma

45

The big picture

The name six sigma originates from statistical terminology. Sigma is the mathematical symbol for standard deviation. Six sigma is a measure for the maximum number of defects that is allowed in a system. At the six sigma level, 99.999998 per cent of all products must be good, i.e. have to fall within the tolerance limits. This implies that no more than 3.4 defects are produced in 1 million opportunities. This level can be achieved by reducing the variation of the process and controlling it. To reach this quality level, the processes must be improved. However, process and quality improvements are not the ultimate goal – financial improvement is the goal.

Six sigma first became rooted at Motorola. To confront heavy Japanese competition, in 1987 Motorola started to focus on quality improvement. The engineers at Motorola decided that the norm they were using, of defects per 1,000 units, was no longer appropriate. They therefore decided to measure the defects per million. Allied Signal and General Electric have perfected the method. These firms have realised huge benefits by saving billions of dollars while improving customer satisfaction. Nowadays, six sigma projects are implemented not only in manufacturing firms, but also in the service industry.

Six sigma claims that focusing on reduction of variation will solve process and business problems. By using a set of statistical tools to understand the fluctuation of a process, management can begin to predict the expected outcome of that process. If the outcome is not satisfactory, other statistical tools can be used to further understand the elements that influence the process.

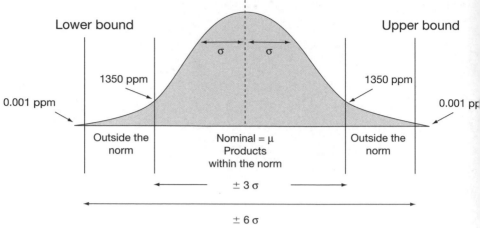

Figure 45.1 The six sigmas

When to use it

Six sigma is used to improve the operational performance of an organisation by identifying and dealing with its deficiencies. Six sigma projects help to achieve better financial results by improving quality and process reliability. Every six sigma project has to focus on financial improvements and cost savings. The six sigma philosophy suggests that top management should not authorise a project that does not have a savings target of at least $175,000.

Six sigma is a top–down method where management has to communicate the goal of each project and audit it. The organisation's employees carry out the projects in a very structured way. The employees have one of the following roles:

- **Executive management champions** – the CEO or other key management team members who have a clear overview of the six sigma projects.
- **Master black belts** – external consultants, who train the black belts and support six sigma projects.
- **Black belts** – the project leaders; they execute overall project management.
- **Green belts** – the project leaders of a part of a project, who implement six sigma projects.
- **Project teams** – each green belt has a project team. These employees are trained in the six sigma techniques.

The infrastructure of a six sigma project is unique for every organisation. Nevertheless, general requirements for successful implementation can be determined:

- A good understanding of statistical tools and techniques;
- Spending adequate resources on the definition phase;
- Spending adequate resources on the implementation phase;

- Effective management leadership and commitment;
- Undergoing a cultural change before implementation;
- Having an effective communication plan;
- Providing adequate training for the improvement teams;
- Having black belts with the ability to facilitate.

How to use it

Six sigma includes five steps: define, measure, analyse, improve and control (commonly known as DMAIC).

1 Define – first of all, a selection of the processes that must be improved has to take place, and the goals for improvement should be defined (SMART).[1]
2 Measure – after the definition phase, data are collected to evaluate the performance of the current process for future comparison.
3 Analyse – the difference between the current state and the desired state is determined in this phase.
4 Improve – the process is subsequently optimised based on the analysis.
5 Control – the new improved processes should be controlled and formalised.

Final analysis

Six sigma comprises hard and soft techniques. The harder ones involve a structured, problem-solving approach, statistical process control tools (applied using DMAIC methodology), and project management techniques. The softer ones involve people management, creativity and improvement motivation.

Benchmarking is used in six sigma projects. The important characteristics of the product, the client, the internal process and the manufacturing system are compared with the products and processes of competitors. This is useful for financially oriented management, because the comparison at process level makes it possible to use six sigma techniques.

In six sigma projects, it is important to have vision and enthusiasm, but a requirement for successful projects is a well-defined infrastructure for training, support and project co-ordination.

Reference

Breyfogle III, F.W. (2003) *Implementing Six Sigma: Smarter solutions using statistical methods*. Hoboken, NJ: John Wiley & Sons.

Note

1 SMART = Specific, Measurable, Acceptable, Realistic and Time-specific.

46

The EFQM
excellence model

The big picture

The European Foundation for Quality Management (EFQM) excellence model helps to establish an appropriate organisational architecture and a corresponding management system with which to build an excellent organisation. The EFQM excellence model is based on the premise that excellent results with respect to performance, customers, people and society are achieved through partnerships, resources and processes. It is result-oriented and has a strong customer focus.

The model explains performance gaps and identifies improvement directions. It is a non-prescriptive framework, underpinned by so-called 'fundamental elements':

- leadership and consistency of purpose;
- management by processes and facts;
- employee development and involvement;
- continuous learning, innovation and improvement;
- partnership development;
- public responsibility.

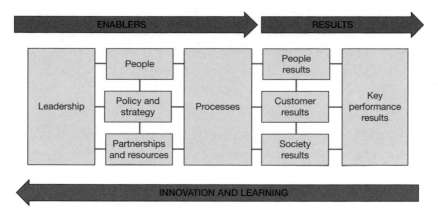

Figure 46.1 The EFQM excellence model
© 1999 – 2003 EFQM

When to use it

The EFQM excellence model is a general model for assessing and designing a company's architecture in terms of best practices. It is based on different cultural and structural elements, with a view to developing an excellent organisation. It can be used by the management of any type of organisation that wants to implement strategy, and redesign and develop organisational structures and processes.

How to use it

The model distinguishes five organisational areas (enablers) and four performance areas (results). The organisational areas are key elements for effectively managing an organisation: *leadership*; *policy and strategy*; *people*; *partnerships and resources*; and *processes*. Key performance results not only reflect how well an organisation is performing, but also measure a company's health from different perspectives: *customer results*, *people results*, *social results*, and *key performance results*.

Leadership – requires managers to:
- develop mission, vision and values;
- be role models of a culture of excellence;
- be personally involved in developing, implementing and improving the organisation's management system;
- be involved with customers, partners and representatives of society;
- motivate, support and recognise people in the organisation.

Policy and strategy – the following criteria are used as a basis to determine excellence:
- present and future needs and expectations of all stakeholders;

- information for performance measurement, research, learning and creativity-related activities;
- continuous development, review and updating;
- deployment via a framework of key processes;
- communication and implementation.

People – play a key role. According to EFQM:

- human resources should be planned, managed and improved carefully;
- people's knowledge and competencies should be identified, developed and sustained;
- people must be involved and empowered;
- there should be dialogue between different people on different organisational levels in the organisation;
- people should be rewarded, recognised and cared for.

Partnerships and resources – excellence requires the management of:

- external partnerships;
- finances;
- buildings, equipment and materials;
- technology;
- information and knowledge.

Processes – Those which are excellent:

- are systematically designed and managed;
- are innovatively improved to meet customer demands and increase value;
- produce well-designed and well-developed products and services that meet customer needs and expectations;
- produce, deliver and service products and services;
- are those that manage and enhance customer relationships.

In EFQM, customer results, people results and society results are measured in *perception measures* and *performance indicators*.

The results the organisation is achieving in relation to its planned performance are collectively called *key performance results* consisting of *key performance outcomes* and *key performance indicators*.

A feedback loop from the performance areas that creates objectives in the organisational areas is essential in order to establish a co-ordinated learning effect. Performance indicators can be developed to measure the effect of the improvements.

Final analysis

The EFQM excellence model is a recognised tool to improve the efficacy and professionalism of a company's planning and control cycle. The EFQM excellence model was co-developed by European top managers of companies such as Renault, Philips and Ciba Geigy. The model provides core elements for the effective analysis, assessment, structuring, improvement and management of an organisation. The EFQM website (www.efqm.org) is a valuable source of information on the use of the EFQM excellence model for self-evaluation, as well as providing a benchmarking model.

The EFQM excellence model is frequently portrayed as a model to assist strategic decision-making. However, it is not a prescriptive model designed to assist with management analyses.

References

The EFQM Excellence Model for self-appraisal. (1992) EFQM: Brussels, Belgium

Oakland, J. (2000) *Total Quality Management: Text with cases*, 2nd edition. Oxford: Butterworth Heinemann.

47 The theory of constraints

The big picture

The essence of the theory of constraints (TOC) is that the output of any given production system is determined by its weakest link. Every system has constraints that prevent a firm from fulfilling its ultimate goal: making money. The theory of constraints states that by removing the largest constraint (the bottleneck), the output of the entire system will be increased. By removing the new bottleneck resulting from the previous action, the output of the system may be further improved. The TOC searches for the bottleneck in the system and tries to eliminate it. This is achieved because a production line cannot work faster than its slowest workstation. If it tries to, inventory will accumulate. It makes use of the drum–buffer–rope principle to control the pace of the production system. The bottleneck acts as the *drum* (determines the pace), by means of the *rope* the materials are planned, and the *buffers* prevent the bottleneck from going dry.

In their book *The Goal*, Goldratt and Cox (1984) illuminate this principle with a line of boy scouts. They cannot march faster than the slowest person (the constraint). If they try to, the line will extend in length (see this as inventory) as people get ahead of the constraint. The line can be held together by allowing the bottleneck to determine the pace. The performance of the entire line can be improved by making the slowest person walk faster.

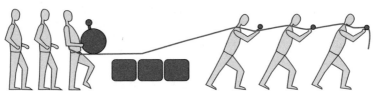
Figure 47.1 Theory of constraints illustrated

When to use it

The TOC is used to maximise the output of a production system. The goal is to generate money. Goldratt and Cox focus on different financial and operational indicators that contribute to the goal:

- Output (throughput) – the difference between inbound and outbound cash flow.
- Inventory – all financial means invested in the system for acquiring assets, which should be sold.
- Operational costs – all costs made by the system for transforming inventory into output (e.g. labour costs, material costs, depreciation).

Goldratt and Cox state that to generate as much money as possible, the output of the system should be maximised. The result is an operational focus devoted more to improving the throughput and throughput time, than merely to reducing costs. If applied correctly, the TOC may prevent a common mistake made as a result of efficiency thinking: instead of maximising the use of the most expensive machine to discount the smallest price per product, it may be more effective to increase the output of an old, depreciated machine (the bottleneck).

How to use it

TOC focuses on system improvement. A system is defined as a series of interdependent processes. An analogy for a system is the chain: a group of interdependent links working together towards the overall goal. The constraint is a weak link. The performance of the entire chain is limited by the strength of the weakest link. In manufacturing processes, TOC concentrates on the process that slows the speed of the product through the system.

There are five steps in the theory of constraints:

1 Identify the constraint(s) in the system (identification of the constraint)

   The constraint is identified by various methods. The amount of work that is queuing in a process operation is a classic indicator of a constraint. Another example occurs when products are processed in batches.

2 Determine how the constraint(s) can be breached (exploitation of the constraint)

   Once the constraint has been identified, the process is improved or otherwise supported, to achieve its utmost capacity without major expensive upgrades or changes. In other words, the constraint is exploited.

3 Make everything subsidiary to the decision made in step 2 (subordinate other processes to the constraint)

When the constraining process is working at maximum capacity, the speeds of other subordinate processes are paced to the speed or capacity of the constraint. Some processes will sacrifice individual productivity for the benefit of the entire system. Subordinate processes are usually found ahead of the constraint in the value stream. Processes after the constraint are not a major concern – they are probably already producing below capacity because they have to wait for the constraining process.

4 Strengthen or breach the constraint(s) in the system (elevate the constraint)

If the output of the overall system is not satisfactory, further improvement is required. The firm may now contemplate major changes to the constraint. Changes can involve capital improvement, reorganisation or other major expenditures of time or money. This is called elevating the constraint, or taking whatever action is necessary to eliminate it.

5 As soon as a constraint is breached, return to step 1 (repeat the cycle)

Do not let inertia introduce a new constraint in the system. Once the first constraint has been broken, another part of the system or process chain becomes the new constraint. Now is the time to repeat the cycle of improvement. The performance of the entire system is re-evaluated by searching for the new constraint, exploiting, subordinating and elevating it.

By focusing on constraints, this methodology produces positive effects on the flow-time of the product or service through the system. Reduction of waste increases throughput and improves throughput-time. When the constraint is improved, variation is reduced and quality is improved. Constraint focus does not require an intimate knowledge of data analysis, or that a large number of people understand the elements of the system. Understanding by a few people with the power to change things is all that is necessary. The effort can be localised with minimum involvement of the workforce.

When performing the steps, bear in mind that there are two kinds of constraints:

● Internal constraints: limitations within the boundaries of the system and the organisation which prevent the goal from being achieved. For example, insufficient capacity, but also managerial and behavioural restrictions are internal constraints.

● External constraints: limitations outside the boundaries of the system, which prevent the goal from being achieved, for example, declining demand, overcapacity and competition.

Goldratt makes frequent use of a current reality tree (CRT) with un-desired effect (UDE) for finding the bottleneck and determining the optimal solution. These techniques are illustrated in Goldratt's book *It's Not Luck,* and are similar to the methods used in *root cause analysis* (see p. 224).

Final analysis

Searching for and determining constraints is one of the key elements of the theory of constraints. In this way, frequent inventory, failure and stoppage are examined. However, one should not only consider the technical and logistical aspects of bottlenecks. The organisational and information aspects are also important.

TOC methodology operates on several assumptions:

- As in the case of lean (see p. 147), the organisation places a value on the speed at which its product or service travels through the system. Speed and volume are the main determinants of success.
- Current processes are essential to produce the desired output.
- The product or service design is stable.

Value-added workers do not need to have an in-depth understanding of this improvement methodology. Suggestions by the workforce are not considered vital for the successful implementation of the theory of constraints. Organisations with a hierarchical structure and centralised knowledge value this approach.

The main critics of TOC concentrate on the fact that bottlenecks may shift, as many different products may be produced by the same system. Depending on the process times, the bottleneck may vary for different products. Moreover, different types of product introduce variability that can only be buffered by time, capacity and inventory. The TOC considers capacity only. However, if variability is neglected, large increases of work-in-progress (and consequently throughput-time) may occur, which are in direct conflict with the goal.

References

Goldratt, E.M. and Cox, J. (1984) *The Goal: A process of ongoing improvement.* Great Barrington, MA: North River Press.

Goldratt, E.M. (1994) *It's Not Luck*, Great Barrington, MA: North River Press.

48

Vendor managed inventory

The big picture

Vendor managed inventory (VMI) is a means to optimise supply chain performance in which the supplier is responsible for maintaining the retailer's inventory levels. The supplier has access to the retailer's inventory data and is responsible for generating purchase orders.

When firms in a supply chain decide to collaborate, the resulting level of collaboration generally extends beyond a better exchange of information; the co-ordination activities and processes also improve (on a reciprocal basis). One example of this type of collaboration is VMI, in which a buyer agrees to authorise a supplier (i.e. a vendor) to manage the entire replenishment process, and to give him the responsibility for controlling the retailer's stock levels. In simple terms, the supplier is given the task of keeping the retailer's warehouse stocked with the supplier's products, so that they can both focus on the more important question of how to sell more products to the end-consumer more efficiently. This changes the supplier's focus from getting the retailer to buy more, to helping the retailer to sell more.

To achieve this, the retailer provides the supplier with access to inventory and demand information (either physically, or via highly automated electronic messaging systems), and sets targets for availability. The supplier periodically takes re-supply decisions regarding order quantities, shipping and timing. As a result, instead of waiting for the retailer to re-order, the supplier initiates replenishment transactions. VMI is an efficient replenishment practice that enables the supplier to respond to demand without the biased effect of purchasing decisions in the retail chain (e.g. the bullwhip effect). Moreover, VMI is designed to cut or at least minimise supply shortages, as well as reducing the costs of all the supply chain members. Accordingly, the measure of a supplier's performance is no longer delivery time, but the availability of inventory and inventory turnover.

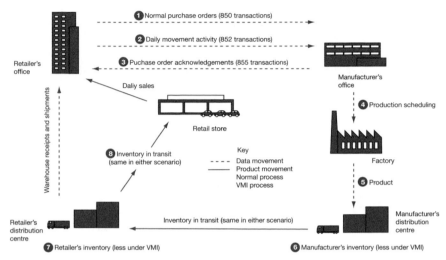

Figure 48.1 Vendor managed inventory

When to use it

Some researchers stipulate that VMI is especially suitable in relatively stable environments with little demand uncertainty and high-volume standard items. However, both empirical and simulation studies indicate that VMI is also much more efficient than traditional replenishment methods for low-volume products with high demand variability, although the implementation of VMI in this type of environment is more laborious.

VMI is a particularly promising opportunity for suppliers, as it allows them to have less excess capacity and achieve high production efficiencies without increasing inventory or reducing order fulfilment goals. Moreover, when resource capacity is scarce, it is extremely useful to know which deliveries can be delayed without causing lost sales for the retailer.

How to use it

We have identified various general, and some supplier- and retailer-specific implications of VMI. All the participating firms must realise that a successful VMI implementation depends heavily on inter-organisational relationships. If VMI is considered as a purely technical solution, which does not take the social and human aspects of the people involved into account, it is unlikely to deliver the promised benefits. Indeed, VMI requires effective teamwork and the committed participation of all the firms involved. VMI will obviously fail without the necessary relationships, supply chain metrics and the right organisational structure.

From a retailer's perspective, the decision to adopt VMI can be made without concern for the supplier's relationships with other customers. In addition, retailers may be reluctant to abandon purchasing activities, as purchasing is generally regarded as one of the core competencies (see p. 20) of the firm. Accordingly, organisation incentives and metrics must be aligned with VMI goals. For example, sales bonuses are often tied to short-term sales goals that are inconsistent with VMI. In addition, retailers should monitor the supplier's performance by their own service level to the customers, as this is the ultimate objective of efficient replenishment. Nevertheless, VMI resolves the problem of conflicting performance measures at both inventory and customer service level.

For suppliers, the major advantage is that VMI mitigates uncertainty of demand, allowing smaller buffers of capacity and inventory. The supplier has better opportunities to co-ordinate shipments to different customers, and can schedule – either postpone or advance – shipments according to production schedules, customer inventory situations and transportation capacity. The frequency of shipments is usually increased in VMI.

Co-ordination of replenishment orders and deliveries across multiple retailers helps to improve service. A non-critical delivery for one retailer can be diverted for a day or two to enable a critical delivery to another retailer. Similarly, a smaller than usual replenishment to one retailer may enable a larger than usual shipment to another retailer in direct need. With the ability to balance the needs of all partners, the supplier can improve the system's performance without jeopardising any individual retailer. Retailers benefit from the assurance that their most critical needs will receive the closest attention. Without VMI, the supplier has a difficult time prioritising shipments effectively.

An interesting side-effect of VMI is that the delivery service also improves for other retailers who are not engaged in VMI, but who buy from a supplier who is engaged in VMI with other retailers. This is the result of the supplier's ability to plan production more efficiently, and consequently improve delivery services in general. In addition, sales are increased as a result of improved service levels due to better product availability. Accordingly, profitability is increased for all of the firms in the chain.

The benefits of VMI are numerous for both supplier and retailer

Dual benefits:

- Data entry errors are reduced due to computer-to-computer communications. The speed of the processing is also improved.
- Both parties are interested in giving better service to the end-customer. Having the correct item in stock when the end-customer needs it benefits all parties involved.

- A true partnership is formed between the supplier and the retailer. They work together more closely and strengthen their ties.
- Stabilisation of the timing of purchase orders (which are generated on a pre-defined basis in practice).

Retailer's benefits:
- The goal is to achieve an improvement in fill rates from the supplier and to the end-customer, a decrease in out-of-stock probability, and a decrease in inventory levels.
- Planning and ordering costs will decrease due to the responsibility being shifted to the supplier.
- The overall service level is improved by having the right product available at the right time.
- The supplier is more focused than ever on providing an excellent service.

Supplier's benefits:
- Visibility of the retailer's point-of-sale data makes forecasting easier.
- Promotions can be more easily incorporated in the inventory plan.
- A reduction in retailer order errors (which would previously probably have resulted in a return).
- Visibility of stock levels helps to identify priorities (replenishing for stock or a stock-out). Before VMI, a supplier had no overview of the quantity or the products that were ordered. With VMI, the supplier can see the potential need for an item before it is ordered.

Final analysis

While VMI was already popular with Wal-Mart and Procter & Gamble in the late 1980s, it has recently received a lot of attention only because of the emergence of sophisticated information and communication technologies that enable real-time data transfer. Indeed, since the implementation of VMI at the above-mentioned firms, it has become increasingly popular in various industries, and has gained the attention of firms such as Kmart, Dillard Department Stores, JCPenney, Campbell Soup, Johnson & Johnson and Barilla.

The electronic information exchanged between supplier and retailer is the most critical part of VMI implementation. Indeed, successful implementation of VMI often depends on integrated information systems, including computer platforms, communications technology, product identification and tracking systems. Dissimilar protocols and uncommon product numbering will therefore hinder the adoption of VMI.

Reference

Paquette, L. (2003) *The Sourcing Solution: A step-by-step guide to creating a successful purchasing program*. New York: AMACON.

Notes

1 For more information on the prisoner's dilemma, we refer to
   http://en.wikipedia.org/wiki/Prisoners_dilemma
2 For more information on the chicken game, we refer to
   http://en.wikipedia.org/wiki/Chicken_(game)

[PART THREE]

Operational models

ese models help to change organisations and implement best ractices. In addition, this category covers models that help to ptimise operational processes and activities. They address the ho, what, when' questions when analysing and implementing excellent organisations.

The balanced scorecard (BSC)

49

The big picture

The balanced scorecard (BSC) was developed by Kaplan and Norton in 1992 as an alternative to traditional performance measurement approaches that focus solely on financial indicators, and are based purely on a company's past performance. The balanced scorecard is a top–down method for defining an organisation's goals and objectives. Key drivers within each perspective are based on the organisation's mission and vision, which clarify its long-term vision. Thus, an organisation is able to monitor its goals, strategy and objectives, and make any necessary corrective measures promptly.

When to use it

The BSC can be used as an alternative to traditional financial accounting methods that have become less appropriate for the operational running of a company. The balanced scorecard measures a company's performance across four perspectives: *financial*; *internal business processes*; *learning and growth*; and *customers*. Financial measures are complemented by non-financial measures that drive long-term financial success and ask the questions:

- What is important for our shareholders?
- How do customers perceive us?

- Which internal processes can add value?
- Are we innovative and ready for the future?

The balanced scorecard is used to monitor organisational performance transparently and via multiple measures. It enables management to take appropriate corrective action when necessary, which will lead ultimately to substantial and lasting performance improvement.

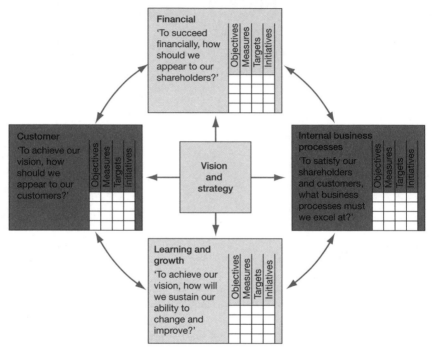

Figure 49.1 The balanced score card

How to use it

To create a balanced scorecard, a company first has to define its mission and vision, as this determines the success factors and key performance indicators from four different perspectives:

Financial perspective. Managers still need timely and accurate financial data to manage their business. Important indicators are return on investment (ROI) and added economic value, however, other measures can be added depending on the characteristics of the company, and of the industry in which it operates.

Customer perspective. Customer service and satisfaction are viewed as important issues for all organisations, as poor customer performance ultimately leads to a company's decline – dissatisfied customers will find other suppliers to fulfil their needs! Measuring satisfaction, retention, market and account share provides an insight into how customers perceive the company. Possible indicators include customer profitability, return policy, handling service calls, market share in target segments, and claims and complaints handling.

Internal process. Indicators for this perspective give management an insight into the effectiveness of their operations. Quality, response and cycle time, costs, new product development, time-to-market, but also break-even time realised, and new sales as a percentage of total sales, are indicators for measuring the performance of a company's operation.

Learning and growth. Indicators for the Learning and Growth perspective provide an insight into how successful human resources management and knowledge, and innovation management are. Possible indicators are employee satisfaction and retention, revenue / value added per employee, strategic redundancy in job skills, new ideas per employee, and information availability relative to need.

Do's

- Use the balanced scorecard to articulate your strategy, to communicate your strategy, and to help align individual, organisational and cross-departmental initiatives to achieve a common goal.
- Refresh the balanced scorecard as often as needed, so that you can focus on and monitor the right goals.

Don'ts

- The balanced scorecard is not a tool for controlling behaviour or evaluating past performance.

Final analysis

There is nothing new about the call for measuring non-financial indicators, but Kaplan and Norton (1992) have to be given the credit for advocating the impact of balanced measures from different perspectives. A CEO is likely to be biased towards financial measures, although nowadays, the management of a company based solely on financial indicators is inadequate. The balanced scorecard forces a company to focus on a balanced set of key performance indicators which are recognisable throughout the organisation, and which will lead ultimately to substantial and lasting performance improvement.

However, it is not an easy task to find a correctly balanced set of performance indicators. Note that an appropriate number of indicators in a balanced scorecard for top-management is 12 to 16 if there is full consensus in a company's management team regarding these indicators. In addition, the main indicators have to be broken down into underlying indicators that can be acted upon by middle and lower management. Otherwise, there is a risk that employees will focus only on the few overall goals on the scorecard. Finally, the balanced scorecard has to be updated regularly, depending on the type of business, to prevent the wrong measures being carried out.

References

Kaplan, R. and Norton, D. (1992) 'The Balanced Scorecard: Measures that drive performance'. *Harvard Business Review* January / February 1992 Vol. 70 Issue 1 pp. 71–80.

Kaplan, R. and Norton, D. (1996) *The Balanced Scorecard: Translating strategy into action*. Cambridge, MA: Harvard Business School Press.

Belbin's team roles

50

The big picture

Belbin (1985) distinguishes nine complementary roles of successful business teams that can be classified as:

People-oriented roles	Cerebral-oriented roles	Action-orientated roles
1. co-ordinator	4. 'plant' / creator / inventor	7. shaper
2. team worker	5. monitor / evaluator	8. implementer
3. resource investigator	6. specialist	9. finisher

1   The *co-ordinator* is a mature and confident person. They probably bring experience as a chairperson or leader of some kind to the table. This person clarifies goals, encourages decision-making, and delegates tasks, but can, however, be manipulative or bossy, especially when they let others do work that they could and should do themselves.

2   The *team worker* is co-operative, mild, perceptive and diplomatic. Put succinctly, everybody's friend. The team worker listens, builds, balances and averts friction. Their inherent indecisiveness surfaces in crunch situations. The doers in the team tend to think the team worker talks too much.

3   The *resource investigator* is an enthusiastic, communicative extrovert who

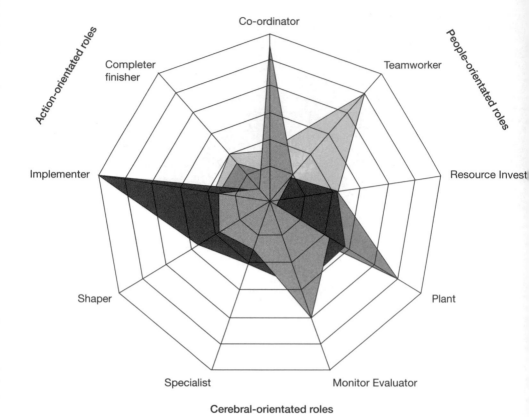

Figure 50.1 Belbin's complementary roles plotted

explores opportunities and develops contacts that they think will benefit them at some stage. Although opportunistic and optimistic, the resource investigator tends to have a short attention span and quickly loses interest.

4 The *'plant'* is Belbin's name for the creator or inventor. The plant is creative and imaginative, even brilliant at times. Their unorthodox thinking helps to resolve difficult problems. The plant ignores incidentals and is too preoccupied to communicate effectively. The problem is that this self-aware genius has a tendency to irritate other team members.

5 The *monitor* evaluates actions and ponders the strategy. This person is sober yet discerning, and keeps track of progress. They oversee all options and judge accurately, but lack drive and the ability to inspire others.

6 The *specialist* is a single-minded, dedicated self-starter. The specialist provides rare knowledge and skills, therefore their contribution is limited to a narrow front. This person enjoys technicalities and needs to be told to get to the point.

7 The *shaper* is challenging, dynamic and thrives on pressure. They have the drive and courage to overcome obstacles, see no evil and hear no evil. The shaper might annoy people in their zealous to efforts get things going.

8 The *implementer* is a disciplined, reliable, conservative and efficient person who turns ideas into practical actions. Once at work, the implementer will keep going and stick to the plan. This person might be a little rigid and unwilling to adopt alternative approaches or solutions along the way.

9 The *finisher* is meticulous, punctual, conscientious and anxious to make sure that everything turns out perfectly. The finisher delivers on time, but sometimes worries too much. They certainly hate to delegate work, feeling that nobody else seems to understand that it has to be perfect.

When to use it

Analysis of (the roles of) team members using the Belbin model is especially useful in situations where a team must be created that can undertake an assignment requiring a certain set of skills and combination of roles, or to optimise co-operation in an existing team.

In order to make use of the model, members of a prospective team should first determine which roles they can and want to fulfil. Each member should subsequently be assessed to see whether, and to what extent, they could play one or more of the nine roles.

Such an assessment is in itself beneficial, in that it encourages individuals to take a closer look at their own strengths and weaknesses, those of the other team members, and their co-operation. These can then be exploited or corrected as necessary, resulting ultimately in a more flexible, complementary, and stronger team.

How to use it

The assessment can be done in various ways:

- self-assessment (apply scores, rank, rate or distribute weights), possibly supervised by a third party;
- team assessment (let the team work on a small assignment or game, and let the members grade each other);
- assessment by an unprejudiced individual such as a mentor, a former team member, or perhaps a co-worker or supervisor.

With a profile of each team member's ability to fulfil one or more roles, it is possible to detect the potential under- or over-representation of certain roles in the team. If necessary, management may decide to use this information to pay greater attention to certain roles during the execution of team tasks, and to make arrangements regarding the way in which the team members work together.

Final analysis

The way Belbin observes teams and the roles of team members assumes that there is an objective basis for assessing team members, but this is open to debate. A team assessment based on Belbin's team roles is nonetheless a very useful exercise.

People will recognise themselves and team dynamics in this model. While the different roles are complementary, it can be fatal to have too many representatives of the same type of role in one team: too many co-ordinators in the same team results in a clash, and having two monitors in the same team may hold up a team's progress because they keep waiting for others to take action.

The model does not address the importance of interpersonal relationships within a team. Many teams that look good on paper fail to function properly in practice because they do not 'click'. The reverse is also true: for example, a person who has no history of being a co-ordinator may rise to the occasion and fill a vacuum.

Reference

Belbin, R.M. (1985) *Management Teams: Why they succeed or fail*. London: Heinemann.

The branding pentagram

51

The big picture

The branding pentagram is a model that helps to translate corporate strategy into branding policy by stating the branding principles, 'loading' the brand, choosing the desired positioning, and translating branding into everyday actions.

When to use it

The branding pentagram is useful for organisations that are willing to develop or improve their branding. It serves as a framework to define the brand and its strategy:

- *Who* is the product or service for?
- *What* does the product or service do?
- *How* is it useful to me as a client?

A brand is the complete set of signals that surround a product, service or company. Branding is the process of managing these signals in a structured and consistent way. The branding pentagram is a framework for evaluating and elaborating five integral factors that influence branding strategy. The pentagram consists of five inter-related points:

1 Principals of branding;
2 Positioning;
3 Consistency in brand carriers;
4 Embedding the branding; and
5 Planning and control cycle.

By covering these five points, an organisation not only states its brand(s) and branding policy, but also incorporates relevant branding activities into the organisation's daily practice.

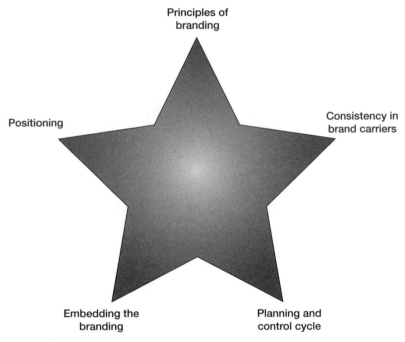

Figure 51.1 The branding pentagram

How to use it

The five points of the pentagram can be addressed by elaborating on the following aspects, in the following order:

1. Principles of branding

The principles of branding consist of:

- Brand mission: Which goals do I eventually want to achieve with the brand?

- Desired brand perception: What are the core values of the brand?
- Brand architecture: What are my choices regarding the brand portfolio?

2. Positioning

The positioning of the brand can be chosen based on:

- Segmentation: Which segmentation criteria are used?
- Target group: Which target group(s) is the brand aimed at (client / end-user)?
- Position: How does the brand distinguish itself compared to (the critical success factors of) the competitors? This should be measured both in terms of the product offered (the proposal to the clients) and the performance of the organisation (the clients' perception).

3. Consistency in brand carriers

To maximise the effect of the brand, there must be consistency in the way the brand is carried. Consistency in brand carriers can be created by creating consistency in the way the brand is carried by the different products and services of the organisation, and by how the brand is 'carried out' and spoken of by the employees of the organisation or the employees of an intermediary. Further consistency can be guarded via the different means the organisation uses to communicate.

4. Embedding the branding

This starts by ensuring consistency. The brand policy needs to align consistently with underlying functions and responsibilities. Responsibilities and authority for branding should be assigned to one of the management team or board members. A person should be appointed who will have direct responsibility for branding. Branding should be embedded by anchoring it in the organisation's culture and the behaviour of its employees.

5. Planning and control cycle

This starts with the formulation of SMART (Specific, Measurable, Achievable, Relevant, Time-specific) targets of brand policy for both the short and the long term. Next, the planning and control cycle can be developed by determining the measuring method. The method must enable measurement of the degree of realisation, and the evaluation of the measured degree(s) of realisation. Furthermore, this method must give input and initiation to adjustment based on the evaluation.

'Branding' is optimal when the *real* brand experience is equal to the *desired* brand experience. In such a case, the branding confers a sustainable, competitive advantage. Conversely, unsuccessful branding has a negative effect on a firm's competitive advantage.

Final analysis

Where brands are concerned, bear the following in mind:

- Brands, and therefore branding are subjective by nature.
- Many of the world's best brands are companies, rather than specific products. A brand can just as easily be a service, an organisation or even an aspiration.
- Brands can take many forms and are not just names, nor are they restricted to physical products.

The model does not fill in the branding strategy of an organisation. It merely serves as a framework on which a company can build. The use of the model is therefore limited to *which aspects* should be borne in mind when elaborating a brand strategy, not *what the content* of the aspects should be.

Reference

Baker, M. and Hart, S. (1999) *Product Strategy and Management.* Harlow: Pearson Education.

Change quadrants

52

The big picture

The basic premise of the model is that the most appropriate change strategy depends on whether an organisation is *warm* or *cold*, and whether the motivation for change is *warm* or *cold*. A cold organisation is one where rules, regulations, systems, structures and procedures drive direction, control and co-ordination to get results; there is little or no intrinsic willingness to (out)perform. In a warm organisation, it is shared norms and values and a common understanding of direction that make the organisation work.

A cold motivation for change is an objective response to a situation or emergency, such as a near bankruptcy, a drastic drop in market share, revenues, profits or an unavoidable (new) competitive threat. A warm motivation for change, on the other hand, is driven primarily by personal and professional ambitions. Based on the various warm / cold combinations of organisation and change, there are four possible change strategies: *intervention*, *implementation*, *transformation* and *innovation*.

When to use it

The change quadrants can be useful in determining the change agents; identifying active participants in the change process; and establishing the scope and timing of change, in order to maximise the success of the change efforts. The model is used to determine the right change strategy, given the type of change and the type of organisation in which the change is being proposed. The model of change quadrants is drawn up based on interviews with key figures within the organisation. This qualitative analysis is the key to determining the most suitable strategy for change.

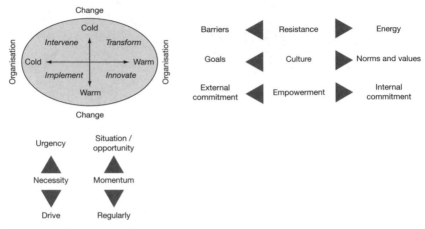

Figure 52.1 Change quadrants

How to use it

By analysing both the type of organisation and the type of change motives, an appropriate change strategy can be determined according to the table below.

Warm organisation that is willing	Warm organisation that is obligated
Adopting the energy and ambition to create a long-term vision and realising it. Motivation to build something new together. Openness to bottom–up creativity. Final goal is open to change. RENEWING	Efficiently using available ideas according to the final goal. Participation is based on clear final goals. Large participation but because of time pressure it is not always possible to have a say. TRANSFORMING
Cold organisation that is willing	**Cold organisation that is obligated**
Mobilising the organisation to make the use for change clear. Top–down, driven by ambitions of management. Moving the employees through middle managers. IMPLEMENTING	Top–down design and implementation of change. Employees are being asked for a say only concerning operational consequences of the definite final goal. INTERVENING

Figure 52.2 Four strategies for change

Final analysis

The change quadrants model is often used in conjunction with other models and change management approaches, for example Kotter's (1990) eight phases of change (see p. 140).

In addition to the change quadrants, the style and preferences of management should also be reflected in the change management approach. A mismatch between organisation and proposed change, combined with the feelings and personal style of management could obstruct the process. Bear in mind that a 'cold' change is easier to plan and communicate than a 'warm' one, and that many organisations believe themselves to be 'warmer' than they really are.

On the flip-side of the 'prescription' for warm or cold change, organisations should not exclude the option of 'warming up' or 'cooling down' before going through a change process, whether it be warm or cold.

Reference

Kotter, J.P. (1990) *A Force for Change: How leadership differs from management.* New York: Free Press.

53

Discounted cashflow

The big picture

This is a valuation method used to estimate the attractiveness of an investment opportunity. Discounted cash flow analysis (DCF) is an evaluation of the future net cash flows generated by a capital project by discounting them to their present-day value. It uses future free cash flow projections and discounts them (most often using the weighted average cost of capital) to arrive at a present value, which is used to evaluate the potential for investment. If the value arrived at through DCF analysis is higher than the current cost of the investment, the opportunity may be a good one. DCF converts future earnings into today's money.

When to use it

DCF is used for capital budgeting or investment decisions:

- to determine which investments projects a firm should accept;
- to determine the total amount of capital expenditure; and
- to determine how a portfolio of projects should be financed.

A relevant cost is an expected future cost that will differ from alternatives. The DCF method is an approach to valuation, whereby projected future cash flows are discounted at an interest rate that reflects the perceived risk of the cash flows. The interest rate is reflecting by the time value of money (investors could have invested in other opportunities) and a risk premium.

How to use it

The discounted cash flow can be calculated by projecting all future cash flows and making a calculated assumption on what the current value of that future cash flow is according to the following formula:

$$\sum_{1}^{n} \frac{\text{Future cash flows}}{(1 + \text{discount rate})^n}$$

The discount rate can be determined based on the risk-free rate plus a risk premium. Based on the economic principle that money loses value over time (time value of money), meaning that every investor would prefer to receive their money today rather than tomorrow, a small premium is incorporated in the discount rate to give investors a small compensation for receiving their money in the future rather than now. This premium is the so-called risk-free rate.

Next, a small compensation is incorporated against the risk that future cash flows may not eventually materialise, and that the investors will therefore not receive their money at all. This second compensation is the so-called risk premium, and it should reflect the so-called opportunity costs of the investors.

These two compensating factors, the risk-free rate and the risk premium, together determine the discount rate. With this discount rate, the future cash flow can be discounted to the present value. See the box for a calculation example.

Time	t	t + 1	t + 2	t + 3	t + 4 ... n
Investment	−15.000	−5.000	−5.000		
Cash flows		2.000	4.000	4.000	5.000
Total cash flow	−15.000	−3.000	−1.000	4.000	5.000
Discount rate = 10%					
Discount rate	0	0.91	0.83	0.75	0.68
$(1 / (1 + 10\%)^n)$					
Net Present Value (NPV)	15.000−	2.727−	826−	3.005	34.151
NPV total	18.602				

Final analysis

DCF models are powerful, but they do have their faults. DCF is merely a mechanical valuation tool, which makes it subject to the axiom 'garbage in, garbage out'. Small changes in inputs can result in large changes in the value of a company. The discount rate is especially difficult to calculate. Future cash flows are also hard to forecast, especially if the largest part of the future cash inflows is received after five or ten years.

Reference

Brealey, R.A. and Myers, S.C. (2003) *Principles of Corporate Finance*, 7th edition. London: McGraw-Hill.

Kaizen / Gemba

54

The big picture

Kaizen literally means change (*kai*) to become good (*zen*). Key elements of kaizen are: quality, effort, willingness to change and communication. The Gemba house, as the basis of kaizen, has five fundamental elements:

- teamwork;
- personal discipline;
- improved morale;
- quality circles; and
- suggestions for improvement.

Based on this foundation, kaizen focuses on the elimination of *muda* (waste and inefficiencies), the 5-S framework for good housekeeping and standardisation.

When to use it

Kaizen can be used to solve several types of problems: process inefficiencies, quality problems, large inventories and delivery and lead-time problems. Employees are encouraged to come up with suggestions during weekly meetings (kaizen events) for small and large improvements. Kaizen suggests eliminating *muda* (waste and inefficiencies) first. The types of waste are:

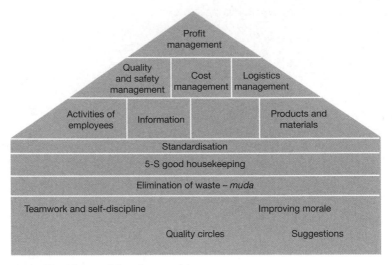

Figure 54.1 The Kaizen / Gemba model

- **Defective products.** Defects in quality prevent customers from accepting the manufactured product. The effort to create these defects is wasted. New waste management processes must be added in an effort to reclaim some value from an otherwise scrap product.

- **Over-production.** Over-production is the production or acquisition of items before they are actually required. It is the company's most dangerous waste, because it hides production problems. Over-production has to be stored, managed and protected.

- **Transportation.** Each time a product is moved, it runs the risk of being damaged, lost, delayed, etc., as well as being a cost with no added value. Transportation does contribute to the transformation to the product that the consumer is disposed to pay for.

- **Waiting.** Refers to the time spent by the workers waiting for resources to arrive, the queue for their products to empty, as well as the capital sunk into goods and services that have not yet been delivered to the customer. It is often the case that there are processes to manage this waiting.

- **Excess inventory.** Whether in the form of raw materials, work-in-progress (WIP), or finished goods, excess inventory represents a capital outlay that has not yet produced an income for either the producer or the consumer. If any of these three items are not being processed actively to add value, it is waste.

- **Motion.** In contrast to transportation, motion refers to the worker or equipment, and is represented by damage, wear and safety. It also includes the fixed assets and expenses incurred in the production process.

- **Extra processing.** Using a more expensive or otherwise valuable resource than is required for the task, or adding features that are included in the design but are not needed by the customer. There is a particular problem with this factor. People may need to perform tasks for which they are over-qualified to maintain their competency. This training cost can be used to offset the waste associated with over-processing.

After the reduction of waste, good housekeeping based on the 5-S method is put forward, which comprises:

- *Seiri* – tidiness. Separate what is necessary for the work from what is not. This should help to simplify the work.
- *Seiton* – orderliness. You can increase efficiency by making deliberate decisions regarding the allocation of materials, equipment, files, etc.
- *Seiso* – cleanliness. Everyone should help to keep things clean, organised and looking neat and attractive.
- *Seiketsu* – standardised clean-up. The regularity and institutionalisation of keeping things clean and organised as part of 'visual management', is an effective means of continuous improvement.
- *Shitsuke* – discipline. Personal responsibility for living up to the other four Ss can make or break the success of housekeeping.

The last building block of the Gemba house is standardisation. Standardisation of practices and institutionalisation of the 5-Ss will make it easier for everyone in the organisation, including newcomers, to improve continuously, including newcomers. Top management plays an important role in guarding and acting for the widespread implementation and co-ordination of kaizen, the 5-S method and the standardisation of work.

Correct implementation of the kaizen concept will lead to:

- **improved productivity;**
- **improved quality;**
- **better safety;**
- **faster delivery;**
- **lower costs;**
- **greater customer satisfaction; and**
- **improved employee morale and job satisfaction.**

How to use it

The following steps should be taken in kaizen events:

- Define the problem and the goal of the event.
- Analyse the facts.
- Generate possible solutions.

- Plan the solution.
- Implement the solution.
- Check and secure the solution.

It is important that the solution is checked and secured. In the final phase of a kaizen event, people start to seek opportunities for new kaizen events, which may hamper the process of embedding each improvement into operational practice.

Final analysis

The kaizen philosophy resonates well with the speed of change at operational levels in the organisation. The sustainability of the improvements proposed and implemented by people on the work floor is perhaps the strongest argument in favour of kaizen. Its sheer simplicity makes implementation easy, although some cultures may not be as receptive to the high level of self-discipline that the Japanese are able to maintain.

Kaizen has more potential in incremental change situations than in abrupt turnarounds. A culture focused on short-term success and big 'hits' is not the right environment for kaizen. Co-operation and widespread discipline at all levels of the organisation are the absolute keys to its success.

Reference

Imai, M. (1997) *Gemba Kaizen: A commonsense, low-cost approach to management*. London: McGraw-Hill.

Mintzberg's management roles

55

The big picture

At the beginning of the twentieth century, the French industrialist Henri Fayol described the task of managers as being a combination of organising, co-ordinating, planning, controlling and commanding. Mintzberg, however, was not convinced that these five activities cover what managers actually do. Based on facts uncovered by extensive research, Mintzberg drew up a series of self-study questions for managers. By considering these questions in the light of the 'facts' as opposed to the 'myths' about the way in which they tend to work, managers are encouraged to find ways to circumvent potential problems.

Mintzberg identifies ten roles of managers, using formal authority and status as a starting point. These roles are divided into three inter-personal roles, which in turn give rise to three informational ones, followed by four decisional ones, as shown in the table.

Myth 1:	Myth 2:
Managers are reflective, systematic planners.	Effective managers have no regular duties to perform.
Fact:	**Fact:**
Managers work at an unrelenting pace; their activities are characterised by brevity, variety and discontinuity; they are strongly oriented to action and dislike reflective activities.	Managers perform a number of regular duties, including ritual and ceremony, negotiations, and processing soft information linking the organisation to its environment.

Myth 3:	Myth 4:
Senior managers need aggregated information, best provided by a formal management information system.	Management is a science and a profession.
Fact:	**Fact:**
Managers prefer verbal media, telephone calls and meetings to documents.	Managers' programmes (scheduling time, processing information, decision-making, etc.) are locked inside their brains.

Figure 55.1 Myths in management

When to use it

The idea is that, as a manager enacts their role, these aspects will come together as a *gestalt* (integrated whole) reflecting the manager's competencies associated with the roles. In a sense, therefore they act as evaluation criteria for assessing the performance of a manager in their role.

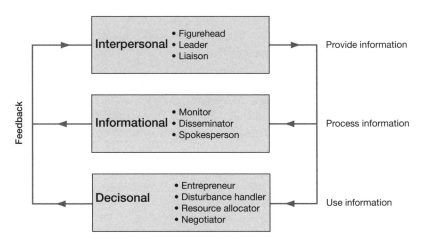

Figure 55.2 Mintzberg's management roles

Interpersonal	
Figurehead	Because of status and authority, the manager is the symbol of the organisation for social, inspirational, legal and ceremonial duties.
Leader	The manager leads the organisation. This role is at the heart of the manager–subordinate relationship and managerial power. The manager defines the activities and the structures and context within which subordinates work, encourages and disciplines them and tries to balance subordinate and organisational needs for efficient operations.
Liaison	This is the manager as an information and communication centre. Networking skills to shape and maintain internal and external contacts for information exchange are essential.
Informational	
Monitor	The manager seeks / receives information from many sources to evaluate the organisation's performance, well-being and situation. The role involves building and using an intelligent information system, by building contacts and by facilitating subordinates to provide relevant information.
Disseminator	The manager brings external views into their organisation and facilitates internal information flow between subordinates (factual or value-based). The role includes sharing and dissemination on the one hand and converting and assimilating information on the other. Communication skills – both internally and externally – are crucial for this role.
Spokesperson	The manager informs others outside their own organisation on behalf of their own organisation. For outsiders, the manager is the expert in the field in which their organisation operates. The role involves representative skills and the ability to interest others in the organisation.
Decisional	
Entrepreneur	As initiator / changer, the manager designs and initiates much of the controlled change in the organisation. Gaps are identified, improvement programmes defined and a series of related decisions are taken initiating activities to achieve actual improvement. The role involves designing and co-ordinating change programmes, including delegating responsibilities and empowering employees.
Disturbance handler	The manager takes charge when the organisation unexpectedly 'hits an iceberg' and where there is no clear programmed response. Disturbances may arise from staff, resources or unexpected events. The role involves calming, evaluating and resolving matters.
Resource allocator	The manager oversees allocation of all resources (monetary, staff, reputation, etc.) and setting organisational priorities. The role involves scheduling time, programming work(load) and authorising actions.
Negotiator	The manager takes charge over important negotiating activities with other organisations on behalf of their own.

Figure 55.2 Mintzberg's ten managerial roles

How to use it

The main value of the model is that it provides managers with a frame of reference. Consider your own work: which roles do you fulfil? Go through the roles in turn, and give yourself a score out of ten for each one. Low scores indicate weak areas, i.e. those to which more attention must be paid.

Mintzberg's management roles are not intended to be prescriptive. Rather, they serve as a looking-glass, providing managers with an insight into how they spend their time, on which activities and through which roles. Drawing attention to potential problems can go a long way towards remedying them. By dispelling the myths and highlighting the real nature of their work, managers can focus on how they can avoid the pitfalls and work in a more effective manner.

Final analysis

Despite the exponential growth in the number of management schools, according to Mintzberg, most of them focus on imparting knowledge in specialist areas such as accounting or marketing, rather than the skills needed to manage: resolving conflicts, establishing information networks and disseminating information. The model claims that managers need to be organisational generalists and specialists because of system imperfections and environmental pressures. At present, therefore, it is only by being introspective that managers can successfully learn 'on the job'. A number of studies have confirmed Mintzberg's theory, but they also show that the focus on specific management roles changes according to the hierarchical position of the manager.

References

Fayol, H. (1949) *General and Industrial Management*: London. Pitman Publishing Company.

Mintzberg, H. (1983) *Structure in Fives: Designing effective organizations*. Englewood Cliffs, NJ: Prentice-Hall.

Mintzberg. H. (1990) *Mintzberg on Management: Inside our strange world of organizations*. New York: Free Press.

Risk reward analysis

The big picture

The risk reward analysis charts potential rewards of strategic options against the associated risk. The result is an assessment of the attractiveness of strategic options, serving as a basis for decisions to allocate resources. The risk reward analysis works in the same way as a risk return analysis for evaluating financial products such as bonds and options.

Figure 56.1 The risk reward analysis model

When to use it

The risk reward analysis can be performed at any level of detail. The CEO could do it on the back of an envelope, or he might ask a team of analysts to perform a full-fledged analysis, including extensive market research, ROI calculations, scenario development and sensitivity analysis. The fundamental steps remain the same.

By using this tool one can compare completely different types of projects and combinations of projects. Combining projects may add up to a balanced resource allocation that fits the acceptable risk profile of the company. However, the model is not able to show variance in risk and reward if certain strategic options are combined in different models. The inter-connectedness of strategic options is not taken into account.

How to use it

Management and / or analysts should draw up a list of viable strategic options and their potential rewards. For example, options might include international market development; new product introduction; professionalising the purchase department; and outsourcing production. Together, investments, additional savings and / or reduced costs represent a potential reward that can be quantified. In addition, the choice might be rated based on qualitative factors such as improved image, expansion of strategic long-term freedom or the development of capabilities in an emerging field (e.g. technology).

A thorough analysis must be carried out for each strategic option to assess the associated risk. Factors to consider in this respect include the level of investment, industry threats, cut-off from other options, effects on supply chain relations and exit barriers.

Once all the options are plotted in the risk reward analysis chart (see figure 56.1), a brainstorming session is useful to find ways to reduce the risk associated with options that have high-reward potential. In a similar vein, methods must be found to increase the reward of relatively safe options. The risk reward analysis can be extended with a third dimension to become a risk reward *resource* analysis. The amount of resources required is then represented in the diagram by bubble-size. Options that require large amounts of resources are plotted with larger bubbles than options that require fewer resources. This enables one to trade off risks, rewards and resources or to find the best options.

Ultimately, the objective is to balance risks, rewards and resources according to the company's desired risk profile. Organisations with an aversion to risk will focus on decisions for the long-term continuation of the organisation, and will therefore accept fewer possible rewards. A more entrepreneurial, risk-seeking company might accept higher risks as it chases higher rewards. Nevertheless, there should be a positive balance between the two.

Final analysis

One of the prevailing pitfalls in strategic management is that decisions are made with limited information and a lack of multiple perspectives. Inaccurate, optimistic or unrealistic predictions about the potential rewards of strategic options push risk analysis into the background. The estimated risk on the other hand, tends to be under-estimated. The result is an over-valuation of the strategic options.

The drawback of the model is that the evaluation of the dimensions, risk, reward and possible resources, is the result of a complex interaction of factors. The weight of each factor and the inter-relation between factors are generally affected by emotions.

To maximise the effect of the use of the risk reward analysis, it is advisable to compare the possibilities extensively to minimise the number of strategic options. Furthermore, it is recommended that the details of all potential risks and rewards are sufficiently analysed. The greatest pitfall is to oversimplify the situation and not pay enough attention to the inter-relatedness and complexity of factors.

Reference

Sperandeo, V. (1994) *Trader VIC II: Principles of professional speculation.* Hoboken, NJ: John Wiley & Sons.

57

Root cause analysis / Pareto analysis

The big picture

Root cause analysis (RCA) is a class of problem-solving methods aimed at identifying the root causes of problems or events. It is based on the Ishikawa diagram (also fishbone diagram, or cause and effect diagram) named after its founder Kaoru Ishikawa (see figure 57.1). The Ishikawa diagram shows the causes of a certain event. It was first used in the 1960s, and is considered one of the seven basic tools of quality management, along with the histogram, Pareto chart, check sheet, control chart, flowchart and scatter diagram. This principle is used in root cause analysis and tries to explain the variations in a particular process. The analysis is generally used at the beginning of a business process redesign (BPR) project (see p. 97), or a quality management programme, for example with the EFQM excellence model (see p. 180). We have therefore ranked the model as operational.

When to use it

RCA is used to explain the variation in any process (or outcome of a process). A certain amount of variability is normal and does not necessarily cause significant disturbance. However, unwanted variation can cause serious losses or damage, delays and reduced productivity, especially if it occurs in critical processes. The first essential step is to find the causes of variation and to quantify the effect. The main causes, that are generally easy to solve, should be taken care of first. The technique is particularly valuable for the analysis of critical processes that show undesirable variance.

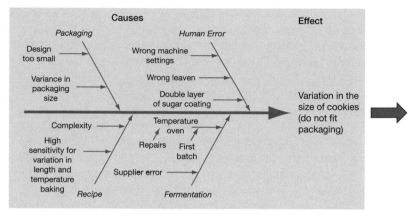

Figure 57.1a Cause effect diagram

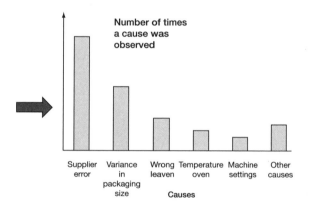

Figure 57.1b Pareto diagram

How to use it

RCA usually starts with the formation of a project team, including managers, suppliers, customers and employees. Next, the team defines the problem and decides which variation causes the most critical disturbance in the system under study. Then the team maps out the process and identifies the issues that can cause variance in the data- evidence-gathering phase. Next, issues that contributed to the problem are identified and their root causes found. However, the root causes might not be immediately evident, in which case brainstorming techniques are required. Subsequently, the root causes identified (usually large in number) are illustrated on a whiteboard in order to discuss and sharpen the findings. Recommendations for solutions then have to be developed and actually implemented.

The root causes can be organised by categorising them, and by distinguishing between main root causes and smaller effects. This provides the input needed to draw a 'cause and effect' diagram. The diagram provides an overview of the possible causes of variation. It is essential to study the possible root cause in the diagram in detail, to see the extent of the cause of variation. The Pareto diagram is often used to present the findings. Analysing root causes generally shows that 80 per cent of the variation is caused by 20 per cent of the causes.

Final analysis

Root cause analysis is not a single, sharply defined methodology; there are many different tools, processes and philosophies regarding RCA. To maximise the effect of the use of RCA, it is advisable to start with the most critical processes and / or the most disturbing variances. This ensures that success will propagate the broader use of the model. However, try to avoid finding causes of variation that have only a small effect on the lead-time, productivity or costs.

Reference

Blanchard, K.H., Schewe, C., Nelson, R. and Hiam, A. (1996) *Exploring the World of Business,* New York: W.H. Freeman.

58

The six thinking hats of de Bono

The big picture

De Bono's thinking hats represent six ways of thinking about strategies. Edward de Bono (1985) states that human cognition and thought consist of different types, approaches and orientations. Most people develop thinking habits that make them think in a limited way. De Bono believes that by defining the various approaches, people can become more productive and collaborative.

When to use it

The six thinking hats model forces us to shift from our normal way of thinking. As such, it helps us to understand the full complexity of a decision and see opportunities we would otherwise have missed; important decisions can be viewed from a number of different perspectives. The premise of the model is that people make better decisions if they are forced to move outside their habitual ways of thinking. This technique allows necessary emotion to be brought into what would otherwise be a purely rational decision. Thus, more creative and lateral thinking is encouraged. Furthermore, the technique can be used to speed up decision-making.

Hats	Focus	Typical questions
White	• Information / facts • Lacking information • Different kinds of information	• What information would we like? • What information do we need? • What information is available? • What information is lacking and how do we get it?
Red	• Feelings • Intuition	• What feelings do we have? • Are we committed to the subject? • What does our intuition say?
Black	• Downsides • Why it will not work • Pitfalls	• What are the risks? • What are the difficulties? • What are potential problems? • Does the idea suit the way we work?
Yellow	• Advantages • Optimism • Why it would work • Finding opportunities	• What are the advantages? • What are the good aspects? • How would it be feasible? • What are the potential opportunities?
Green	• Possibilities • Growth • New ideas • Creative thinking	• What other possibilities are there? • Can we challenge the existing situation?
Blue	• Management of communication • Summary and conclusions	• What are focal points? • Can we summarise? • What conclusions can we draw? • How do we proceed?

Figure 58.1 De Bono's six thinking hats

How to use it

The six thinking hats can be used in a meeting, a workshop or a brainstorming session, but it can also be used by individuals. Each thinking hat refers to a different style of thinking. If applied in a group, each participant wears the same hat at the same time.

De Bono distinguishes the following thinking hats:

- **White Hat (factual)**: With this hat, one can focus on available data. Analyse the information and see what can be learned from it.

- **Red Hat (emotional)**: With this hat, one considers the problem with intuition and emotion. Try to imagine how other people would respond emotionally, and try to understand these responses.

- **Black Hat (critical)**: With the black hat, one looks at all the bad points of the decision. Look in a cautious and defensive way: why would it work? Highlight the weak points in a plan.

- Yellow Hat (positive): With the yellow hat, one has to think positively. Look from an optimistic point of view and try to see all the benefits of the decision.
- Green Hat (creative): With the green hat, one thinks in a creative way. Create solutions to a problem in a free way of thinking.
- Blue Hat (process control): A blue hat is worn by the chairman of the meeting or workshop. The session leader intervenes in the process and says when to change hats.

Final analysis

This model allows for various ways of thinking, i.e. it allows a problem to be considered from a variety of perspectives. De Bono claims that the key to the successful use of this model is to choose a deliberate focus *during the discussion*. A particular approach has to be chosen that suits the needs of a particular stage in the discussion. Hence, a discussion may start with one hat to develop goals and objectives, while another hat may be used to collect reactions and opinions. By choosing a deliberate focus during each stage of the discussion, all people will simultaneously be focused on the same aspect of the 'problem', and thus be more collaborative in solving it and working towards a 'solution'.

Reference

Bono, E. de (1985) *6 Thinking Hats*. London: Little, Brown.

59

The Deming cycle: plan–do–check–act

The big picture

The Deming cycle or plan-do-check-act cycle (PDCA cycle) can be used as a method for structuring improvement projects. It refers to a logical sequence of four repetitive steps for continuous improvement and learning: *plan*, *do*, *check* and *act*. Planning ('plan') the improvement of an activity should be followed by execution of the activity ('do') according to the plan. One should then measure and study ('check') the results and the improvement. Action should then be taken ('act') towards adapting the objectives and / or improvement. The consequent learning should be implemented in planning the new activities.

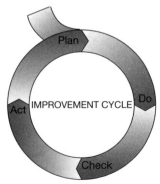

Figure 59.1 The Deming cycle four repetitive PDCA steps

When to use it

The PDCA cycle allows an organisation to manage improvement initiatives in a disciplined way. When confronted with this model for the first time, many will realise that they are steering, but not really managing their organisation. It can be used to structure and discipline the process of continuous improvement. Pictorially, the process of improvement may look as if we were rolling the PDCA wheel uphill (see figure 59.2). Each problem-solving cycle corresponds to a PDCA cycle.

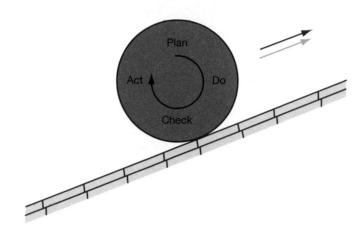

Figure 59.2 Continuous improvement with successive PDCA cycle

It is important to teach all the managers who have to work with this improvement method how to use the cycle. By making explicit use of the PDCA cycle, people will become aware of the improvements and benefits. This will encourage people to continue with the improvement projects. The cycle can be applied to different subjects, for example to achieving a mission, objectives, control points or in training.

How to use it

Go through the four steps systematically when pursuing improvement in specified activities:

1. Plan

Plan ahead for change. Analyse the current situation and the potential impact of any adjustments before you do anything else. Predict the various results expected, with or without the theory. How can you measure the impact? When has the desired result been achieved? Plan to include result measurement in the execution. Make an implementation plan with assigned responsibilities for participants.

Experience shows that it is useful to ask the following questions:

- What are we trying to achieve?
- How can this be linked to the higher purpose of our organisation?
- Who is / are going to be affected?
- Where will it happen?
- When will it happen?
- What is the step-by-step procedure?
- How can we measure the improvement, if at all?

2. Do

When executing the plan, you *must* take small steps in controlled circumstances in order to be able to attribute improvements (or failures) to the planned changes in the activity.

3. Check

Check the results of your experiment. Was the desired result achieved? If not, why not?

4. Act

Take action to standardise the process that produced the desired result, or in the event that the result proved to be other than what was desired, use the experience as input for new attempts at improvement.

Final analysis

Many organisations are unable to specify objectives, activities and desired results, let alone manage their own improvements systematically and consistently, with or without the PDCA cycle. In addition, it requires discipline to practise the whole PDCA cycle, to stop fire-fighting, and to stop undertaking only plan-do-plan-do. There have been several adaptations of the PDCA cycle. For example, *Plan* can be split into: determine goals and targets, and determine methods of reaching goals. *Do* can be split into training and education, and implementation. The PDCA cycle constitutes an important part of the kaizen thinking described in this book (see p. 213).

Reference

Walton, M. and Deming, W.E. (1986) *The Deming Management Method*. New York: Dodd.

60 Value stream mapping

The big picture

Lean (see p. 147) focuses on adding value for customers and eliminating non-value-adding steps (waste). Value stream mapping is used in lean environments to map and analyse both the value-adding and non-value-adding activities and steps in information flows and processes. It visualises which activities add value for a customer, and which activities do not. Because of its fixed structure, it is often possible to find substantial improvement potential and corresponding improvement actions.

When to use it

Value stream mapping is used in lean environments to identify opportunities for improvement in lead-time, as it identifies slack, waste and other non-value-adding activities. Mapping the processes involves making a diagram in which the processes, the material flows, the information flows on and all other important data (e.g. inventory levels, processing times and batch sizes) are visualised with the help of standardised frameworks and symbols; see Rother and Shook (2003). This map is the starting point for designing a desired future value stream that is lean.

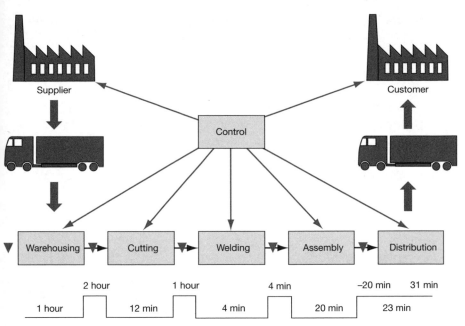

Figure 60.1 Example value stream map

How to use it

The first stage in value stream mapping is the preparation of the *current state map*. Analysing the material flow in its current state provides information about value- and non-value-adding activities (for example, machine time, unnecessary space, amount of rework, distance travelled and inefficiencies).

In the second stage, information from the current state map is used to prepare a desired *future state map*, where waste is eliminated, and the number of non-value-added activities is minimised. Questions that must be answered during this step are, for instance:

- What is the 'takt-time' (the desired time between units of production output, synchronised to customer demand)?
- Is it possible to introduce continuous flow?
- Can production be controlled with a pull system?

An important aspect to bear in mind during this stage is the need to adjust the production system to meet customer demand, while keeping the processes flexible. The third and most important stage is to take action to change the manufacturing process from its current state to resemble the desired state as closely as possible. Thereafter, the process can start at the beginning again.

A stepwise plan could look as follows:

1 Identify which product (group) or service (group) needs to be analysed. Compose a team of process-owners and employees who are involved in the different steps in the process.

2 Analyse the current state and translate this into a general process scheme.

3 Collect supporting data for the process scheme (e.g. throughput, throughput-times, employees).

4 Formulate the ideal process based on the demands of the customers. (In this step, use parameters such as minimal work in progress, short setup times and a list of improvements needed to arrive at the ideal future state into account.)

5 Determine an action plan for realising the improvements needed to arrive at the future state. This action plan should contain priorities for the different improvements; actions that are coupled to persons, a clear time path and the involvement of sponsors.

6 Monitor progress, and start again at step 1.

Final analysis

Value stream mapping comprises more than just eliminating waste. It is about the reduction of variability and levelling equipment utilisation. The core aim of value stream mapping is to process exactly what the customer wants. Therefore, the customer's demands and wishes have to be reviewed and assessed first. The data required for analysing the value stream may not always be present or available, perhaps because data are not systematically collected, or because it is the first time the administrative process is being analysed in this way. The consequence is that the analysis is more time-consuming due to extra data collection activities.

Another important condition is that everybody respects the agreed method of working, so that the design of the ideal process yields the desired results. This sounds simple, but practical problems often arise because people are used to a certain level of freedom in performing their activities. This option is now substantially restricted. Initiative will now have to be channelled differently. Instead of improvising, using the existing working method, one should now think of how the existing working method may be continuously improved.

Determining the desired future state is an important starting point for improvements. The action plan is an enabler that starts the implementation of the improvements. However, the new situation often requires new rules, and sometimes it requires new behaviour. If these two elements are not carefully taken into account in the action plan (and implementation), there is a risk of reverting to the old situation. Making the current state and future state maps is a waste of time unless the necessary follow-up action is taken.

Reference

Rother, M. and Shook, J. (2003) *Learning to See: Value stream mapping to add value and eliminate* muda. Cambridge, MA: Lean Enterprise Institute.

Appendix: Model matrix / categorisation of models

	Strategy and organisation	Finance and governance	Marketing and sales	Operations, supply chain management and procurement	Innovation and technology management	HRM, leadership and change
Strategic						
Ansoff's product market grid	X					
BCG matrix	X					
Blue Ocean Strategy					X	
Competitive analysis: Porters's five forces	X					
Core competences	X					
Greiner's growth model	X					
Kay's distinctive capabilities	X					
Market-driven organisation			X			
Off-shoring / outsourcing	X					
Roadmapping					X	
Scenario planning	X					
Strategic dialogue	X					
Strategic human capital planning						X
Strategic human resource management model						X
SWOT analysis	X					
The value chain	X					
Value-based management		X				
Value disciplines of Treacy and Wiersema	X					

	Strategy and organisation	Finance and governance	Marketing and sales	Operations, supply chain management and procurement	Innovation and technology management	HRM, leadership and change
Tactical						
7-S framework	X					
Activity-based costing	X					
Beer and Nohria – E & O theories						X
Benchmarking		X				
Business process redesign				X		
Competing values						X
Core quadrants						X
Covey's seven habits of highly effective people						X
Curry's pyramid			X			
DuPont analysis		X				
Factory gate pricing				X		
Henderson and Venkatraman – Strategic alignment					X	
Hofstede's cultural dimensions						X
House of purchasing and supply				X		
Innovation circle					X	
Kotler's 4Ps of marketing			X			
Kotter's eight phases of change						X
Kraljic's purchasing model				X		
Lean thinking / just-in-time				X		
MABA analysis			X			
Milkovich's compensation model						X
Mintzberg's configurations	X					
Monczka's purchasing model				X		
Overhead value analysis		X				
Quick response manufacturing				X		
Senge – The fifth discipline						X
Six sigma				X		
The EFQM excellence model	X					
Theory of constraints				X		
Vendor managed inventory				X		

	Strategy and organisation	Finance and governance	Marketing and sales	Operations, supply chain management and procurement	Innovation and technology management	HRM, leadership and change
Operational						
Balanced scorecard		X				
Belbin's team roles						X
Branding pentagram			X			
Change quadrants						X
DCF		X				
Kaizen / Gemba house				X		
Mintzberg's management roles						X
Risk reward analysis	X					
Root cause analysis / Pareto analysis				X		
Six thinking hats of de Bono						X
The Deming cycle: plan–do–check–act				X		
Value stream mapping				X		

Strategy and organisation

Ansoff's product market grid

BCG matrix

Competitive analysis: Porter's five forces

Core competencies

Greiner's growth model

Kay's distinctive capabilities

Off-shoring / outsourcing

Scenario planning

Strategic dialogue

SWOT analysis

The value chain

Value disciplines – Treacy and Wiersema

7-S framework

Mintzberg's configurations

The EFQM excellence model

Risk reward analysis

Finance and governance

Value-based management

Activity-based costing

Benchmarking

DuPont analysis

Overhead value analysis

Balanced scorecard

Discounted cash flow

Marketing and sales

Market-driven organisation

Curry's pyramid

Kotler's 4Ps of marketing

MABA analysis

Branding pentagram

Operations, supply chain management and procurement

Business process redesign

Factory gate pricing

House of purchasing and supply

Kraljic's purchasing model

Lean thinking / just-in-time

Monczka's purchasing model

Quick response manufacturing

Six sigma

Theory of constraints

Vendor managed inventory

Kaizen / Gemba house

Root cause analysis / Pareto analysis

The Deming cycle: plan–do–check–act

Value stream mapping

Innovation and technology management

Blue ocean strategy

Roadmapping

Henderson and Venkatraman's strategic alignment model

Innovation circle

HRM, leadership and change

Strategic human capital planning

Strategic human resource management model

Competing values

Core quadrants

Covey's seven habits of highly effective people

Hofstede's cultural dimensions

Milkovich's compensation model

Belbin's team roles

Mintzberg's management roles

Beer and Nohria – E & O theories

Change quadrants

Six thinking hats of de Bono

Senge – The fifth discipline

Kotter's eight phases of change

Activity-based costing

Ansoff's product / market grid

Balanced scorecard

BCG matrix

Beer and Nohria – E and O theories

Belbin's team roles

Benchmarking

Blue Ocean Strategy

Branding pentagram

Business process redesign

Change quadrants

Competing values

Competitive analysis: Porter's five forces

Core competencies

Core quadrants

Covey's seven habits of highly effective people

Curry's pyramid

DCF

DuPont analysis

The EFQM excellence model

Factory gate pricing

Greiner's growth model

Henderson and Venkatraman – strategic alignment model

Hofstede's cultural dimensions

House of purchasing and supply

Innovation circle

Kay's distinctive capabilities

Kotler's 4P's of marketing

Kotter's eight phases of change

Kraljic's purchasing model

Lean thinking / just-in-time

Off shoring / outsourcing

Overhead value analysis

Scenario planning

Senge – The fifth discipline

Six thinking hats of de Bono

Strategic dialogue

Strategic human capital planning

Strategic human resource management model

SWOT analysis

The value chain

Value disciplines of Treacy and Wiersema

7–S framework

MABA analysis

Market-driven organisation

Milkovich's compensation model

Mintzberg's configurations

Mintzberg's management roles

Monczka's purchasing model

Quick response manufacturing

Risk reward analysis

Roadmapping

Value-based management

Index

Read on...

80273719090

Key Management
Ratios
The 100+ ratios every manager needs to know

ISBN: 9780273719090
September 2008

Drawing data from 200 companies worldwide, this book brings clarity and simplicity to its explanation of every measure and shows how they all link together to drive your business. Its unique approach remains as classic as ever, bringing a simple and visual understanding to a complex subject.

80273722038

Key Marketing
Metrics
The 50+ metrics every manager needs to know

ISBN: 9780273722038
December 2008

A comprehensive, up-to-the-minute introduction to over 50 valuable marketing metrics. This book shows you how to use these metrics to maximise the return on your marketing investment and identify the best new opportunities for profit.

Linda

UK and decided to write after
the worst tea lady in the Bank
now lives and works in Sydney. S
film, TV and stage and teach
She is married with two children.

te tale of a teenager in trouble'
Daily Telegraph

ulously entertaining'
Achuka

Kelp

varm-hearted and
unny'
an

d quite hilarious'
Mail on Sunday

and bizarreness are delightful'
Guardian

. A genuinely funny novel'
Daily Telegraph

Linda
Aronson

MACMILLAN CHILDREN'S BOOKS

First published 2004 by Macmillan Children's Books
a division of Macmillan Publishers Limited
20 New Wharf Road, London N1 9RR
Basingstoke and Oxford
www.panmacmillan.com

Associated companies throughout the world

ISBN 0 330 48254 8

1 3 5 7 9 8 6 4 2

A CIP catalogue record for this book is available from
the British Library.

Typeset by Intype Libra Limited
Printed and bound in Great Britain by Mackays of Chatham plc, Kent

For Daniel Platt-Nolan

Acknowledgements

This novel took a long while to write and I am indebted to many people. For their patience, good humour and warm encouragement as the delays got longer I must thank everyone at Macmillan Children's Books UK and Penguin Australia, but most particularly Laura Harris, Dmetri Kakmi, Rebecca McNally, Gaby Morgan and Polly Nolan. Thank you for your faith in me. For their day-to-day support during the entire process I have as usual to thank my long-suffering family and my agents Geoffrey Radford and the late, much-missed, Tony Williams. For lending me their London flat in which to bury myself and write, special thanks go to Annie Platt and Daniel and Michael-James Platt-Nolan. Writers Ken Methold and Charles Harris combined astute technical advice with endless hospitality. Dr Kerryn Parry-Jones of the Wildlife Animal Rescue and Care Society of New South Wales invited me to visit the ARC flying fox sanctuary and helped me construct, in Jacinta Frye, a conservationist who would drive the saintliest of fellow-conservationists completely crazy. When the novel reached a reasonable draft, Lisa and Mark Aronson proofread and gave insightful feedback. They were followed in this process by Daniel Platt-Nolan, whose rigorous analysis and detailed advice were absolutely invaluable. Thank you to each and every one of you. I owe an enormous debt to you all.

1

It's eight-fifty-two on Tuesday morning and I'm holding a pair of chilled sheep's eyes. To be precise, I'm standing behind the curtains of the stage in the school hall holding a pair of chilled sheep's eyes because it's World Recycling Day.

It's not because I'm going to recycle the sheep's eyes.

It's because I'm in a drama presentation being put on in Assembly to make people feel guilty about plastic shopping bags wrecking the planet. To be honest, this isn't because I care about plastic shopping bags or the planet. It's because Suzie McLaren cares, and I'm trying to get her to go out with me. Which is why I'm doing everything I can to impress her, including volunteering to be in this way dumb drama presentation she made up.

Not that I've got a chance.

You get the picture of my love life if I tell you that my most recent relationship was with a girl called Kristen on holiday at Surfers. We spent three days walking round together a metre apart and trying to think of things to talk about. She then told me the only reason she was going round with me was because I was the only boy available. I couldn't really complain because the only reason I was going round with her was because she was the only girl available.

You see, Suzie is the best-looking girl in Year 8, and every boy from Year 7 to Year 9 is after her, including me. It'd be hard enough even if I wasn't short, chunky and the dream of every pimple cream manufacturer across a couple of continents. But to make things even more difficult, Suzie is a Clone.

You know Clones.

Clones are those amazingly clever, good-looking, clear-skinned, kind students who are brilliant at everything, from sport to dealing with smelly old people on speech nights. They're a Principal's dream. There's a whole mob of them in Year 12 and a sprinkling across the rest of the school.

When they're not raising money for the poor they're winning medals at State Sports Festivals. When they're not winning medals at State Sports Festivals, they're playing the piano in Assembly or going in debating championships or doing genius-level maths and worrying if they miss out on half a mark. I think of them as Clones because they're just too perfect to be human. I reckon the Government Education Department grows them in secret labs from the toenail clippings of fashion models and the navel fluff of dead professors or something so as to make the rest of us improve.

I mean, I don't want to sound slack, but if you're a genius you should at least have the decency to be weird, like my mate Bogle. And if you're really totally good-looking you should at least give the rest of us a chance by being like my other mate Pricey, who looks like he's lead singer from a boy band and is the nicest guy you could meet, but let's face it, is no rocket scientist. And if you're like me, plain ordinary, you should have a chance with someone like Suzie. I say, *should*; whether you do is a different matter.

There are three Clones in our class, which is unusual. There's Melissa Miller, who plays State level tennis and got a gold medal in the Schools Junior Science Competition. There's Jesse Park, who goes to University to do extra maths in the holidays and can't decide whether he should be a surgeon or a member of the Australian cricket team. And there's Suzie, Super-Clone, who I've been crazy about for ever and who's stunning and nice and brilliant at absolutely everything.

It all started two weeks ago. I whip in late to

Assembly, and, right at the only place I can sneak into line – there she is! The number of times I've tried to arrange this – and suddenly it happens. She smiles and shifts to give me a place. I'm dumbstruck. In my fantasies, this is where I strike up a fascinating conversation and she's totally impressed. In real life I suddenly remember I've got a zit the size of a peanut on the side of my nose facing her direction. As casually as I can, I clamp my hand over that side of my face, spreading my fingers.

I'm breaking out in a cold sweat. Bogle and Pricey are turning round and doing thumbs-up and 'go for it' gestures.

I sneak looks at her and rack my mind for something to say.

The Principal's raving on about how World Recycling Day is coming up and we should all think about recycling. And Suzie suddenly puts up her hand. Right in the middle of the Principal talking. This is the sort of thing Clones do. Anyone else would be put on detention for five years, but the Principal just stops respectfully and says, 'What is it, Suzie?'

To which Suzie flicks back her shining black hair and says, 'Well, Mr Cobbett, I feel we should do more than *think* about recycling. We should have special activities to educate people about it.'

4

The whole school stirs with surprise. A big rumble of approval goes up from all the teachers. Clint Pocky, class member most likely to end up a serial killer, does an armfart. Suzie starts into all this stuff about giving out prizes for good ideas on recycling and special certificates for the class who picks up most rubbish in the school grounds. I'm staring at her ear lobe like I'm hypnotized. She catches me looking up at her and beams. At that moment she says, 'And I'm sure there are heaps of people who'll volunteer.'

I'm gone. My hand shoots up. I volunteer for everything, from picking up rubbish in the school grounds to promising to busk in the shopping mall to raise funds for koalas with nasty diseases. I volunteer for so many things I lose count.

The result is that for the last two weeks I've gone to about three meetings a day and picked up two tonnes of rubbish. The idea is that I'll get to talk to Suzie. What actually happens is that I end up stuck with Jesse and Melissa, the other two Clones, while Suzie dashes off to a meeting to raise money for a community bus or do extra maths or read newspapers to old people at Yarradindi Retirement Village.

I haven't talked to Bogle and Pricey for days. The worst thing is that I've got caught up in all the other stuff that Clones do. And I'm exhausted.

Because the thing about Clones is that they do three times as much as everyone else.

So now that I'm an Honorary Clone, I end up getting sucked into things like Debating and Student Representative Council and, as of tomorrow, Big Kids, Little Kids, which is this thing where miniature thugs from Yarradindi Primary come to our school during lunch break for extra help with their reading.

It sounds like a con to me. It sounds like the teachers at Yarradindi Primary finally stumbled on a way to stop Year 3 gangsters setting light to their school during lunch break.

This is to send them to set light to our school during lunch break.

To cap it all, Fridays is Chess Club.

Let me tell you, you don't know what humiliation means until you're beaten at chess in four moves by an eight-year-old Clone who won't start the game until you have admired their Donald Duck pencil.

It's held in the Geography room with all the Clones bussed in from local schools. Everybody has to play several games. If you get defeated in the early rounds, you're out. I always get defeated in the early rounds. My first partner's normally a girl with a fluffy headband and a T-shirt with fairies on it. She takes five moves to wipe me out.

6

My second partner's got a runny nose and a handkerchief featuring Thomas the Tank Engine. He takes four moves to wipe me out.

My third partner's a Year 4 genius who at least has the decency to look like a toad. Last week he gets me in four moves and says, 'All you need is practice.' Patronizing little geek. I drawl, 'Ah well, you see, if you play chess too much, your willy drops off and rolls around in your underpants.'

His eyes widen. 'No way . . . !'

But even when I get to see Suzie, there are problems. The main one is my height. Because Suzie is so much taller than me, I need to stand on things to be at her eye level. So I've started pretending that I normally jump absent-mindedly on to low walls and seats while I'm having a conversation.

Now what happens is that on the few chances we get to meet I'm wrecked because I'm constantly jumping up on walls and leaping for low-hanging branches so I can hang there chatting while my arms feel like they're being ripped out of their sockets.

I keep swearing to myself I'll give all this up, but I can't. I take one look at Suzie and, before I know it, I'm volunteering for something else.

Which is why I'm standing here behind the curtains on the school stage, clutching these clammy sheep's eyes. If Suzie wanted me to, I'd clutch the clammy sheep as well. The presentation's called 'Earth, Our Home', and it's all about how rich countries are wrecking the world.

I couldn't care less if it was about the three bears. The point is, it gets me near to Suzie, and there's this cool bit where Suzie, who's playing the part of 'Conservation', puts her arm around me and says she'll teach me how to see. This is way cool because she's so tall I fit right into her armpit and get to take giant, dizzying whiffs of deodorant mixed with fabric softener through her cardigan.

You see, I'm playing the part of 'The Rich Countries'. All I have to do is hang around behind the curtains while Suzie raves on about how people are blind to pollution, particularly plastic bags. Which is where I come in. Because, in a really dramatic bit, my eyes get gouged out by 'Greed', which is played by Natasha Frye, class whacko.

Natasha's an environmentalist.

With the emphasis on mental.

At the moment she's out in front of the curtain, rabbiting on about soya beans. This has nothing to do with the play, but Natasha refused to take part in any presentation about the planet unless she could give a speech about vegetable protein.

She's only been at Yarradindi High for a couple of weeks. On her first day she released Year 7's stick insects back into the wild. On her second, she got put on detention for refusing to shut up in Biology about how other Greenies like her have proved cows' farts are destroying the atmosphere.

I check my watch. I'm getting nervous. Not that I have to do much. I have to wait for Natasha to say, 'I am Greed, and I rule the world!' and throw out her arm dramatically. I then come on and say, 'Yes. Pollution is necessary so that rich countries can stay rich.' At this point, Natasha pretends to poke my eyes out. I scream, 'I've lost my eyes!', let the sheep's eyes plop horribly on the stage with a little plastic bag of watery red paint for blood, and then wait for Suzie to clamp me under her armpit.

The eyeballs were Bogle's idea after he and Pricey came in to watch a rehearsal. They got them from the butcher's for us two days ago. We were worried they'd go off, so Mrs Bailey, our drama teacher, suggested we put them on a saucer in the staffroom fridge. This was a mistake, as they've gone all rubbery. Also, Mrs Wong came in at recess for her strawberry yogurt and nearly had a heart attack.

I sneak a look out through the gap in the curtain. We're getting near to where I come on. I get the plastic bag of blood out of my pocket. My heart's thumping at the thought of being in a clinch with Suzie. Natasha says, 'I am Greed!'

That's it! I'm on! In a few seconds I'll be in

Suzie's armpit! I burst through the curtains. I'm early. Natasha's just saying, 'I rule the world!' She throws out her arm dramatically and gets me full in the chest.

'Oomph!'

I reel back, winded. The sheep's eyes fly out of my hand. They hit the stage, bounce high in the air, arc out over the sea of faces and land right in the middle of Year 7.

2

Everyone screams.

Suzie yells, 'What are you doing?'

I'm gasping and wheezing. There's nearly a riot. The whole school's killing themselves laughing. I can't get away from Natasha! My watch strap's caught in her wild mop of frizzy blonde hair. I wrench my arm. She shrieks. The fake blood goes everywhere. Jesse's trying to untangle us. Somewhere up the back of the hall I can see the eyeballs flying through the air. People are chucking them around. Teachers are yelling and fighting their way through to the troublemakers. I catch Suzie's look of desperation.

I remember my lines and shout, 'I've lost my eyes!'

Cunningham, class psychopath and man-mountain, yells, 'No you haven't, they're up here by the fire extinguisher!'

Suzie's fighting back tears. Melissa's trying to sing a song about a dolphin dying because it's swallowed a plastic bag. One of the eyeballs flies up, smacks high up on a window and rebounds into the crowd. Clint Pocky, professional vandal, is pretending to eat the other one. Caroline Dillinger, class dobber, shouts, 'Mrs Bailey, Clint Pocky's pretending to eat an eyeball, Mrs Bailey!'

At which point Clint Pocky stops pretending to eat it and starts trying to stuff it down her back.

It's pandemonium.

Suzie runs off the stage in tears. Cunningham's laughing so much he's rolling on the floor like a beached whale, having a suck of Ventolin between laughing. Natasha's screeching as Jesse pulls at her hair. I could kill her. I deliberately wrench my entangled hand so it yanks at her frizzy mop.

I shout to Suzie, 'I'm sorry!' but she's gone.

Finally, when about forty people have been put on detention and the eyeballs have been confiscated, Mrs Bailey finds some scissors. She cuts my watch strap away from Natasha's head.

Half way through the hacking, I see something tucked up Natasha's sleeve. It's some kind of native mouse.

What a complete loon.

At last we're free. I rip the chunk of frizzed hair away from my watch strap and rush off to find Suzie.

*

I could die. I find her hunched over in the little room behind the stage. Her beautiful, shiny black hair swings down, screening her face, but you can see she's crying. Melissa and Jesse are trying to play it down. I stand on a crate and say that nobody in the audience really noticed. The truth is, the whole school thinks it's the funniest thing in living memory.

The lunch bell rings. Pricey and Bogle come up, killing themselves laughing.

Bogle says, 'That was so cool! That was the funniest!'

Pricey adds, 'My stomach's aching, man. When did you think of doing that?'

Great. Even my friends reckon I did it on purpose.

I make an excuse and head off after the Clones. I wish the ground would open and swallow me up. People are falling about, laughing. A whole mob of Year 10s come up, going 'Baaa' and asking me where I've left my eyes.

Clint and Cunningham come up, snorting with glee. Cunningham always gives off this weird, biscuity smell. He leans his big meaty gut over me and wheezes, 'Ay, when you chucked them eyeballs at the Principal . . . !'

Clint Pocky says, 'Tonight. Wanna come up the station sidings and do some graffiti?'

It's already turning into a legend. Suzie holds her head high, but her lips are trembling. She keeps saying the most important thing is that people remember the play.

Remember it. How could they ever forget? How can I ever forget?

Natasha Frye is hanging round near by with her normal sour frown. 'Look . . . Ian, I'm really sorry about what happened.'

'Yeah, so am I.'

Sorry, be blowed. She's one of the few girls in the class who are as short as I am, so I can stare her in the eye. I glare at her with total hatred.

The rest of World Recycling Day passes in a blur of total embarrassment. I keep apologizing to Suzie, but what use is an apology? There's a lunchtime competition to pick up the most rubbish from the school grounds and put it in hessian sacks lent by the Council. The prize is a fifty-dollar CD voucher, donated by the Yarradindi CD Mart, home of Year 12 gangsters.

A Year 10 team's in the lead with twelve sacks. This is until Mr Thompson twigs that as soon as one of them hands in a sack, another one's whipping round to the back of the pile, collecting it and handing it back in again at the front.

After school I hover near Suzie, Melissa and Jesse. I'd really like to walk home with them, but I haven't got the nerve. I peel off. I watch their three perfect shapes disappear down the street.

That stupid, idiotic Natasha. The drama presentation was my only chance with Suzie, and she wrecked it. In front of the whole school. Even the teachers were laughing. I mean, total humiliation.

I set off angrily for home. Someone's changed the street sign 'Fifth Avenue' to 'Filth Avenue'. As I stride through the shopping mall I have a flashback to one of the eyeballs bouncing off the piano and landing in Josh Tate's lap. I die with embarrassment. I have another flashback. It's Cunningham holding the two eyeballs up to his ears like earrings. Now it's Clint Pocky – putting the two eyeballs next to each other on his butt, so it looks like his bum's got eyes. I mean, why me? This is so slack. I could kill Natasha.

Some loony woman is standing next to the butcher's with a placard saying: 'Save native animals, don't eat them'. She's been doing this for weeks. She offers me a pamphlet. I ignore her and walk past. As if one Greenie idiot per day isn't enough.

Constable Platt patrols near by to keep an eye on her. He's Yarradindi's only policeman. He's irritable. He's always irritable when police work keeps him away from his hobby farm. This means every time you see him he's irritable except for when he's selling fruit at his roadside stall. Then he does this big welcoming act and pretends he didn't bellow at you for riding your bike through the pedestrian walkway in the shopping mall instead of wheeling it (when there are, like, two pedestrians there).

I stride up to the back gate behind our health food shop, kick it open viciously and find myself face to face with an emu, peering over the back of a strangely tilted and bouncing horse trailer.

Wait a minute.

An emu?

3

Of course. It's the Pockys. The Pockys live next door to us. To be exact, Syd and Granny Pocky live next door to us and run a motorbike repair place. The Pocky family's got about three hundred members. They're usually responsible for anything unlikely or violent in Yarradindi. This time, they're just about to open an emu farm on a swampy bit of land they own, downwind of Yarradindi tip.

This is against everybody's advice, because emu farms are well known for going broke and leaving people with five million emus that nobody wants.

It still doesn't explain why the emu's in a horse trailer in our back yard. I stare at it. It's like a scrawny-looking ostrich. It blinks its ping-pong-ball eyes, tips its head and stares back. There's a cheerful gargling roar.

'Aaah – shutta gate a case a emu escape, a flighty begga – aaah!'

It's Syd Pocky. Syd's the grandad of Clint Pocky from our class. He's a chunky little bloke with a bald head, blue shorts, a black singlet and a long line of tattoos up his arm. He looks exactly like Clint will look by the time he's sixty, unless Clint gets murdered in some kind of gang warfare, which is completely possible.

Syd's OK. In fact, he's a great mate of our family, despite the fact that we can't understand half of what he says. He and the Cannibals rescued me from the bush once when I got lost. The Cannibals are our local bikie gang. They're a bunch of old men and women who ride round Yarradindi dressed in black leather outfits with studs, assisting the needy – whether the needy want it or not.

They're always in and out of our health food shop for food and herbal remedies because they're all worried about their high blood pressure and varicose veins and they love to chat about them. In fact, I'd say I know a lot more about varicose veins than I need to.

I come into our yard and close the gate. I realize the horse trailer is tilting and bouncing because it's being jacked up by Granny Pocky, Syd's wife. She's small and skinny and dressed exactly like Syd except for the bald head. Her strength always amazes me. So does the crocodile tattooed in her cleavage.

'G'day Ian! We got a flat!'

She beams and pumps away at the jack. The horse

trailer bounces and tilts, and the crocodile jerks in a web of leathery brown wrinkles.

Syd explains that the horse trailer is in our back yard and not theirs because their dog Ripper was going ballistic at the smell of emu. My dad said they could park it at the back of our place.

All the noise has brought Dad out from our shop. My dad's an accountant. He used to work in Sydney until he got made redundant. This is why we packed up and moved to Yarradindi to set up our health food shop. Since our name is Rude and Dad has a sorry sense of humour, it's called 'Rude Health'. He keeps telling me I should be grateful we didn't open a hi-fi shop called 'Rude Noise'.

Dad is Syd's accountant. He's the accountant for all the Yarradindi Cannibals. Dad's a sort of part-time member himself, although Mum doesn't approve for safety reasons.

Soon Syd and Dad are deep in conversation about the emu farm. I keep trying to get away, but each of them is trying to get me on their side to convert the other one.

Dad's worried the farm will lose the Pocky family money. Syd isn't bothered because he reckons he has the secret of success. The secret is that you don't just run an emu farm. You run an emu farm with a theme park attached. This way, you get income first of all from the emu meat, oil and leather. Then you get income from tourists coming to see the emus. Finally, you get income from tourists when they're so bored by looking at emus that they're prepared to risk their lives by going on fun rides built by Terry Pocky.

Terry is Syd's son, Clint's dad and the world's worst handyman. While the Pockys don't question for a minute that all the things that happen to Terry and his work are amazing examples of bad luck, everyone else knows that if you employ Terry to do a job, it will fall apart, explode or somehow self-destruct, usually injuring Terry in the process.

Our worst experience was last year. Terry was fixing our roof when he touched a live electric wire and nearly electrocuted himself. Everyone except Terry was terrified. Once he regained consciousness, he insisted it had done him a power of good because when he was unconscious he had an out-of-body experience and found his car keys.

So, as you can understand, the idea of a theme park built by Terry is pretty scary to everyone apart from the Pockys, who've been working out at the farm for weeks, putting up fences and incubation sheds and special pens, most of which immediately fall down.

The place is to be called Yarradindi Emu World, and it's opening next Sunday. As well as the theme park, it will contain a cafe selling emu food products (prepared by Granny Pocky), a shop (selling touristy emu products), seventy pairs of breeding emus (to be named after Australian celebrities) and a wide range of motorbike exhaust pipes (which have nothing to do with emus, but Syd got them cheap and is finding them hard to sell).

A big feature is to be a giant concrete emu positioned at the farm gate. It's going to be built by Crusher Pocky, Syd's other son. Crusher's just left the army, where he was a commando and took up pottery to calm his nerves. He knows fifteen ways to kill people, not including sticking his thumb in your pressure points. Crusher's got Clint's exact face, except inflated with a bicycle pump and covered in blond whiskers and big hairy sideburns.

Syd raves on about the emu in the horse trailer. It's the first to arrive at the farm. It's a male, in fact it's the father of their flock. According to Syd, it's got the face of a champion and cost peanuts.

Dad tells him the reason it cost peanuts is because nobody wants to buy emus.

It's amazing to see my dad worried like this because he's usually the world's greatest optimist.

But Syd's unconcerned. He just launches into a cheerful speech about how emu meat is low-cholesterol and we'll live to see the day when most people go into McDonald's for a Mac Emu and fries. He's going to tell all this to the local newspaper when they interview him tomorrow about emu farming.

By now, Granny Pocky's got the horse trailer completely jacked up and is unscrewing the nuts on the flat tyre. The emu's standing at forty-five degrees, looking seriously panicked.

Suddenly, there's a loud, blasting 'moo!' It's like a cow attached to a microphone. The emu goes berserk. It probably thinks the mother of all jersey cows is out to get it. But the rest of us know it isn't a cow.

It's Terry Pocky, leaning on the hooter of his ute as he roars up the road. Terry's ute's got a cabin that can take four, mag wheels, black-and-white cowskin seat covers and signs on the side saying: POCKY FENCING AND HOME MAINTENANCE and DON'T BE A LOUSE, LET POCKY FIX YOUR HOUSE.

There's always a barking dog in the tray, thrash music blasting out of the cabin and a bunch of Pocky kids blowing raspberries at pedestrians from the back seats.

The ute screeches to a halt in our side drive. A bunch of under-ten Pockys are beating each other up in the back. Terry lurches out with a spare tyre under one arm. He's lurching not because of the weight of the tyre but because he's got a five-year-old kid attached to his leg.

His T-shirt reads: 'Don't go off your brain, Let Pocky fix that drain'.

He shouts out, 'G'day, Ian! See the emu!' Then

adds to the kid, 'Look, Troy, it's your big friend, Ian! What do you say to Ian?'

Troy looks at me, pulls his mouth into a rubbery sneer, and says, 'Nick off.'

Terry roars with laughter. 'You little shocker! No tae kwon do training for you tonight!'

This is the Pocky equivalent of being sent to bed without seeing *Bananas in Pyjamas*.

Terry hands over the tyre and Granny Pocky swings it expertly into place.

As Mum comes out of the shop, carrying my little sister Daisy, Syd yells, 'Aaah, soona onna way, a tyre a flat a silly begga!' to reassure her.

'No hurry, Syd,' says Mum.

Granny Pocky is now energetically screwing the wheel nuts back into place, the crocodile bouncing.

Terry grins. 'No one changes a tyre like Mum!'

He chats on about the emu farm. He reckons it's almost finished. There are just a few jobs to be done, then Bruce Willis can be set up in style.

Wait a minute.

I ask, 'Bruce Willis?'

Terry nods towards the emu. 'This bloke. The founder of our flock. I told you, we're naming 'em after Aussie celebrities!'

Dad says, 'But Bruce Willis is American.'

Terry hoots with laughter. 'Yeah, everyone thinks that!'

4

I look at Dad. Dad looks at me. We don't follow it up.

The tyre is in place. Syd attaches the horse trailer to the back of his old maroon Falcon. Granny rummages in the glove box of the Falcon until she finds a Mintie for Daisy. Terry and the junior Pockys pile back into the ute. Meanwhile Bruce Willis is looking at me out of the back of the horse trailer. In fact, he's staring at me like crazy. I tip my head. He tips his head. I tip my head the other way. Bruce tips his head the other way.

This is weird. Still, weird things have a habit of happening to me. It's not that I'm accident-prone. It's that wherever I go, strange things seem to have a way of happening around me. Like unintentionally causing accidents to happen to last year's Maths teacher until, luckily, he went to Africa. Now it's being gawped at by some pop-eyed emu.

Terry notices. 'Look at ol' Bruce staring at Ian. Reckon he likes you, Ian.'

Three under-ten Pockys in the back do armfarts and shriek, 'Rudie's in love with an emu, naaaa!'

Syd and Granny get into the Falcon.

Syd invites us to a celebration barbecue at Yarradindi Emu World on Thursday. It's a get-together for family and friends before the Grand Opening to the public on Sunday. Syd reckons the Grand Opening is going to be the biggest thing Yarradindi has ever seen, and we're all lucky beggas because of it.

One of the under-ten Pockys suddenly yells that Ripperson, Terry's dog (and son of Ripper) is lifting his leg against a bag of quick-set cement in the back of the ute. Syd bellows. Terry chucks his sandal at Ripperson, then has to wrestle him to get the sandal back.

Then they're off. Syd tells us to watch out for the posters, which are going up tonight, then toots the horn and heads out of the drive, towing Bruce, who's still staring at me, pop-eyed. Granny waves a fence post in salute. Terry gives us a blasting moo, and follows.

Troy leans out of the back, pulls down his bottom eyelids to show the red and white gory bits and yells, 'Get nicked!'

Dad sighs, 'An emu farm? They'll end up bust in a couple of months.'

Mum shifts Daisy on her hip. 'Who knows?

Maybe they'll make a go of it. At least emu farming's environmentally sound.'

Mum's a bit of a Greenie as well. Normally she'd be totally against people like the Pockys, who are quite cheerful about wrecking the planet, but since they rescued me from the bush she's sort of forgiven them. I think she's also got some idea she'll eventually convert them, which just shows how living with an optimist like Dad can warp your common sense.

Not that Dad sounds like an optimist at the moment.

He snorts, 'Well, it's not financially sound, that's for sure.'

Mum, Dad and Daisy head off inside. I shuffle behind, reliving the day. I could die with embarrassment. How could I have wrecked things like that? I'll be lucky if Suzie ever talks to me again.

How can I ever make up for it?

I stop in my tracks. There is a way. Tonight the Clones are going through the accident ward of our local hospital, singing cheerful Australian folksongs. I got out of it, but it's a chance to see Suzie and take her mind off the eyeballs.

Maybe I could cheer up the accident victims. That would impress her. That's it! I'll cheer up the accident victims. By the time I've finished with them they'll be glad they're in there.

I pelt upstairs, rip off my school clothes, give myself a few blasts of Kleen Superstrength Sporting Deodorant and pull on my best T-shirt and jeans. I check myself out. Pretty pathetic, but it's the best I can do. I tug a few bits of hair over the pimples on my forehead, shout a quick excuse to Mum and set off on my bike.

I arrive at the hospital just as Melissa and Jesse pull up in Melissa's mum's car. I stroll over and spring casually on to the low wall behind them. I get a really overpowering waft of Kleen Superstrength, but they don't seem to notice. They're laughing and chatting about some maths problem. They sound like they're speaking a foreign language. I haven't got the foggiest idea what they're on about, but I smile knowingly.

They burst into laughter. I burst into laughter.

The amazing thing about Clones is that they just assume other people are brilliant as well. I've forgotten my word sheet for the songs. Melissa says I can have hers because she's memorized them.

Clones are flocking in from all the schools in the district. I'm laughing and chuckling with them. This is cool. I'm starting to feel like a Clone myself.

Another Clone comes up and starts laughing about the website he's running for people who are really interested in algebra. All I have to do is keep laughing.

And then the smile drops off my face. My heart sinks.

Because I see Suzie getting out of a car. And getting out of the car after her are three giants.

They must be footy players. Their shoulders are huge. Their legs are so long it takes the rest of them about twenty seconds to unfold and follow the feet out of the car. Worse still, their blazers are covered in braid and badges. There's so much metal attached to their ties you wonder how they can hold their heads up. These guys are all Captains of one sort or another. Worst of all, they're all incredibly good-looking. These are not Clones. They're Super-Clones.

Suzie waves and leads across the handsomest. She says, 'Ian, this is Dan from St Joey's, he's Year 9 Captain of Drama.'

I could have guessed this because Dan has 'Year 9 Captain of Drama' on an embroidered label on his blazer.

It's just below 'Year 9 Captain of Cricket', 'Year 9 Captain of Tennis' and 'Year 9 Captain of Chamber Music'.

Suzie explains that St Joey's is doing an entry in the Schools State drama competition. This year's topic is 'Youth for the Environment'. Because they're a boys-only school, they need girls, and the rules say that girls from other schools are allowed.

Dan says, 'We always need girls, but it's not often we're allowed.' They all break into manly chuckles. Suzie says it's cool because this play will take the message of World Environment Day to the public of the whole State. What's more, unlike ours, it's got music and songs.

Brilliant. So now Suzie's in a play with three Iron Men. If I didn't have much of a chance before, now I'm cactus.

We head off along the corridor, singing, 'Give Me a Home among the Gum Trees'.

Three Pocky kids appear out of Casualty and make rude gestures. Some old lady in a flowery dressing gown starts trailing along beside us, singing tunelessly.

This is terrible. The Captains are crowding round Suzie, trying to get the spot next to her. The second one turns out to be called Jug. I try to make a joke out of it. It turns out the reason he's called Jug is because his father owns a luxury car dealership near the bus station, and Jug is short for the Jaguar he's going to get when he's old enough to drive.

Suzie explains that the rehearsals are going to be held at our school because we've got the best hall.

As if. They're being held at our school so the Captains get maximum access to girls, particularly

Suzie, the ratbags. I feel jealousy soar up in me like a flame. I quickly say I'll help with the curtains.

Now Captain Number Three is yacking on. He's called Harris. He's telling some story about nearly missing his event in the interstate swimming finals. Shame he didn't drown. I bet he's only saying it to make sure we all know he's a champion swimmer. Now Dan's on about how he forgot some exam and arrived late. The point of this seems to be to let everyone know that he still topped the class. But maybe not. Maybe he's really just making conversation.

My heart sinks as I realize that, on top of everything else, the Captains, are, would you believe, *nice*.

This is the last straw. I accidentally-on-purpose tread on Dan's foot. He doesn't even notice. I jump on his foot. He still doesn't notice. I accidentally poke him in the chin with my word sheet. He beams down and apologizes. I feel like a mosquito trying to bite a Mercedes Sports. I go all round the hospital, stabbing and prodding him to keep him away from Suzie. Finally he notices something is happening.

He smiles warmly and says, 'Hey, I seem to be getting in your way, mate. Why don't you stand next to Jesse.'

I can hardly say no. Brilliant. He's in line with

Suzie and I'm stuck with Jesse, who's busy telling me how he's got his computer hooked into some mega computer that's trying to pick up signals being sent to us by aliens.

You wonder what's in it for the aliens. Imagine coming fifty million light years from the Planet Zog to find Cunningham scratching his armpits.

Imagine coming fifty million light years from the Planet Zog to find Jesse droning on about his computer.

He's annoying at the best of times. Now I'm so ticked off about the Captains, he's driving me bonkers.

He looks like he just walked out of one of those ads for 'back to school bargains' that show a bunch of toothy students thrilled to death because they've got dorky new shoes and a set of ring-pull binders. His hair's short and wavy blond. His eyes are brilliant blue with white eyelashes. His skin's ridiculously clear, apart from a designer pimple on the side of his chiselled nose. And his shirt – it's always white and gleaming!

It's always white and gleaming because *he never sweats*. This is more proof he's manufactured from dead professors' ear wax. I reckon if you yanked his hair, the whole top of his head would come off to show some little computer motherboard thing whizzing and crackling inside his skull.

To cap everything, Suzie gets a lift home with Jug in the family Merc. I watch them roar off into the distance. It's now eight o'clock, I've still got homework to do and I spent about five seconds next to Suzie the whole evening.

Why wasn't I born a Clone? Why aren't I blond and good-looking and unpimply and clever at everything and nice? Of course, it's easy to be nice when you're perfect. It's only when you're struggling to survive that you're horrible.

I stride angrily through the shopping centre. There are posters up everywhere for the Grand Opening of Yarradindi Emu World. That was quick.

They've got a big picture of Syd beaming and winking as he pretends to strangle Bruce Willis, plus the words 'Fun, educational – and tasty!'

I stop to read one. Attractions include free entry, a bouncy castle, an emu sausage sizzle, a motorbike parade, plus exhilarating joyrides with the Cannibals up and down the freeway. I bet they're exhilarating. Last Christmas the Cannibals gave free joyrides at the St Brigid's Christmas Fête, and the St John's Ambulance Brigade had to treat three people for shock and one man for a broken toe because Skull, co-leader of the Cannibals, accidentally rode his Harley over the man's foot.

'Go, Rudie!'

'Whoo-hoo, the Rude Man!'

Bogle's in the shopping mall with Pricey. They're heading for the supermarket and some mid-evening meat squeezing, which is Bogle's main hobby. Meat squeezing involves sneaking up to the butcher's section and having a good prod of the plastic-wrapped joints of meat. I tell them about the Captains. I ask them to come over to my place to take my mind off it. They look at each other. Bogle suggests we go and check out the new line of organically grown legs of lamb. I pass.

So much for my chances of joining the beautiful people. Even my mates reckon I'm less interesting than pre-packed meat. I probably am, now I'm obsessed with Suzie.

It's really late, but I take the back streets and go via Suzie's house so I can stare at it. I have to make sure nobody sees me in case they think I'm a stalker and dob me in to Constable Platt. I stand down the street and look for a few seconds. It's dumb, but it sort of helps. It would be so cool if she liked me. Fat chance.

As I come up to our shop, the noise of motorbikes is deafening. The Cannibals have arrived for their weekly gang conference plus decaf cappuccinos.

They've all been helping out at the emu farm, Dad included. Now Mum and Dad are flat out, serving. Syd's helping behind the counter, gargling at double volume to make himself heard. He's deep in conversation with Skull. Skull's ropeable because Yarradindi Council has just banned the Cannibals' Christmas Santa Ride on the basis that the noise upset the kiddies.

He'd be even more ropeable if he knew that it wasn't the noise that upset the kiddies. It was Troy Pocky telling them that the stag's head Gutsa had strapped to the front of his bike to represent a reindeer was Rudolph's actual head.

I grab a sandwich and head to my room. How can I compete with the Captains? Dan looks like he just walked off a billboard for Calvin Klein underpants. What's worse, he's everybody's ideal big brother. Except if he *was* your big brother, he's so perfect you'd be driven to a life of crime in self-defence.

Maybe I can think of some spontaneous funny comments to say to Suzie tomorrow. I rack my brains all through my homework, but a voice keeps nagging away. Is she going off me? More to the point, was she ever on me? And the real question: have I got the slightest chance at all, now that the Captains are on the scene?

I stare gloomily at myself in the bathroom mirror as I clean my teeth. Look at that gut. I'm not even interesting ugly. I'm just plain ugly. Plain

Rude. Why don't I just admit defeat? Suzie's from a different species. I'm like that stupid emu, just gawking after something I can't get.

No! I slap down my toothbrush. I've picked up three garbage trucks full of rubbish, I've been humiliated at Chess Club, I've got the whole school calling me 'Eyeballs'. All for Suzie. And if that big St Joey's boofhead thinks he can get her just because he's Captain of Everything.

I WILL FIGHT BACK.

I'll get Suzie. I'll be as good as the Captains.

I stride back to my room and throw myself on the bed like a superhero.

But inside me a small voice is saying, 'Yeah, mate – but how?'

5

Next day I'm up early. I've got to outgun the Captains. I've got to find Suzie before she goes to her morning Duke of Edinburgh meeting.

I get trapped by Syd and Dad outside our back door. Syd and Granny have just bought up a truck-load of emu products from the farm that went bust. Syd's raving on to Dad about how emus are a gold mine, with Dad saying, 'But, Syd . . .' every few seconds.

Syd explains that emus are a gold mine because they have low-fat meat, beautiful feathers and beautiful leather. Not to mention eggs you can carve and put as beaut decorations on your mantel-piece or give to friends for weddings or Christmas. What's more, they also produce oil, which Syd reckons does everything from curing arthritis to waterproofing space shuttles.

Also, if you're totally cool, you can wear one of their claws hanging round your neck on a chain. To prove this, Syd is wearing one. He shows how you can use it to pick your teeth and clean out your nails.

The only way you can escape from Syd is to agree with him, so I do. He grins, gargles, 'Aaaaah. Know a fashion, a clever begga . . .' and presents me with an emu claw on a chain all of my very own.

I act like I've just won the lottery.

I bike like a maniac to school.

'Go, Rudest.'

'Whoo-hoo, the Rude Man.'

It's Bogle and Pricey. Bogle's building a mobile phone from a kit he sent away for, except it's not working. The only thing working is the ringer, which Bogle's programmed to make all sorts of weird noises. When you get a text message it blows a raspberry.

Bogle makes it do about five raspberries. Pricey's crying with laughter. This is quite normal because you've only got to get Pricey laughing for about two seconds before he's got tears running down his face.

I talk my way past them and get trapped by Jesse.

He yells, 'Hey, Ian!' beams and says, 'Are you making a solar car this year?'

I look sharply at him. Is he taking the mickey?

He knows I can hardly knock a nail into a piece of wood.

Caroline Dillinger walks past and sneers, 'Oh yeah, like Eeyun Rude could build a solar car.'

Cunningham thunders up, shouts, 'Eyeballs!' and gives me a rabbit punch in the shoulder. Clint Pocky yanks my shorts up my bum in a mega-wedgie and yells, 'Rudie's in love with an emu.'

Where's Suzie?

I head for the library and almost collide with Melissa, Clone 3, outside the music department.

She's standing there, engrossed in her St John's Ambulance book. This is a bad sign because Melissa's totally obsessive about First Aid and always wants to practise her bandaging on you or tell you about what you do if someone has a heart attack next to you at the bus stop.

Melissa lives in this world of horrible accidents.

She once spent a whole lunch break telling me about a school where some kid got the end of their nose cut off in woodwork and some other kid who did First Aid saved the day by finding the end in the middle of a heap of wood shavings so the surgeon could sew it back on again.

I veer away. Too late.

'Hi, Ian. I'm just reading about what you do if someone has an asthma attack during a football match. The main thing is to keep calm.'

She goes on to tell me about what you do if someone falls off apparatus in the gym and knocks themselves unconscious, what you do if the bus driver drops dead at the wheel, and what you do if your mother accidentally slices her thumb off while using an electric carving knife, which apparently is very common at Christmas.

Suddenly, it's Suzie! My stomach backflips. I'm all shaky. I suck in my stomach and spring on to the library steps. It's so cool to be next to her. I'm racking my brains for the right spontaneous funny comment, but she's frantic.

'Ian, where were you? Didn't you remember?'

Don't tell me I've forgotten her birthday.

'It's Big Kids, Little Kids. With Yarradindi Primary. It's our chance to *really do something* for Troubled Youth.'

I beam and get as close to her as I dare.

'But don't worry, I took all the details for you. It's on tomorrow. You're helping a little boy called Jet and I've got one called Brad. They've both got problems with authority, and a reading age that's three years behind their class. But here's the really exciting thing, Ian. They actually *volunteered* to come here. They *want* to improve. So. Isn't that cool?'

I make excited noises.

My own theory is that they volunteered because

they heard Suzie was involved, the little perverts. But Suzie's really rapt in the whole thing, so I'll go along with it. I'll go along with anything really.

We set off. Luckily there's a low wall running alongside the path that I can balance on. Suzie rattles on about the problems of Troubled Youth and how lucky we are to have good homes instead of sitting in corners heartbroken.

I agree because it's so exciting to be near her, but I must say, I've never seen any Yarradindi Primary kids sitting in corners heartbroken. I've seen them running along inside the school fence, shouting swear words and chucking peanut butter sandwich crusts at passers-by, but they don't look troubled. In fact, they look like they're having the best time.

I'm desperately trying to think of a way I can rubbish the Captains without sounding like I'm doing it, but nothing comes to me so I just sigh, nod sympathetically and say solemnly, 'That's it, Suzie. Sometimes, well . . . we just don't know how lucky we are.'

On impulse, I stare deep into her eyes. I nearly die with terror. But she stares back, beams in approval and murmurs, 'Yes, Ian. That's right.'

What? This is fantastic. Suzie is smiling into my eyes again! I said something to impress her.

I lose my balance and topple off the wall in amazement. And then it happens. Like it did in

Assembly. It's because she's smiling at me. I go all sort of dizzy and stupid. But this time, I start to lie. And they're not just little lies. They're classics. They're total porkies.

I go into this big rave about how much I care about Troubled Youth. I'm going way over the top, but it works. I guess it's because Suzie's a Clone and Clones never need to lie, so they can never imagine anyone else doing it.

She says I must have a way with children. I say I do. And animals. I say animals are strangely attracted to me. I say they love me. I say whenever I walk down the street dogs and cats flock round me and little birds come out to play.

Before I know it, I've whipped out Syd's emu claw on a chain and said that it's a gift I bought specially for little Jet, my Troubled Child. I explain how I'll use it to tell him about emus. Then, as a masterstroke, I bring in the planet. I tell her how I'll use it to introduce him to the idea of protecting our environment and saving our native wildlife.

I sound like an ad for Greenpeace. I end up by saying, solemnly, 'You see, Suzie, it's our planet. The responsibility lies with all of us.'

This is something I read on the side of a box of organically grown cauliflowers at our shop, but it comes over really impressively.

Suzie stares at me, full of admiration, nods

seriously and says, 'You think a lot about the planet, don't you, Ian?'

I stare back into her gorgeous face.

I say, huskily, 'Well, we all have to think about the planet, Suzie.'

She puts her hand on my arm. 'We do, Ian. We do.'

YES.

This is amazing. All I need to do is rave on about loving animals and the planet and how much I care about horrible little Yarradindi Primary mini-thugs. I nearly laugh out loud with triumph and delight. Suzie McLaren, who I totally fancy, is impressed with me. *I've found the answer.*

I spend the whole day asking Jesse serious questions about ozone so Suzie can overhear. In English I turn the discussion round to how children who can't read are going to turn into criminals. Clint Pocky jabs me in the leg with a compass and hisses, 'Who you calling a criminal?'

But Suzie's really getting into it. She's smiling at me! I could explode laughing with relief and excitement. She's nodding her head earnestly and saying, 'Mm.' I'm on top of the world. In Science, Mrs Parker starts to talk about how the planet needs a wide range of plants and animals in the ecosystem.

Suzie's nodding her head. I find myself nodding my head. Suzie's going 'Mm' and nodding. I'm going 'Mm' and nodding. Suzie sees me nodding – and smiles.

I beam and suddenly, without realizing it, I shout, 'Absolutely!'

There's a silence. Everyone turns and stares. Mrs Parker looks at me in a puzzled way and says, 'What was that, Ian?'

I have no idea what she just said, but Suzie's looking, so I say earnestly, 'Sorry, Mrs Parker, it's just that I feel very strongly about this issue.'

Mrs Parker brightens.

'Oh that's interesting, Ian. Why do you feel so strongly about cuttlefish?'

6

'I . . . I, well, I . . .'

Suzie's looking straight at me.

'Well, you know, if you didn't have cuttlefish in the world . . .'

I'm dying. What the hell use are cuttlefish?

I gulp. 'I mean, without cuttlefish . . . without cuttlefish . . .'

People are starting to giggle. Suzie is smiling expectantly.

Andy Bogle yawns and murmurs, 'Of course, you give budgies cuttlefish to sharpen their beaks.'

I seize on it like a drowning man.

'That's right! Budgies . . .'

'Thank you, Ian . . .'

I can't stop. There has to be something I can say to impress Suzie. I rave on helplessly about the beak-sharpening habits of budgies – and parrots. I'm just starting into cockatoos when luckily someone smells gas because Clint Pocky and Cunningham have turned on all the Bunsen burners. By the time windows are opened and Clint and Cunningham get sent to the Principal, the bell's gone.

That was close. This lying is way too dangerous, but what else can I do? It's the only way I've come up with to get Suzie's attention.

But the test is really coming up now because school's nearly finished and the Captains are turning up for the rehearsal at three-thirty.

I'm exhausted. Sometimes I think it'd be really nice to be back in the old days before Suzie. Just hanging out with Bogle and Pricey, with nothing to worry about except homework and what pizza to order and how to get the shop assistant with the big boobs in the video shop to bend over and pick something up. I look at my watch.

Captains, here I come.

We head for the hall. I feel like I'm going to be executed. The Captains are already surrounded by a group of giggling girls from St Brigid's. Dan's playing some flash classical music on the piano, making weird faces and tossing back his mane of shining hair.

Suzie calls out, 'Hi, Dan!'

He stops, beams, says, 'Hi, Suzie!' Then turns to me with genuine pleasure and says, 'Whoa, Ian! How's it going?'

I feel like socking him on the nose. He strolls off

with Suzie. I jog behind. They don't even know I'm there. I leap on to a chair and ask Suzie what topic she's choosing for her environmental studies project. Dan joins in with suggestions. I haven't got a hope. Even if I get rid of him, there's still Jug and Harris. And three nights a week these three are going to be turning up at school, trying to crack on to Suzie.

I think of Suzie's armpit. I choke. I could cry. If only I could stop this drama thing. If only I could turn back the clock.

The accompanist arrives. It's a girl from St Brigid's.

Dan claps his hands and shouts, 'Listen up, everyone, this is Jessica Lee. She's playing the piano for us.'

Jessica sighs, puts the music on top of the piano and says, 'That's the thing, Dan. My mum won't let me.'

There's silence.

Dan says, 'Well, don't you know anybody else?'

Jessica shrugs. 'I've rung everyone. They've all got music exams.'

Suzie blinks. 'But there's got to be a pianist somewhere. And if we don't start rehearsals tonight, there won't be time.'

Everyone starts talking. For every name that comes up there's some reason why the person can't do it. I'm hardly listening at first because I'm so depressed. But then it dawns on me. This is fantastic. There's no way they'll find an accompanist tonight. Of course, any one of the Captains could play, but then there wouldn't be the singers to do the main parts. If the play's off, I get rid of the Captains. All I'll have to do is rave on to Suzie about small children, animals and my deep love for the planet.

Finally Harris gets up and says, 'This is dumb. We're wrecked. We might as well pack up and go home.'

I could cheer.

'I can play the piano.'

It's Natasha Frye, standing in the hall doorway.

I say, 'Thanks, Natasha, but we need a proper pianist.'

'I am a proper pianist.'

Suzie gives a pained smile.

'Natasha, thanks, but this is really hard music to play . . .'

Natasha sniffs, goes up to the piano, takes the music – then plays it like some kind of genius.

She finishes, and everyone bursts into applause. I can't believe this. Whacko Natto does it again.

Suzie hurries over to her. 'Natasha, you're excellent. That was fantastic! Will you play for us?'

Natasha doesn't crack a smile. 'On one

condition. My family runs a wildlife refuge. Someone will have to look after my bats.'

Dan says, 'You mean, you just want someone to help your mum and dad with the animals?'

'Not just anyone. We're very fussy about who we let near our animals. We need someone who's got a genuine commitment to the environment.'

Dan says, 'I'll do it.'

Natasha shakes her head. 'No, we need someone with a background in environmental protection.'

Harris interrupts, 'Like who?'

Natasha folds her arms.

'Ian Rude.'

My mouth has dropped open. Everyone's staring at me.

I burst out, 'But no. I can't. You see. I . . . I . . .'

I stare round desperately. I can't think of an excuse. I've just spent the whole day acting like a Greenpeace documentary.

Natasha sniffs. 'My parents are very fussy about who cares for our animals. Ian's OK because his parents run a health food shop and he's really into protecting the environment.'

Suzie's rapt. She hurries over to me. 'But this is fantastic, Natasha. Ian really *loves* animals.'

I'm dying. *Bats?* Is she kidding?

Suzie's going on, 'And as for the environment,

Ian's into conservation and the planet like you wouldn't believe.'

No, I wouldn't believe, that's the problem. She beams at me.

Natasha unfolds her arms. 'Well that's settled. All you have to do is feed the bats and other animals, clean up their cages and help generally. You'll need to have the injections, of course . . .'

A desperate laugh spurts out of me. 'What, in case I get rabies?'

'No, Lyssavirus from the bats. Many people think it's rabies, but it's not. But it's very rare for humans to get it. There are only a couple of recorded deaths.'

'Deaths!'

'Statistically that's nothing. You're in more danger crossing the road.'

'And I have to have a needle?'

Natasha looks at me. 'Actually, it's a course of three . . .'

Suzie's smiling at me with hope in her eyes. I'm frantic. For a start bats stink. And they piddle on you when you walk underneath. I have a vision of a bat landing in my hair. I see bats going for my throat, crawling all over my chest.

I can't help myself. I burst out, 'I'm sorry, I haven't got the time, I . . . I . . .'

There's a silence. I catch sight of Suzie's agonized

face. She stares into my eyes. I'm gone. I have to please her.

Before I can stop myself, I say, super-casual, 'But hey. Look. I'll do it.'

It's like I'm outside of my own body, watching myself. I've just committed myself to nursing a bunch of reeking bats. I've traded sheep's eyes for rabies.

Suzie beams. 'Are you sure?'

Natasha frowns even harder than usual. 'You realize you'll have come over to my place tonight to learn what you have to do?'

I stare at her fanatical face. I stare at Suzie standing next to Dan. I imagine Suzie in his arms. I imagine Suzie clamped to his badge-loaded tie, staring up at his clear cheeks and open, manly face.

With a sinking heart I realize that for the whole time I'm being piddled on and bitten by the local wildlife, that's the picture I'll have in my mind.

I say, 'That's cool. I'll do it. It's OK.'

Suzie's thrilled.

Dan clamps a firm hand on my shoulder. 'Thanks, mate. We won't forget this.'

Goodbye, peace of mind; hello, bat droppings.

And thank you, Natasha Frye.

7

The rehearsal starts. I can't go ahead with this, but I've got to.

Suzie keeps beaming at me. Dan keeps beaming at me. Now Jug and Harris smile manly, sympathetic smiles and clap me on the shoulder.

Then Mr Lee, the drama teacher from St Joey's, turns up to run the rehearsal and Dan tells him what I've offered to do. So he starts smiling manly, sympathetic smiles and clapping me on the shoulder as well.

The rehearsal kicks off with everyone singing rousing songs about loving the world.

At this moment I hate the world. Particularly the bit Dan's standing on. I can't believe I'm leaving Suzie alone with the Captains. The rest of the rehearsal passes in a blur of discussions about dolphins and the hole in the ozone layer.

Natasha Frye sits at the piano, frowning. Afterwards, she takes me to Dr White's to get my first anti-bat needle. She says it won't hurt. It hurts like hell.

She's waiting outside in the waiting room. I could deck her. I say, 'You know I'm not doing this for you, don't you?'

She says, 'No, you're doing it to impress Suzie. That's fine. As long as the animals are looked after.'

What a sour piece of work she is. We stare at each other. Checkmate.

We head for her house in silence. Posters for the emu farm are up everywhere. Just as we're passing the Odeon, there's a long toot from a car. It's Suzie with her mum. She's off to her tennis lesson. She waves. I catch a glimpse of her armpit and feel a deep stab of pain.

The armpit. Never again.

The Fryes' house is on the outskirts of town. It's in the middle of a scraggy-looking paddock filled with tin sheds and rusty rolls of chicken wire. Right round the outside is a huge fence, like you get round a tennis court. You'd have a job trying to play handball in between all those sheds and junk, let alone tennis.

There's an old Land Rover in the drive. It's got two bumper stickers. One's for the World Wildlife Fund and another one reads: 'Friends of the Hooded Eel'.

We stop at a rusty gate in the tennis court fence.

Natasha opens it and whispers menacingly, 'Now. Don't say anything about me playing the piano for the play. The story is, I'm doing extra maths at school and you're coming here to do my jobs because you love native animals.'

'Why can't I say anything about you playing the piano for the play?'

She glares. 'Just do it, Ian.'

She strides in, ushers me through and bolts the gate behind me. Suddenly, there's a metallic crashing noise coming from somewhere behind the sheds. This is followed by fierce barking noises and a man yelling something.

Without warning, a psycho with a beard shoots out from between two sheds and pelts towards us. He's being chased by a huge, barking, one-eyed kangaroo. He bellows, 'The shed! Get in the shed!'

Natasha screams, 'Run for the shed!'

We pelt towards the nearest shed. The kangaroo's after him, doing its barking. The man joins us. The three of us hurl ourselves into the shed, close the door and push our shoulders against it.

The man yells, 'Brace yourself!'

Something hits the door with huge force. The whole shed shakes. Things are squawking and flapping. I realize the place is full of owls in cages.

The man yells, 'Push!' We push against the door as hard as we can. There's another thump.

I whisper to Natasha, 'What's it doing out there?'

'He's reared up on his tail, kicking the door with his feet. It's the male fighting position. They can tear out a man's stomach with those claws.'

Another thump. Any more of this and the door's going to give way. Silence.

Holding my breath, I look sideways. On one side of me Natasha is frowning darkly at the door with her teeth bared in anxiety. On the other side the man's frowning darkly at the door with his teeth bared in anxiety. They look identical, except the man's got a beard.

There's a lone hoot from one of the owls. The place smells of warm bird poo.

I go, 'Excuse me . . .'

'Shhh.'

They're listening intently. I listen intently. This is insane. I'm being kept hostage by a demented one-eyed kangaroo with two whacko Greenies in a shed reeking of owls. If I died in here nobody would ever find me.

Natasha says, 'Dad, this is Ian. Ian, my dad. Ian's very interested in native wildlife.'

Mr Frye nods politely, like we just met at the bus stop.

There's a loud grunt from the kangaroo outside. Mr Frye holds up a hand for silence. We stand, straining our ears. Finally, ever so slowly, Mr Frye sighs, relaxes and moves away from the door.

He looks at me, tugs his beard nervously and puts out his hand to shake mine.

'Sorry about that. I was repainting the "Please don't open the gate" sign, ready to warn you, but we had a hatching crisis. And that . . .' he nods his head towards the door and sighs wearily, '. . . is Noddy.'

He opens the shed door about two centimetres, peeks out then turns back to us, smiling tightly.

'It's OK. We can go. He'll be round the back by now.'

He's got to be joking. Natasha shoves me out.

We scuttle off to the house, picking our way between the rickety buildings. I keep checking over my shoulder, but Noddy seems to have disappeared. Mr Frye is trying to put my mind at rest about him, but I notice he's looking over his shoulder, too.

As we head past an animal graveyard covered in tiny crosses, he explains that Noddy was orphaned and lost his eye in a road accident when he was a baby. He was brought up by an elderly couple who trained him to hop round Yarradindi shopping centre begging for scraps.

This was cute when he was tiny. It's a different matter now he's nearly two metres tall and likes to lurk behind the life-size statue of Ronald McDonald and snatch toddlers' chips.

Things came to a head about a year ago. Noddy whipped out from the side of the hot bread shop and grabbed a Big Mac from a lady on crutches. Not surprisingly, she fell over. She also sent a whole load of other pedestrians toppling like dominoes, including the mayor, who sprained his ankle. Constable Platt said Noddy was a public nuisance and had to be put to sleep.

This is where the Fryes came in. The Fryes are not only interested in rescuing animals. Being complete lunatics, they also specialize in taking on animals that nobody else wants.

So they said they'd adopt Noddy. They promised he'd be enclosed at all times and, at great expense, installed the tennis court fence. This was an incredibly nice thing to do. Unfortunately, nobody explained that to Noddy.

So Noddy hates the Fryes because, from his point of view, they're just these horrible people who've kidnapped him, jailed him and stopped him going out for lunch – and he's constantly trying to get them.

By this time we've reached the back door of the house. Mr Frye sighs, grabs on to his beard, and says wearily, 'Yes, Ian. We're hoping to make a breakthrough with Noddy, but . . . I'd have to say, it's a challenge.'

At that point a middle-aged woman clutching a big cardboard box of apples crashes backwards out through the door like she's been shoved. She totters with the enormous box, collides with two bales of straw, screams, drops the box and collapses in a heap on the doorstep. Apples go bouncing everywhere. She looks up and sobs, 'She's mad. She's criminally insane. I tried to give her apples for the bats and she waved a knife at me and told me I was a traitor to the Green movement.' Her voice drops to a hoarse gasp. 'I cannot work with that woman.'

Mr Frye doesn't blink. He says mildly, 'Hello, Mrs Thacker, how nice to see you. This is Ian. He's helping us with the animals.'

Mrs Thacker looks at me, snorts, 'I hope your parents know you're in close contact with Jacinta Frye, the woman's a lunatic!' and stalks off. Mr Frye smiles brightly and starts putting the apples back in the box.

Meanwhile Natasha's bundling me towards the back door. We go through a porch stacked with bales of straw and sacks of animal pellets and enter the kitchen. The first thing I notice is that the curtains are practically ripped to shreds. The next thing is that every surface is covered with junk and pamphlets. The third thing is that a cupboard next to me flies open and a woman looms out with a carving knife. She says, 'Is Thacker still out there? Because if she is, I'll finish her off.'

It's the woman from the shopping centre who had the placard about eating wildlife. She's wearing a T-shirt and open cardigan with a fur scarf tucked inside. Her chest is moving of its own accord. I blink. Her open cardigan jerks and wriggles. The brown fur scarf swings out. From the bottom of the scarf an upside-down, doggy little face appears.

It isn't a scarf at all, it's a bat!

8

I give a croak of horror. This woman's got a bat the size of a small cat hooked on to her T-shirt. The bat swivels and peers at me with beady little eyes. It looks me up and down. It's checking me out. It gives an ear-piercing chirp.

Natasha is putting on a plastic apron. 'That's Horace, Mum's pet flying fox. Calm down, Horace.'

But Horace doesn't calm down. Horace is now squawking like crazy, swarming over Mrs Frye's chest, his beady little eyes fixed on me. He's got a big groove down the middle of his piggy, deformed little nose. He starts darting his head out at me, trying to nip me.

Mrs Frye snorts with laughter. 'Look at him. Isn't he priceless the way he hates males? Quite a few bats are like that, but I think flying foxes are the worst.'

At that moment Mr Frye appears with a giant see-through plastic bag full of meat scraps. Horace sees him and goes absolutely berserk, squawking, swinging out and trying to nip him. Mrs Frye is laughing happily, like Horace is totally lovable.

Natasha shouts, 'Go, Ian! Go through to the kitchen!'

I stumble off to the kitchen with Horace still squawking behind me. Dirty dishes spread out of the sink all across the benches. There are little baskets all over the place. Mr Frye follows me with the bag of meat scraps and slaps it on the table.

He smiles a bit too brightly and says, 'Don't worry about Horace. He's just jealous. It's quite common for male bats to become deeply bonded with female carers. And for females to bond with males. My wife brought Horace up from infancy, you see. You'll probably find it happening to you when you get your first baby bat. Cute, isn't it?'

At that moment Mrs Frye enters with Horace, who sights Mr Frye, gives a ferocious screech, swings out from her chest and spits a big pellet of gunk at him.

It lands on his arm. It looks like a mixture of snot and fruit. Mrs Frye roars with laughter, scolds Horace, unhooks him from her cardigan and hooks him on the kitchen curtains. He immediately goes swarming up to the pelmet, shrieking and swearing.

This is definitely not what I call cute. In fact, if the little beggar spits on me, I'll throttle him.

Mr Frye's face has set in a sort of rigid grin. He's

wiping the gunk off himself. He says calmly, 'Will I chop the meat for the eagles, dear, or will you?'

Mrs Frye takes the bag. 'I'll do it. You help Natasha with the babies. Ian, clear a space on that little table to chop fruit. Just chuck those pamphlets anywhere.'

Meanwhile Horace's screeching has set off strange miniature screeching from the baskets. Natasha has joined us. She opens the fridge, gets out a couple of tiny babies' bottles full of milk, goes to the baskets and gets out two really small, wrapped-up baby bats. She sticks them both in the crook of one arm and gives each of them a bottle. Horace sees this and comes swarming along the curtains towards her.

Natasha shouts, 'Get lost, Horace. This isn't for you!'

Horace still keeps coming, chirping and darting at the bottles.

Mrs Frye's ripped open the plastic bag of meat scraps. There's a big hairy hoof tucked down one side. She's slicing it all and putting it into plastic bowls, humming to herself. By now, Horace's shrieks are deafening.

Mr Frye suddenly gives a strangled roar and rips Horace off the curtains. Literally. Horace comes off, still attached to a big lump of curtain, screeching like a maniac and trying to bite. No wonder the curtains are in shreds. Mr Frye heads off through a door at the end of the room, with Horace struggling and screeching even louder.

The weird thing is that Natasha and Mrs Frye carry on like nothing has happened. Now Mrs Frye is slicing up some big dangly bit of meat. I don't even want to think what that is. She catches me looking.

'Don't worry about Horace. He'll be fine. Mr Frye's only putting him in the hospital cage for a while.'

It's not Horace I'm worried about. Anyway, if it was up to me, Horace'd be in the hospital cage permanently. Even better, he'd be chucked back wherever he came from.

I say, 'Where did you get Horace?'

'In the rainforest behind the house. His wings were torn, so he can't fly, and he's got a deformed nose. It's probably why he's so aggressive.'

It's a relief to know the little runt can't fly up and go me in the neck. I watch Natasha feeding the little bats. Mr Frye walks back in, looking furious. He grabs a baby bat and starts feeding it. He looks up, smiles brightly and says, 'This will be you as soon as you've had your full course of injections.'

Well, whoopee do.

The evening's a nightmare. Mr Frye and me have to chop three million mouldy melons while Natasha bottle-feeds more baby bats and Mrs Frye hauls handfuls of intestines out of the plastic bag and starts whacking into them with a meat cleaver.

Mr Frye tells me to go and get Sophie the python's dinner out of the freezer and put it in the microwave. It turns out to be three deep-frozen baby mice. We defrost them on medium-high.

Meanwhile Mrs Frye keeps up a running commentary about wildlife protection and how Erica Thacker should be sacked as President of the Yarradindi Wildlife Protection Society and replaced by Mrs Frye, whose first job would be shutting down the new emu farm. Because, she says, while hacking meat off from round the hoof, if emus are protected animals in the wild, how come they can be turned into sausages because they happen to be born on a farm?

Don't tell me she's taking on the Pockys.

I wish her luck.

She raves on about a horrible old couple blasting through the wetlands on a three-wheeled Harley. I get an image of Syd roaring and gargling through the bush, with Granny Pocky clinging happily to his back.

Good job she doesn't know my dad's a trainee Cannibal.

We stagger out with buckets of chopped fruit to cages where the bats hang upside down like umbrellas and snort lumps of snot and fruit skin three

centimetres from your shoulder. The pong is spectac-
ular. We finish the bats and start on the other
animals.

Forget all your ideas about cute and cuddly
wildlife. The Fryes' animals are horrible. There are
possums who hide behind logs, then rush out and
spit at you. There's Stan the eagle, who goes for your
eyes. Not to mention Sophie the python, who once
got Mrs Frye in a death grip and had to be prised off
by Mr Frye with a garden fork.

We move from cage to cage, treading in assorted
animal poo and getting snarled at. It's appalling.
Now we're outside the cage of Bobby, the Hairy-
Nosed Wombat. He smells like a rubbish tip in a
heatwave.

Mr Frye beams and says I can feed him. I force a
smile and tiptoe in. Bobby charges at me, baring his
teeth. I chuck his food at him and whip out of the
cage, swearing under my breath. Mr Frye explains
that Bobby is an endangered species. No wonder he's
bloody endangered, he needs a good kick up the
bum.

He looks at me, his lip curled, growling. Behind
Mr Frye's back I do a rude signal at him.

After an hour of scrubbing dirty plastic con-
tainers under a cold tap in the yard, Mr Frye says I
can go, then adds, 'But first, a treat.' He leans over
and whispers, 'The shrikes!'

Eh? I've no idea what he's on about, but it's obvious I'm supposed to know, so I beam and say, 'Wow!'

We head off over the paddocks towards some bushland. It turns out shrikes are birds and Mr Frye is recording them for some international survey so they can see what species are dying out. There aren't enough scientists to do it all, so people like Mr Frye are helping.

Noddy looks up from grazing and grunts resentfully.

Mr Frye's bird-watching place is a tiny shack made out of bits of old corrugated iron. There are slits at eye level all round and a solar-power cell thing on top. As we approach, Mr Frye stops and puts his finger to his lips to silence me. He starts walking in long, tip-toey strides. He looks like a big stalking bird himself, the dopey old coot. I copy him. We look like two total dorks.

We go in. A big cloud of mosquitoes flies up in the air. Set on a shelf are three ancient reel-to-reel tape recorders, a set of battered speakers and the oldest audio-cassette player I've ever seen. A tangle of cables goes everywhere.

Mr Frye smiles triumphantly. 'Old but service-able. It's on a time clock. All solar-powered of course.'

I'm getting eaten alive by mozzies.

'Sit on that bench – that orange matter is just fungus. Now, I'll play back through this machine the range of activity between five-thirty and six this morning. That's when they're most active. Of course, I can listen in live at any point, should I want to.' He chortles. 'Sometimes I do. Just for the hell of it.'

Boy, does he need to get out more. I sit on a fungus-encrusted bench. I can feel the damp seeping into the seat of my shorts.

He flicks a switch. There's a slight hiss, then some distant chirping. That's it. That's what we've come here for. We sit listening to assorted chirps and squawks until my entire backside is soaking and I'm freezing. Mr Frye's face is alight with enthusiasm. Finally, when I think fungus is about to start growing on me, he sighs, smiles, and says I really have to go.

I shoot out and nearly collapse because I've been sitting so crunched up I've got pins and needles. Natasha says she'll see me out. We have to pass Noddy grazing behind the fence. He looks up and glares at us with his one good eye.

Natasha says, 'Walk slowly. We've got to show him he doesn't scare us.'

He sure scares me.

We get to the gate.

She blinks. 'You come again the day after

tomorrow. And remember. You're coming because you love hurt and defenceless animals.'

Noddy growls and rattles the fence.

No way am I keeping this up. By the time I get home it's nearly eight-thirty and Mum and Dad are furious because I hadn't told them about going to Natasha's so they thought I'd be back from the rehearsal by six. Since I hadn't answered their text messages they thought I was either dead, kidnapped or lying unconscious in a ditch.

Now it turns out I'm still alive they take the opportunity to rip into me for keeping on coming home late. I tell them I've taken up helping at a wildlife refuge. Mum says if I'm interested in cleaning out animal pens, I could start by tidying my room.

I eat my dinner as they get to gale-force hysteria. I wish Suzie could know what I'm going through for her sake. At least I've got something to impress her with tomorrow. I can talk about what I did at the Fryes'. Plus my great love for all at Yarradindi Primary.

Suddenly, there's a knock on the back door. It's a bit strange someone calling this late at night. Dad opens the door and looks around. There's no one there.

Suddenly, Syd Pocky jumps from round the corner yelling, 'Aaaah! Surprise a silly beggas!'

9

He certainly does surprise us because he's dressed in tight, yellow leather trousers, topped with a matching waistcoat covered with leather fringes. He's an amazing sight.

He looks like Christina Aguilera's grandad.

'Aaaah – suit a emu leather! Crusher made – a clever begga, aaah!'

We're all struck dumb. This is not a problem since Syd talks non-stop about the latest venture from Yarradindi Emu World: emu leather fashions. Apparently the bankrupt emu farmers who were selling the emus and the emu souvenirs were also selling off a whole heap of emu leather at bargain prices. Syd and Granny took one look at it and realized the huge market for leather clothes in the bikie world.

In the space of a few minutes, this suit was designed by Terry. It was made by Crusher Pocky, who's apparently a whizz on the sewing machine, but we're never supposed to mention it.

The suit comes with three different styles of trousers. It's the first of a whole range of clothes to be made under the Yarradindi Emu World label. There are going to be hats, jeans, skirts, vests, dresses and shirts and, as we're neighbours, we get a discount.

Syd puts his leg up on a chair to point out the colour, strength and fineness of the leather.

Mum asks him to sit down and have a cup of tea. He says he won't because the trousers pinch a bit. Mum orders a belt. Dad orders a hat. They all look at me. I say I'll wait to see the full range of clothes before I place my order.

Syd tells us all about his interview with the local newspaper. He got photographed with Bruce Willis at the entrance to Yarradindi Emu World. He's puzzled because some strange woman started bellowing at him.

It turns out that Mrs Frye rushed up in the middle of the interview with a placard reading: 'The World Needs Emus'. Syd agreed. He said he's giving the world as many emus as it can take. In fact, a whole mob of them are arriving at the farm tomorrow, and as soon as they're fat enough they'll be available, plastic wrapped, in a range of burgers, fillets and sausages.

This brings us to the names for the new emus. Syd refuses to believe that Brad Pitt isn't

Australian. I give up. By the time Syd goes, it's ten o'clock. I stagger to my room, exhausted. I scrub the bits of rotted melon from my fingernails and think of Suzie. It was going so well until that drama presentation and the sheep's eyes. And now the Captains have turned up. If only I could get her on her own. Maybe the Big Kids, Little Kids thing could be the start of something.

Maybe we could tutor our kids together. Maybe we could take them to the park for an educational trip and show them how plants get rid of carbon dioxide. Knowing the Yarradindi Primary kids, they'd probably be more interested in how to rip the plants up by the roots, but it's worth a try.

As I get into bed, I catch sight of a timetable Suzie organized for me through the Student Representative Council Committee on School Hygiene. Next week, I'm scrubbing graffiti off the canteen wall, organizing a team of Year 7s to chisel chewing gum off the underneath of desks, and running a raffle in support of the Yarradindi elderly.

There's got to be an easier way to get a girlfriend.

I wake up next morning to Daisy screaming her head off as Mum tries to calm her down. She got her finger stuck in the door. I take over because I'm good at situations like these. My tactic is to tell Daisy her favourite story, which for some reason is

Goldilocks.

I've always hated Goldilocks. I mean, how slack can you get? Breaking into the poor old bears' place and scoffing their porridge. Smashing up their furniture. She reminds me of Natasha Frye. Barging into people's lives and wrecking everything. The bears should have ripped her into three and eaten her in place of the porridge. But it does the trick for Daisy. I finish just in time to pack my bag and shoot off to school before I get cornered by Syd, who's out the back, telling Dad about the new emus. They're both wearing emu leather cowboy hats.

I sprint in through the gates just as Suzie's springing through the air and scoring a goal at netball practice. She is unbelievably good-looking. While I walk her to the changing rooms, she tells me how helpful Dan the Captain is being about extra rehearsals.

I bet he is.

She asks me how it went at the Fryes'. Of course I lie. I make it sound as hard as possible. I describe myself staggering for miles with buckets of food. I describe Natasha's animals queuing up to be patted.

I sneak a look sideways. She's nodding sympathetically.

I feel really slack. She's such a nice person, she just can't imagine someone stacking it on to get attention. Like I say, when you're a Clone, you don't have to stack it on to get attention.

The Clones are like champion surfers who ride along on top of a giant wave, admiring the view of the beach. Meanwhile all the normal slobs like me are underneath, getting dumped by five tons of water and dragged along the seabed and getting their knees and elbows scraped off to the bone.

Except, of course, the Clones don't even know that the stuff they do is hard. They just stand there, beaming vaguely and waiting for the rest of the world to catch up.

It's kind of infuriating and likeable at the same time.

I bring up Big Kids, Little Kids as we head off to class. I say how cool it would be if our Troubled Children could learn together outside of school. I say how she and I have really got to commit ourselves. I'm just about to suggest a trip to the park when Suzie says, 'I know. We could take our Little Kids to the opening of Yarradindi Emu World on the weekend.'

I stop in my tracks. No way. I can just imagine it. The kids'd be mugged on the bouncy castle by Clint Pocky and I'd have to try and rescue them so as to look good in front of Suzie.

I hastily change the subject to the best way to teach our Little Kids their multiplication tables.

Suzie says it's only really the seventeen-times table that's hard, and goes back to the idea of a trip to Yarradindi Emu World.

I didn't even know there was a seventeen-times.

I have to get her off the idea of going to Yarradindi Emu World. Even if I can keep the kids off the bouncy castle, Yarradindi Emu World's no place for a first date. I can just imagine it. I'm standing there, trying to get romantic, and Syd's gargling in the background about how soothing emu oil is for those troublesome cracks between your toes.

At lunchtime we head to Room 32, where the Big Kids are supposed to assemble to meet the Little Kids. Mrs Gonzales is waiting. Mrs Gonzales has got the most amazingly big nose. It's got varicose veins. When she gets angry the end of it goes all red.

The Big Kids are a mixture of Clones, Year 12s who want to be social workers, suck-ups like Caroline Dillinger, and psychopaths the Principal thinks might benefit from the responsibility.

As the psychopaths sit up at the back, ripping bits off a Year 7 mural about conserving rainforests, Mrs Gonzales hands out piles of kiddies' picture books. She reminds us that our task won't be easy. She says these children often have unhappy families. She says we're to expect aggression and respond to it with kindness and firmness.

They'll learn from us that learning can be cool. They'll learn from us that when you're angry and frustrated you don't have to respond with violence. The main thing is – we're role models.

A Year 9 psychopath farts. Caroline Dillinger turns to him and whispers, 'If I hear you do that again, I'm dobbing.'

He whispers back, 'OK, next time I'll do it silent.'

Someone sitting by the window yells out that they're arriving. We all rush over. A white minibus pulls up outside the Principal's office. The Yarradindi Primary kids are marched in by three burly teachers.

Brad is one of the first to be called out. He's dark, scrawny – and, boy, is he pleased to get Suzie. A fat kid called Conan gets a two-metre-tall Year 11 psychopath with a wispy beard, and nearly faints. I'm looking everywhere for Jet. Which one is he?

Jet is a girl. She's got green streaks in her hair, a nose ring and a shiny pink plastic koala-shaped backpack. She comes up to me and puts out her hand. As I take it, she stamps on my foot, gives me a Chinese burn on the wrist and hisses, 'Dob, and I'll say you punched me!'

10

We split up into our pairs and sit down at the desks. Suzie waves at me, beams, nods towards Brad and mouths, 'Isn't he cute?' Brad's eyeballs are hanging out on stalks.

I smile at Suzie. Jet's staring round the room, chewing gum and picking her nose. Given the nose ring, this is even grosser than it sounds. I remind myself that her parents probably hate her. Mind you, they could have a point.

I catch Suzie watching me. I beam angelically into Jet's scowling little face. I open a picture book and say loudly, 'All right, Jet, I'll read a bit, then you read a bit.'

I read, ' "My grandma has a great – big – cookie jar. It is orange and green and she keeps it on a shelf in the pantry." Your turn, Jet.'

Jet blinks, flicks a bogey across the room and reads in a really loud voice. ' "My grandma has a great big bum. It is orange and green and she keeps it on a shelf in the pantry." '

I snatch the book away from her. She grabs my pencil case. I try to grab it back, but she whips it away, then gets out my compass and stabs it into the desk. I make a grab for it. She stabs an HB pencil into my hand, then sticks the top end up her nose and wiggles it to get snot on it so I can't grab it. We're wrestling for the pencil under the desk.

This is terrible. I can't even deck her in case Suzie or Mrs Gonzales sees.

The next minute she tears the corner off a page of the book, rolls it up and chucks it at Caroline Dillinger at the same time as doing a big hoicky cough.

Caroline Dillinger gets hit by the paper, thinks it's a gob of phlegm, shrieks, then dobs me in to Mrs Gonzales for letting Jet do it.

Mrs Gonzales tells Jet not to be a naughty girl. Jet blinks innocently and says she's sorry.

The minute Mrs Gonzales has turned her back, Jet hands me the pencil, rummages in her pocket and gets out a pink bobbly liquorice allsort. 'Want this?'

Suzie's watching. So are all the Yarradindi Primary kids.

I say, 'Well! Thank you, Jet,' in that sort of loud, wide-eyed voice your aunties use when they're trying to be your favourite relative.

And pop it in my mouth.

76

All the Yarradindi Primary kids burst into snorty laughter.

Jet chants, 'You ate it. It's bin in my sock. You ate a sweaty liquorice allsort.'

Suzie bursts out laughing. I instantly chuckle like a saintly uncle. I take the liquorice allsort out of my mouth and put it in my hanky.

I beam. 'Now, Jet, that wasn't very nice . . .' and I hiss in her ear, 'Do that again and you're dead meat.'

She looks at me and hisses, 'Pay me and I'll be nice.'

'Get lost.'

'Five dollars or I run out and kick that teacher with the big schnozz.'

She pinches me on the wrist. I pinch her on the wrist back.

She hisses, 'OK. That girl you're hanging out for. Four dollars and I pretend I like you.'

This is one smart monster. She glares at me. I glare back. I can't take the risk.

I mutter, 'One-fifty.'

She smiles smugly and puts out her hand. I slip her the coins. She puts them carefully in her pocket, then folds her arms and says in a loud voice, 'Oh, so *that's* the word for "grandma". I get it. What a good teacher you are, Ian.'

Suzie beams. Mrs Gonzales beams.

For the rest of the lesson Jet's pretending she can hardly read and making loud comments about my teaching ability. Across the room, Brad is behaving like a little angel.

Correction. Suzie reckons he's behaving like a little angel. She's too dense to see he's actually planning to make a move on her and all the grinning and cute colouring-in is him flirting.

What is it with these kids? They're eight and they act like they're about twenty-five. Jet's as tough as an old boot and Brad was probably going steady when he was six. Meanwhile I'm nearly fifteen and the only way I can get near a girl is to babysit bats and get my wrists pinched by feral Primary kids.

Suzie smiles at me and nods approval at Jet, who's so absorbed in colouring that her tongue's half out. I smile back.

What Suzie can't see is that the reason Jet's so rapt is because she's giving Aladdin blacked-out teeth, a semi-automatic and glasses. The bell rings.

Jet picks up her pink koala backpack, blinks sweetly up at me and says loudly, 'Thank you, Ian. Will you be my teacher again?'

Mrs Gonzales beams. Suzie melts. We take the Troubled Children down to the white Council minibus. As Jet gets on, she slips me a bit of paper. 'You can reach me at this number.' She nods towards Suzie and whispers, 'Next time it's three bucks.'

We wave the bus away. Suzie sighs. 'Well. Wasn't that the best thing? They're really going to love Yarradindi Emu World.' Then she adds, 'Ian, after school. Would you like to come over to my place?'

I gasp. I nearly drop down on my knees and thank her. My hands are shaking as I ring Mum to check. I act all casual.

When Mum answers I drawl, 'Ah, Mum, hi. Tonight. OK if I go over to a friend's?'

Mum says, 'No, sorry, it's the Pockys. We're going to their celebration barbecue.'

11

The Pockys? I walk away from Suzie so she won't see me begging and pleading pitifully with Mum. Mum's unshakeable. She says I have to go because Yarradindi Emu World is such a big deal for the Pockys.

As I'm talking, a white Alfa screeches to a halt outside the school gates. It's Jug and Jug's dad, a bald version of Jug. Jug hops out, waves warmly to me, jogs across to Suzie and gives her some music. I hang up, rush back, leap – and swing casually from an overhanging branch. Suzie invites Jug and the other Captains to her place for dinner. He says cool, he'll tell them and they'll all be there by six-thirty.

Meanwhile I'll be celebrating with two hundred maniacs and an emu who can't take his eyes off me.

I'm still hanging there when Jug offers Suzie a lift home in the Alfa, apologizing to me because they're going in the opposite direction to my place. I smile warmly and say it doesn't matter, then drop into a pile of cigarette butts left by Year 12 gang-sters. Jug opens the passenger door so Suzie can get into the back. She bends over and squeezes in, laughing. Jug's laughing like a maniac to cover the fact that he's perving his eyes out.

They roar off.

I go home, feeling murderous.

Mum says, 'Don't look like that. Tonight's special. You can always go to your friend's.'

Yeah, right.

We head to the Pockys in our car, which is not a white Alfa.

Syd's instructions are to turn left at the Big Emu, which Crusher finished this morning and which Syd reckons is already creating tourist interest.

The first sign of the farm is a bit of wood nailed to a tree with the words: 'Emu Farm ahead'. A bit further on there's a sign saying: 'Emu Farm Getting Closer'. Another hundred metres ahead there are two signs, the first an old battered one saying: 'Pocky's Swamp', and the second a brand-new one reading: 'Next Left for Your Big Emu Expeiriense'. Next to the letters is an arrow pointing to an unmade sandy road leading up a hill.

Dad turns left into the road and nearly crashes into several huge lumps of painted concrete toppled around a concrete platform. We stop to look. The biggest bit is a ball about a metre and a half across. It's got bits of chicken wire sticking out of it, plus a couple of tall poles that could be legs. The next biggest is a ball with a triangular bit of chicken wire coming out of one side. A beak?

Dad looks at me. I look at Dad.

I say, 'The Big Emu?'

Dad says, 'What on earth could've knocked that over?'

At that moment there's an amplified mooing, and we see Terry's ute whizzing down the track from up the hill. Terry leans out of his window.

'G'day! Just coming up to tell you to watch out for the Big Emu.'

We all look respectfully at the lumps of concrete.

Terry sighs. 'I clipped it with the trailer half an hour ago. Crusher's ropeable – but what d'ya do? I said when he was making it, the concrete was too dry. It's brittle. Hey presto, the slightest tap and it's over.'

He turns to my little sister Daisy and beams.

'There's a big surprise for kids who've been good!'

That moment there's a huge explosion.

Whooomph!

The ground shakes. A big flock of birds goes

squawking frantically up into the sky. We hear distant cheers and applause.

Dad gasps. 'What on earth was that?'

Terry chuckles. 'Darn kids. They've started without us.' He revs the ute. 'We're blowing up tree stumps.'

As we go bumping up the track after Terry's ute there's a series of ground-shaking explosions, followed by cheers. The birds are going berserk. It's the Pocky equivalent of a fireworks display. It's like being in the middle of a war zone.

Mum leans forward. 'Pete, this is dangerous.'

Dad grins. ' Oh – isn't this what we came to the country for? Peace and quiet?'

Whooomph!

We drive up a hill and round a bend, to see a ramshackle one-storey wooden house surrounded by rusting cars. We're on the flat top of the hill. Down one side of the hill are open paddocks with a few trees, an old barn and a marshy creek way below in the valley. On the other side of the hill it's just dense bush.

There's no sign of Bruce Willis the emu, but there are lots of half-completed enclosures and sheds tilting to one side. A bunch of Pocky toddlers are playing frisbee with a cowpat.

A toilet bowl stands completely alone in the middle of a paddock.

Mum says, 'There's no chance this place can be finished by Sunday, surely?'

Dad shrugs. 'Syd reckons it will, bar the adventure rides, which is probably just as well.'

Down the hill, a mob of Pockys are clustered near some tree stumps, waiting for the next explosion.

As we drive up, Syd pulls a funny face at Daisy and waves us in cheerily. 'Aaah! Come in! Missed a big one, a silly begga, aaaaah!'

From the distance there's a yell, 'Fire down the hole!'

Whooomph!

We get out of the car – and immediately duck because it's raining little clods of earth. From the bottom of the hill there's enthusiastic applause and cheering.

Terry's striding across from the ute to welcome us. He's wearing an emu leather waistcoat. His singlet reads: 'Don't be a Goose, let Pocky fix your Sluice'. 'Come down for a look. We normally use just the one stick a jelly. Doing two today.' He winks at Mum. 'It's by way of a celebration. The old farm hasn't been a working property since me great-grandad's day. But you wait. This'll be the best farm in the area. Not to mention tourist attraction.' He points to the pile of wood and roof iron by the gate. 'See that? That's Dad's idea. That's the Emu Education Centre. We're just getting the display together. Dad's working out a quiz.'

Syd yells, 'Aaah, warra six foot six, live Austraya, gorra wings a khan fly, a-makes a bigga omelette inna world, a cheeky begga, aaah?'

Dad ventures, 'The emu?'

Terry shouts with laughter, 'Got it in one!'

Syd's rapt. ' Aaaah, brainy begga-aaaah!'

He scoops Daisy up and tosses her in the air. We all gasp. Luckily he catches her.

We walk past a wrestling ball of Pocky toddlers.

Terry turns seriously to Dad. 'You see, Pete, it's not the money. It's about getting the kids back on the land.'

Whooomph!

A wombat goes galloping over the hill, pursued by a four-wheeled motorbike crammed with junior Pockys. Syd chats about progress at Yarradindi Emu World. They've had a few setbacks, like the time when the whole family divided into four teams to build a shed. They finished it, then discovered they'd forgotten to put in any door. Now the emus due today aren't arriving until tomorrow.

Terry winces, scratches under his arm and says, 'Darn mozzies. These bites in me pits are giving me murder!' He lifts his arm. A big, pointy tail of red and blond hair pokes out. He scratches luxuriously and sighs, 'Jeez, that's a relief!'

No way am I bringing Suzie to the Opening.

Crusher lumbers out of the barn with a rusty car door tucked under one arm like a newspaper. He's wearing emu leather shorts and his legs look like hairy blond tree trunks. Terry takes us up to see the view. We stare across the valley. It's dense bush all the way to the horizon.

Terry sighs. 'Just take in the silence . . .'

Whooomph!

Syd insists we all go to see Bruce Willis, who's apparently eating like a horse and fattening up a treat. He's in the barn because his enclosure fell down due to inferior foreign fence posts. On the way, Terry's making jokes about Bruce having a crush on me. Sure enough, Bruce takes one look at me and starts ducking and bobbing his head and making drumming noises in his throat. It's really embarrassing. Everyone laughs. Bruce even stops eating, which is amazing because, according to Terry, he hasn't stopped eating since he arrived. He even ate Crusher's elastic knee bandage which was accidentally left on a fence post.

Terry goes to give Bruce an affectionate pat, but Bruce just ducks away and keeps staring and drumming at me.

Terry says, 'Eh! Look at ol' Bruce Willis, he's really taken a shine to Ian.'

Everyone roars.

Clint Pocky comes in, flicks my ear and yells, 'Yay, Rudie's on with an emu!'

Syd hoots, 'Good a Clinta Ian such top mates, a silly beggas!'

Terry nods. 'It's amazing that kids whose families live next door to each other get on so well. Ol' Troy here won't go to sleep unless he's bin told a funny story about his big friend Ian.'

Troy looks at me and blows a raspberry.

To think I could be having dinner at Suzie's.

We come out of the barn to hear the sound of a car frantically hooting. An ancient Land Rover comes straining up the hillside track in a cloud of dust.

Terry tuts. 'Ah no – here we go. Here comes old Scraggy Neck.'

The Land Rover skids to a halt at the gate. There's something very familiar about it. A woman leaps out, yelling and screeching. It's Mrs Frye.

If she sees me here, I'm cactus.

12

I shoot behind the barn. There's no way the Fryes'll let me near the animals if they think I'm a friend of the Pockys. I know I've got to find a way out of looking after the Fryes' animals, but until I do I'm stuck with it or Natasha can't play the piano for Suzie.

So the Fryes' land adjoins the Pocky farm. I should have realized. The Fryes are at the bottom of the hill and the Pockys are at the top.

Mrs Frye's bellowing at Terry, 'What in heaven's name d'you think you're doing?'

Terry grins and leans on the gate. 'G'day. Just shifting a few stumps.'

Mrs Frye's stuttering with fury. 'You vandal! There's three pairs of endangered spotted swamp finches nesting at the bottom of that hill!'

'They'll be right. They'll take it for distant thunder.'

Whooomph!

'I'm reporting you to the police!'

'Don't you threaten me! I'll report you for digging up my road.'

'We were inserting a wildlife tunnel for endangered bilbies! Endangered because of you – you've been running them over!'

Terry bristles with indignation. 'You listen to me, madam, we've been running them bilbies over for two hundred years.'

Dad steps in. 'Come on now, everyone, I'm sure there's a way of settling the matter.'

Mrs Frye turns on Dad. 'Look around you! It's a wasteland. They won't stop until there isn't a single tree or animal on this land. They're chopping down trees and damming creeks and disturbing the wetlands. Do you know, in Australia we are destroying species before we've even discovered them! There are areas of wilderness that have never even been properly examined for new species . . .'

Mum's uncomfortable because she sympathizes with Mrs Frye on this one. 'But it *is* their property . . .'

Terry interrupts. 'I know what this is all about. This is all about you putting your darn wildlife windows round our swamp.'

'Corridors, not windows!' Mrs Frye slaps her hand on her forehead dramatically. 'All we're asking for is a few trees to permit animals to move freely across your land . . .'

The wombat goes shooting past at sixty kilometres an hour, pursued by Clint on the four-wheeled motorbike.

Terry hoots, 'They look like they're moving pretty freely to me! You want a corridor? Just follow him!'

Mrs Frye's purple with rage. 'That is scandalous!'

'Na. It's good for 'em. Keeps 'em fit – keeps 'em frightened of humans. You don't want wild animals getting tame.'

I don't think there's any chance of that.

I feel a sharp pain in my hand. A miniature female Pocky is biting it. It looks like Syd with pink ribbons. I whack her. She whacks back. She keeps whacking me as I desperately try to listen to what's going on.

Dad's trying to persuade Terry and Mrs Frye to break it up. At the same time the Pockys are loudly defending their treatment of local wildlife. They reckon they're savage and will go you as soon as look at you.

Maybe they're right. Maybe they're actually improving the wildlife. Maybe two hundred years of Pocky inhabitation has bred a specially tough species of animals. Certainly, any animals that have survived around the Pockys for a hundred years would have to be the toughest in the area. The koalas probably spend the afternoons kick-boxing.

Now Mrs Frye's getting furious. She says the emu farm will open over her dead body. She says she'll go to the highest court in the land to stop it. She says the Pockys can expect a visit from the Council plus the wildlife protection people, who'll shut the farm down.

Terry's saying he'll take a rifle to anyone trespassing on Pocky land.

Suddenly, Crusher gives a terrible roar and snaps a fence post as thick as a brick across his thigh.

Mrs Frye yells, 'Don't think I'm intimidated!' and shakes her fist.

As she drives off, a roar of fury goes up from the Pockys. Terry yells that Crusher will be after her pressure points, and ten seconds on her carotid and she'll know what it's all about. Syd and Mum are trying to cool people down, but the Pockys are all threatening terrible things to anyone trying to interfere with Yarradindi Emu World.

Ouch! The Pocky toddler is nearly through to the bone of my thumb. My dad jumps up on to a box of beer cans (he's little as well) and says there's no need for people to get upset. He says Mrs Frye was just letting off steam. There's no way she'll really interfere.

This cheers everyone up. Syd chucks a can of kero on the barbie to get it going again. A bit spills and causes a grass fire, which is soon put out by Terry, who thoroughly drenches the area with a hose. He goes on to thoroughly drench everyone standing anywhere near the area, which increases the holiday mood. In ten minutes everything's back to normal.

While the emu fillets, emu sausages and emu patties sizzle away on the barbie, Crusher gathers the junior Pockys for another stump detonation in the gully.

Granny Pocky comes round with emu egg rolls for Mum, Dad and me and a miniature sandwich for Daisy. I really don't want to eat this. I take a gulp. It's OK. It tastes just like a normal egg sandwich, except, as Granny points out, one emu egg serves a family of four.

Granny tells us that the Grand Opening is on her and Syd's wedding anniversary. They got married forty years ago to the day. The Cannibals formed a guard of honour outside the church. Granny wore a black ankle-length leather dress with a slit up each side. Syd's bike was draped in white ribbons. Syd's listening. He gets all sentimental. He shows us a tattoo on his chest that reads 'Syd for Gloria'. Granny shows us a tattoo on her leg that says 'Gloria for Syd'.

Granny says that she's trying to get Syd to renew their vows. This is when people who've been married for ages have a kind of repeat wedding to let everyone know they're still serious. Apparently some married couple on a TV home renovation programme renewed their vows just after they ripped out someone's attic. Now all the wrinklies are doing it.

I think mournfully of what's going on at Suzie's. I get a terrible image of Suzie and Dan walking hand in hand round the garden and getting into a clinch next to the water feature.

Syd suddenly yells, throws his barbecue scraper down and starts gargling wildly. There's a lot of 'Aaaahs' and 'Cheeky beggas'. All the Cannibals get very excited. Granny goes all pink and giggly. The crocodile rolls in her cleavage.

Syd's suggesting that he and Granny have their repeat wedding ceremony at the Grand Opening of Yarradindi Emu World as a gimmick and crowd-puller.

Since my mum's a marriage celebrant, she could run the ceremony. Terry comes up and says he reckons this is a cool idea. All the Pockys start thumping Syd on the back and hugging Granny.

The question is, can it be organized in time? Dad and Lily are given the job of arranging the cavalcade of bikes. Lily, who's a man, is well known for doing wheelies on his Harley all the way along the pedestrian mall. Skull says he'll be fine, now he's back on his medication.

As the Cannibals break up into groups to discuss all this, I manage to squeeze out between them and walk off across the hill. The sun is setting.

Way down below is the Fryes' place with all its sheds and water tanks, linked by a crazy network of pipes. I can see Noddy grazing next to the tennis court fence.

I think yearningly of going to Suzie's. Maybe she likes me. Let's be realistic here – maybe she could get to like me.

A voice yells out, 'So. You're part of this emu farm as well, are you!'

It's Natasha Frye.

13

The last thing I need is a lecture about spotted swamp finches or some such.

She's come over from the Fryes' side of the fence. This isn't difficult, since the fence is down. I turn on my heel, pretend I haven't seen her and hurry off over the other side of the hill towards the farmhouse. She's yelling something about the Pocky Wetlands.

It's weird to hear the Pocky Swamp being called wetlands. Wetlands makes me think of people with binoculars, while the Pocky Swamp makes me think of abandoned cars and teenage Pockys holding people's heads under water.

At the bottom of the hill there's a dilapidated old barn. Good. The ideal place to keep away from Natasha and Clint. What a pair. I flop down and lean against the wall. There's a weird noise. Like a droning. Something's happening inside.

I peek through a dirty old window. A bunch of people are sitting cross-legged in a circle. They're wearing ski masks and chanting. It's like they're praying or something. The leader seems to be a big fat woman wearing baggy trousers made of sacking.

She puts up her hand to stop the others chanting, then gets to her feet. 'With the permission of the Bottle-Nosed Orange Flying Fox, endangered species of this area, this meeting is now opened.'

Across her bum are printed the words: 'Desiree Potatoes. Grade A'. Down her leg it says, '80 kilos unwashed'.

What's going on?

There's a general mutter of conversation. Spud Bum raves on about the ecology and emus and why the Pockys should be planting soya beans. She says she personally lived in a tree for three years to save the environment.

By the size of her it must have been a pretty big tree.

I thought the Fryes were lunatics, but this lot leaves them for dead. What are they doing here? I thought I was on Pocky land, but this must be the Fryes' barn.

A weedy male ski mask starts talking about how he also lived in a tree. He survived on bush tucker and after two years found he could talk to the wallabies. He demonstrates basic greetings in wallaby language and how to say 'The police have just arrested me'.

The police? I'm out of here. This is some loony group the Fryes are involved with. I've had enough Frye insanity for this week. I set off.

Somewhere back in town Suzie's staring into the eyes of Dan the Captain while he tells her how he recently conquered Mount Everest or rescued three families from a burning building.

I wish I could do something heroic. You can't get away from it: the only thing I've got going for me is Big Kids, Little Kids and my love for the planet. Tomorrow I'll have to corner Suzie and get her into the idea of us taking Jet and Brad to the park to experience Healthy Outdoor Activity and Sports, which Mrs Gonzales reckons is really important for Troubled Children.

I'd probably have to handcuff Jet to the basketball net, but it beats having my first date with Suzie at the opening of Yarradindi Emu World with Terry scratching his armpits.

I pass Bruce Willis's shed. Thank heavens he's shut up. Except he isn't. As I turn the corner I see him in a new enclosure, with Terry banging the last nails into a fence post. Bruce catches sight of me and starts drumming. Oh no . . .

Now he's walking beside me on his side of the fence. Terry and a bunch of Pocky kids in emu leather hats are cheering. I shout and shake my fist at him, but he keeps following. Finally I go ballistic and chuck a stone right in front of him. Without stopping, he bends, swallows it in one gulp and keeps on following me.

By the time I find Mum and Dad, the party's breaking up and they're leaving. In fact, everyone's leaving except Crusher, who's now living in the farmhouse. Crusher says, after what Mrs Frye said, from now on he'll do a nightly patrol.

Syd detonates one last load of explosives for the toddlers. They stand around in their little dressing gowns, eyes aglow.

Whooomph!

Dad says, 'Well, as you say, at least emus are good for the environment.'

Mum shifts Daisy on her hip. 'If there's any environment left.'

Next morning I'm up early. I stare at my gut in the mirror as I do my hair. I've got so fat, Wish I had a six-pack. I've got more like a fourteen-pack. The main thing is to keep Suzie's mind off the Captains. I remember this video we had at school on self-confidence. It said to be self-confident you have to believe you're self-confident. I try to believe I'm self-confident.

It doesn't work.

I don't know who makes these videos. They must live on another planet. It's like the video we had in sex education, which said that a teenager's sex life was a wild rollercoaster.

I wish.

A rollercoaster? Mine's more like one of those kiddies' merry-go-rounds with big pink bunnies and Thomas the Tank Engine, puttering slowly round in circles. I try one more time to believe I'm self-confident.

Not looking in the mirror helps.

I head off. Syd's yelling over the back fence to Dad that Crusher's building a brand-new Big Emu and Granny Pocky's gone out to buy the fabric for her repeat wedding dress, which has to be made in a total hurry. To add to the excitement the new emus have arrived.

I get to school. As usual, Suzie's nowhere to be seen. It's really frustrating how at school she's always doing things in every spare moment. Bogle and Pricey come up with Bogle's new version of the mobile phone. Bogle insists on ringing me on my mobile to show how you can talk in whispers on mobile phones and the other person still hears you.

He reckons this proves his theory that all those people who talk loudly on mobile phones to their girlfriends are just idiots. I reckon all it proves is that Bogle's jealous of people with girlfriends. Which goes for all of us. I'm tempted to stay and talk, but I've got to find Suzie. I kind of miss them. It's not that I did anything much with Pricey and Bogle, it's just that I didn't have to be on my guard all the time. I have a quick vision of Suzie's armpit. She's worth it.

I make for the library in case she's putting up signs about something, and I get trapped by Melissa, who wants to tell me what you do if your best friend gets a fish bone trapped in their throat.

She's just about to demonstrate how you grab the person from behind and make them vomit it back up when luckily Suzie comes hurrying up.

My chest seizes with excitement. I'm so off-guard that when I spring on to the cyclone fence to dangle so I can say Hi at eye level I miss my grip, drop on to the asphalt and land sideways on my ankle. It really kills. I try not to hobble. Luckily Suzie doesn't notice.

She's chatting away about the Student Representative Council. This is an incredibly boring thing where people spend hours discussing stuff like whether Year 10 girls can wear skirts with pleats. I don't mind. I could listen to Suzie reading the entire Yellow Pages.

We set off to roll call. Apparently, there's a Student Representative meeting coming up to discuss what shoes Year 7 are allowed to wear. Frankly, I couldn't care if Year 7 came to school wearing cornflake packets strapped to their feet, but I've got to make Suzie think she's got more in common with me than with the Captains.

So I go into all this stuff about how good shoes are essential to growing feet. Suzie's nodding and saying 'Mm' at all the right moments. She interrupts to tell me all about the benefits of school uniform generally. This is cool because with a bit of luck I can turn the conversation from this to uniforms in primary schools. From where I can suggest the two of us take Brad and Jet to the park.

I'm just saying, 'But of course, what all young kids need is Healthy Outdoor Activity . . .' when suddenly Natasha Frye appears.

She says, 'Excuse me, Suzie, I have to talk to Ian about the bats,' and drags me off round a corner.

I'm ropeable.

I hiss, 'What d'you think you're doing!'

'I need you to spy on the Pockys.'

14

'What? Are you demented? Oh. Yes. Silly me. You are.'

'There's only two days to close that emu farm down. I need everything you can get so I can take it to the newspapers and the RSPCA. Photos, letters, documents – anything that can prove the Pockys are being cruel to those emus . . .'

'They're not being cruel. They really like them . . .'

She jams her scowling face up to me.

'It may not matter to you that the Pockys are destroying the rainforest, but it does to me.'

'They are not destroying the rainforest . . .' I tail off as I get an image of Syd blowing up a tree stump.

'Have you seen how they persecute the native animals? And now emus!'

'But emus *are* native animals.'

'Yes, and the Pockys are planning to eat them!'

She's got a point.

She's off again. 'Did you know their property backs on to the largest wilderness area in the State? There'll be dogs getting in, and rubbish being left about. Have you seen how many wrecked cars they've dumped in the wetlands?' She's spluttering with rage. 'There's not even a proper fence in the whole property. This morning a whole bunch of emus arrived and came straight down and ate all our vegetables, probably because they're totally starving to death . . .'

'But emus eat anything.'

She talks over me '. . . and yet the Council's letting them run an emu farm. Look at this.'

She pulls out a copy of the local free newspaper. It's got a picture of Syd standing next to Bruce Willis and the headline: 'Syd Gets the Bird'. Syd is winking and holding a knife and fork over Bruce's head. Bruce is staring, pop-eyed, at the camera, looking like Kermit the frog.

She reads, ' "Syd Pocky, local motorbike celebrity, sees emu burgers as the solution to Yarradindi's failing meat slaughter industry. Syd estimates that Bruce the emu could produce as much as thirty kilos of meat and twenty-eight kilos of fat . . ." ' She splutters, '. . . which is about three hundred hamburger patties and six bottles of hand lotion . . . I mean, how could he? Look at that emu's face.' She jams her face up to mine. 'Yarradindi Emu Farm must be shut down.'

'Well, you do it.'

She stamps her foot in frustration.

'I've tried. I've cut their wire fences. I've turned their water tanks on and left them running. They're so stupid, they either don't notice or they think it's one of their horrible kids.'

She's cut down the Pockys' fences? She really is crazy.

She hisses at me. 'You spy on them. You tell me about any examples of cruelty to those emus.'

'I can't spy on the Pockys. They'd kill me if they found out. Anyway, what am I supposed to spy on?'

She screws her face up savagely and folds her arms.

'Think it over. Help me get Yarradindi Emu World closed down or I don't play the piano for Suzie. You've got till tonight when I get back from the rehearsal.

I'll see you at my place.'

She stalks off down the corridor. It's as much as I can do to stop myself lobbing my copy of *Way Cool Maths, Year Eight* at her. It really annoys me how they try to make really boring school books sound like the most exciting thing in your life. Like, if they stick a few cartoons on the front and call it

Whoa, Man – it's History . . . ! we'll all be fighting to do it. Now Suzie's gone and I've missed my chance to bring up the trip to the park. Great. Thanks, Natasha Loony-Tunes Frye. And if you think I'm going anywhere near the Pockys' place with Crusher patrolling the fences and ready to go for my pressure points, you're dopier than I thought. I mean, what's her problem? Why is she so anxious to shut down the Pockys? What's wrong with an emu farm?

Spying on the Pockys. And now I won't see Suzie now until lunchtime because all the Clones do genius-level maths. Plus my ankle's killing me.

I limp into Maths late. The only place left is next to Caroline Dillinger. She does an exaggerated snort of disgust because I'm sitting down next to her. I do an exaggerated snort back and pull a savage face.

She leans over. 'If you reckon Suzie McLaren would ever go out with you, Eeyun . . . !'

I do a rude gesture. She does a rude gesture. Mr Andropolous sees her and raises his eyebrows, so she turns it into pretending she's coughing and covering her mouth. Great. Good. This is the only good thing that's happened to me in days.

The minute Mr Andropolous turns his back she whispers, 'Suzie McLaren and Dan spent an hour alone at her place learning their lines together – as if. They were making out.'

'And you'd know, Ape Face?'

'More than you, Chunky. Ask her.'

Mr Andropolous turns round and tells us how to work out the surface area of a cone. This is really useful if you need to calculate the size of your ice cream.

Suzie and Dan learning their lines together. This is serious.

I glance over at Natasha. She mouths, 'You and the Pockys.'

I glance over at Caroline. She mouths, 'Get nicked.'

I have to see Suzie. I have to find out what's happening. As if I don't know what's happening. Suzie shut up alone with something out of an Iron Man commercial – what's likely to happen?

For the rest of the class I'm tortured by mental pictures of Suzie and Dan. I've got to stop them being together. I try to concentrate on the maths questions. I read number one. 'Debbie has blown up twenty-three balloons for her little brother's birthday party . . .' I'd say Debbie needs to get a life. How can I prevent Suzie from seeing Dan?

At the lunch bell I hobble off towards the library to catch Suzie coming out of Advanced Maths. This play's the cause of all my problems.

Correction. Natasha Frye's the cause of all my problems. If she hadn't volunteered to be the pianist, there wouldn't be a play at all. And if she hadn't punched me in the stomach during the drama presentation we put on in Assembly, by now I'd be on with Suzie. Still. No point in lingering on it.

I get there as Suzie's coming out with Melissa and Jesse. She's so gorgeous I nearly say something out loud. I can't let Dan take her.

She sees me, beams, says, 'Hi, Ian, coming to lunch?'

I glow. Lunch with Suzie . . . !

And Jesse says, 'He can't. He's got Chess Club.'

Not Chess Club. Please, not Chess Club.

I'll have to get myself knocked out as soon as possible. How fast can I lose three games? I beat all records and lose three games in ten minutes. Toad Face looks anxious. He tells me he's not going to any more tournaments because of the risks. He says he's taking up tae kwon do because he reckons it's safer. I do a flying hobble back to the library lawn, where Suzie normally has lunch. She's gone off to band practice. I go to the music room. I've just missed her.

Finally, I find her beside the basketball courts talking to a bunch of Year 7s about the Student Representative Council and what shoes they're allowed to wear. I quickly join in. Normally I'd spring up and hang on to the wire fence during the discussion, but my ankle's still bad and I can't do the jump. So I stand rocking on tiptoe like it's an absent-minded habit and jabber away about foot fungus.

Suzie looks at her watch and says, 'Oh no, I've got a Leadership Seminar. I know, tell Ian. Ian knows all about it,' and she heads off.

The Year 7s don't miss a beat. They're off again about the individual's right to choose. They say they want the right to wear any shoes they like, including no shoes at all, plus time off for anyone who wants to go to Melbourne for a rock concert.

I say, 'Fine. I'll recommend that to the Principal.'

By the time they've finished cheering, the bell goes and I've lost another chance to talk to Suzie. I'm done for. There's another rehearsal tonight, and every rehearsal means more chance of the Captains getting Suzie.

The rest of school passes in a blur. In Science I try to sit next to Suzie, but she's surrounded. In History the same thing happens. It's like I'm doomed. Last period is French. Suzie's of course in the genius stream that goes to the university for special talks by French people. I'm the first out of class when the bell goes. I limp at top speed to the hall to catch Suzie before the Captains.

I rush in. It's empty. Except for Dan. He's there on his own.

He beams and says warmly, 'G'day, mate.'

I flop on to a bench. He comes up and sits next to me. I could belt him one. Any minute I have to go and look after Natasha's reeking bats, while he's here with Suzie, singing about saving the oceans. Like he cares about the oceans. He's after Suzie's armpit like the rest of us.

He shifts uneasily. 'Can I ask you something? You're a friend of Suzie's . . .' He coughs uneasily and tosses his big, film star's head. 'D'you know if she's seeing anyone?'

15

I blink. I invent a boyfriend who lives in Melbourne. Dan asks his name. My mind goes blank.

I see an old chip packet and say, 'Chippy.'

Dan says, 'Chippy, eh? Weird name.'

Now he won't stop asking about Chippy. I keep trying to change the subject, but he won't let me. I'm inventing stuff as fast as I can go. I invent Chippy's family, his hobbies, his looks. I rattle on about Chippy's brilliant school results and personal bravery. I explain how Chippy saved Suzie from drowning, which is why he and Suzie are probably going to get married. By the time some other kids arrive I'm starting to believe in him myself. Dan stares at me, his eyebrows raised.

I scuttle off at a fast limp. What's happening to me? I'm becoming a compulsive liar. That's another thing they don't mention in all those videos on becoming a teenager. They tell you all about smoking and horrible diseases, and they show animations of hormones sloshing in bucket loads round your innards. They don't say you'll end up inventing a whole fake world to get a whiff of deodorant and fabric softener.

The lie I liked the best was Chippy's older sister. She was leader of a girls' band and was planning to stand for parliament.

I head off to the Fryes. Now all I've got to do is stall whacko Natasha about getting me to spy on the Pockys.

Easy peasy.

Not. If I don't spy, she won't play the piano; even worse, she'll dob me in to Suzie for being a fraud. This is getting insane. And now there's this Chippy thing. The minute Dan asks Suzie about Chippy, she'll tell him it's a pack of garbage. I'll have to catch him and tell him she doesn't like talking about Chippy.

But why wouldn't she like talking about Chippy? After all, he's terrific. Maybe he's dead. Maybe Chippy's dead and Suzie's so heartbroken she can't talk about him. That's ridiculous. If he's dead, Suzie's available. I curse silently. Typical Clone, dying heroically and causing problems for everybody normal. Maybe he's just dying a slow death.

I hear a car horn tooting. It's a red Porsche. It's Jug's dad driving Jug and Harris to the rehearsal. I smile through gritted teeth. Then there's the roar of motorbikes and yelling. It's the Cannibals, led by

Syd and Dad. They stream past in formation, waving cheerfully.

I wave back, then feel terrible. Here I am, thinking about spying on Syd and wrecking his farm just so I can get Suzie. I mean, how can I ruin Syd's farm? He's a friend. How can I betray him? And of course there's the small issue that he'd flatten me.

At the entrance to Yarradindi Emu World, Crusher's out in his leather shorts, repairing the Big Emu with a trowel and a bucket of concrete. He's fattened its legs to make it more stable. It looks like it's wearing trousers.

I get to the Fryes'. Noddy's standing, grasping the fence, under a sign saying 'Yarradindi Animal Refuge. Help our defenceless animals'. He growls throatily and tries to claw me.

I see Mr Frye holding a lettuce and groaning. The groaning's not him, it's the windmill that pumps water for his watering system. He looks up.

'Hello, Ian. I suppose Natasha told you about those emus getting our vegetables.'

I murmur apologetically.

'Our whole crop's gone. Now the windmill's broken and I've pulled my back chasing those birds. Can you get up there and tighten that screw?'

He hands me a screwdriver. I climb up the ladder on the side of the windmill.

I can see for miles. If I look in one direction I can see the town and, beyond it, the ocean. If I look in the other I can see up the hill to the bottom bit of the emu farm. Huge floodlights are being set up so the work can continue at night. A giant excavator's digging an enormous hole for something or other.

Frye looks up and smiles wanly. 'Beautiful view, isn't it. Just rolling hills and pasture.'

Plus floodlights and a ginormous big hole. I don't mention it.

As I fix the windmill, he goes over the last week's events. For a start, Noddy escaped and cornered a bunch of roadworkers who were having chips and Big Macs by the Fryes' front gate. Then yesterday Terry accidentally cut the phone cable with his bobcat and joined the wrong wires together. So the Fryes kept getting phone calls meant for the Pockys and vice versa. The Fryes had a whole morning of people ringing up and offering them cheap chainsaws and pig-shooting holidays before Terry sorted out his mistake.

Back at the Pockys', people were phoning in to ask the best thing to do with injured wildlife. The Pockys were recommending a quick bullet between the ears.

Now Mrs Frye has heard that Terry is thinking of letting his Yarradindi Skydiving Club mates drop people over his land, so it will literally be raining Pockys.

Suddenly there's a yell. 'Michael!'

It's Erica Thacker, the leader of the local conservationists. She's pulled up outside the gate in her Land Rover. She gets out and comes stomping across to us. She's livid.

It turns out that Mrs Frye has been chalking rude messages about Yarradindi Emu World all over the shopping mall. All the shopkeepers are ropeable and have been ringing up Erica Thacker and abusing her because they think she did it.

Mrs Thacker's so furious, she's spraying spit all over us and there's froth in the corners of her mouth.

She says Mrs Frye is giving wildlife carers a bad name. She says Mrs Frye is going to lose the Fryes their licence to run a wildlife refuge. She says that emu farms are ecologically sustainable and conservationists should be supporting them as an alternative to cattle and sheep. She winds up saying that unless Mr Frye stops Mrs Frye defacing people's property, the Frye family is in big trouble, and if you ask her, Mrs Frye is a dangerous menace.

I'd agree with that.

She looks at me wildly, snorts, 'Don't say I didn't warn you you're working with the State's biggest animal welfare lunatics!' and stalks off.

114

Noddy growls and rattles the fence as she passes. Mr Frye smiles brightly at me as if it's the commonest thing in the world to have people claiming your wife's criminally insane.

We head for the house. I can see Mr Frye's mind is racing about his wife, but I don't say anything. I wonder if he knows about those whacko Greenies meeting in his barn?

As we get to the back door, Mr Frye stops me and forces a grin.

'Horace alert. Mrs Frye did say she'd lock Horace up, but if she didn't . . .'

He rattles the back-door handle and listens. Nothing. He smiles encouragingly but signals to me to wait. Very slowly he opens the door. He puts his head around it. Nothing. He beams back at me and goes inside.

Suddenly there's terrible bat screeching, accompanied by yells and curses from Mr Frye. Horace was waiting for him. Through the frosted glass I can see Mr Frye trying to get Horace off his beard. They wrestle furiously round the kitchen. A door crashes.

A few moments later, Mr Frye appears. His hair is sticking out all over the place and his beard is ruffled in clumps.

'All clear.'

This bloke is an absolute saint.

We set to on the fruit chopping. My brain is working overtime. Things are really hotting up between the Fryes and the Pockys. Mrs Frye's doing graffiti all over the shopping centre. Natasha's building up for a raid. There's no way I'm getting involved.

But how can I avoid it? Natasha's arriving back from rehearsal in a couple of hours with this mad thing about me spying. I'm interrupted by Mr Frye plonking down a box of mouldy oranges ready to chop. He's saying how Natasha used to be really into music. Now she's given it up. He's worried she's going to drop out of school. He's worried about her future.

I murmur sympathetically and defrost some baby mice. Personally, I reckon she's got a great career ahead of her as a professional blackmailer.

We head off to the bat cages, loaded with buckets of fruit. I'm racking my brain for ways I can get out of spying on the Pockys. The problem is, there's nothing to spy on. But Natasha's so mental she won't believe that. The only thing that'll satisfy her is proof the Pockys are being cruel to Bruce Willis. Maybe I could make something up.

Oh no, not again. Not more lying. It's bad enough having to cope with Chippy, let alone invent another pack of big ones.

Mr Frye suddenly says murmurs, 'So. What do you think's wrong with Natasha?'

I could give him a list, but it's not what he wants to hear. I rack my brains for something to say. I remember what my gran's been saying about me since I was three.

I say, 'She's going through a phase.'

His face lights up. He's like a drowning man who's been thrown a lifejacket. He wipes a mixture of bat mucus and fruit skin off his arm, beams and says, 'A phase. Yes. I think you're right. She's going through a phase. Thank you, Ian. Thank you.'

Well, he's easily satisfied. I suppose if you've got an insane wife and a crazy daughter, you clutch at straws. As a reward, he offers me the chance to go and listen to the latest shrike-call recordings. The calls this week have been particularly interesting because three males have established nests close together and they seem to be communicating in a very unexpected way. He says it will be the recording of a lifetime.

I say, normally I couldn't resist, but tonight I've got homework. He keeps up a running commentary of thanks and descriptions of Natasha's good points as we feed the rest of the vicious animals we're supposed to be protecting.

Why are they all so vicious? It's not like this in all those nature documentaries about sick animals. I'm supposed to be collecting the dirty plastic bowls from this morning's feeds, but there's no way I'm going inside those cages. I just open the gates and slide the new food in.

Now – whoopee – I'm outside the cage of Bobby the Hairy-Nosed Wombat, who's going to be Bobby the Dented-Bum Wombat if he charges me again. He's nowhere to be seen. He must be in his burrow, under the logs. I unlock the gate. Suddenly, he gives a roar and thunders out from behind me. I chuck the food at him, slam the gate, slip on a pile of old eagle perches and land flat on my back in the compost heap.

Mr Frye rushes over and picks me up. He beams and says, 'Can't let Natasha's boyfriend come a cropper.'

Brilliant. He thinks I'm her boyfriend. I'd rather go out with a man-eating crocodile. Come to think of it, a man-eating crocodile's probably less dangerous. I've put my hand right in a big pile of manure.

By the time Natasha arrives I'm out in the yard, scrubbing ninety plastic buckets under the tap and seething with rage and jealousy.

She says, 'Well? Are you going to spy on the Pockys or am I going to give up playing the piano and tell Suzie you're a fraud?'

At that moment a splinter from the scrubbing brush jams itself down inside my nail. I snap. I start

yelling at her. I call her every name I can think of.
I tell her I couldn't care less about her animals. I tell
her there's no way I'm doing any more of her dirty
work. I don't care whether she dumps the play or
tells Suzie, I've had enough.

I chuck down my scrubbing brush and head off
to my bike. Getting a girlfriend's just not worth all
this. She's yelling after me. I don't care. She's telling
me she's going to ring Suzie. I don't care.

But I do care. I really want Suzie, and the only
things she likes about me are Natasha's animals
and Jet.

I stop. Natasha pounces.

'Right. Are you in this or not?'

In what? There's nothing to spy on at the
Pockys'. But if I don't pretend to spy she'll wreck
any chance I've got with Suzie. I hesitate. A voice
inside tells me I'll find a way out. She's smart, but
she's not as smart as me.

I nod.

'Right. Follow me.'

We go into a shed. She gets a mallet, two ham-
mers, some wire-cutters and two chisels and sticks
them in her Save the Whale backpack.

'What are these for?'

'We're smashing up the Big Emu.'

16

'We're *what*?'

She's striding out to her bike. 'Guerrilla warfare. Part two of a three-pronged attack. We're giving the Pockys a warning of what's to come if they don't close that place.'

'Now you wait a minute. I didn't agree to smash up the Pockys' stuff.'

'They've got to realize what you get if you persecute defenceless animals.'

There's a shriek in the distance as Bobby the Wombat bites Mr Frye.

Before I can say anything, she's off down the drive and heading for the Pockys' gate.

She yells over her shoulder, 'Just say if you want to back out! I've still got my mobile on me!'

I'm left there, shouting protests. This is insane. What do I say if the Pockys turn up while we're caught in the middle of hacking their statue to bits? But I can't risk her dobbing me in to Suzie.

I pedal after her. 'Natasha, you can't do this.'

'Shut up. We haven't got much time. We've got to smash the emu to bits in time to get to the vet's for the possum antibiotics.'

She's completely matter-of-fact about it. She sounds like Mrs De Havilland the Home Science teacher listing what ingredients to put in your sponge cake.

'But the Pockys'll kill you.'

'Shh.'

She suddenly slams on her brakes, jumps off her bike and runs to hide in the bushes. My heart somersaults. I realize why she's hiding. Crusher's still working on the Big Emu Mark II. He's humming as he slaps on bits of concrete with a trowel.

I duck down beside her. As we're watching, he finishes. He stands back and admires his work, then gets in the ute and drives back up the track and over the hill.

Natasha gets up. 'Right, let's do it.'

'No way. What if he sees you?'

'What if I tell Suzie?'

She gets out a huge mallet, marches over to the Big Emu and starts whacking away at it like a maniac. Lumps of wet concrete are flying everywhere. You can see the chicken-wire frame starting to show through.

I can't believe it. This is like some kind of crazy dream. Here we are in the middle of a paddock, blue sky, sun shining – and Natasha's going ballistic at the Big Emu.

She sees me dithering. 'Come on, you big wuss, help me.'

'Get real. He'll come back.'

'Help me or I'll ring Suzie.'

I'm frantic.

'Natasha.'

It's useless. I'll have to do it. The sooner we get this done, the sooner we're out of here. I shoot across, grit my teeth and start hammering away at the Big Emu's left leg.

The noise echoes everywhere. Somebody's got to hear us. We're even annoying the cows! One's mooing like crazy.

Then I realize. It's not a cow.

We scream and dive into the bushes one second before Terry's ute comes screeching in off the highway. It's got a big sign attached to it reading 'Yarradindi Emu World, Where Big Birds Roam'.

Natasha gives a snort of triumph and whispers, 'Let's hear what he says to that!'

Terry stops. He gets out and stares at the smashed-up statue in amazement.

Suddenly, a ute comes down the hill and stops. It's Syd and Crusher. Now they get out and stare in amazement.

The first one to say anything is Terry. He shrugs his shoulders.

He says, 'I told you that concrete was too watery, mate. It's dropped clear off the frame.'

Natasha's mouth drops open. Terry, Syd and Crusher scrape the splattered concrete into a pile, get into their utes, and drive back up the hill.

Natasha jumps up, shrieking with fury. 'Dropped off the frame? Are they idiots? Are they complete morons?'

She lets out a roar, runs to the closest fence and starts trying to chop it with her wire-cutters. This is insane. The Pockys will kill us.

'Natasha, stop. They'll see you.'

She screeches, hurls the wire-cutters to the ground, bellows, 'They're too blunt!' and grabs the lowest wire of the fence. What's she doing now? She gives a bellow and starts yanking it upwards and cursing.

I can't believe this. I'm nearly jumping up and down in panic. 'Are you mad? Stop it!'

She's going totally bananas. She's wrenched the bottom wire right up. She stops, exhausted.

Terry's mooing car horn blasts as he roars down the hill. Oh no! He jams on the brakes. This is it. He'll have seen us! He has seen us! He's going to say something! He leans out of the ute grinning.

'G'day, kids. Youse want a lift into town?'

He stops as he catches sight of the fence Natasha just wrecked. My heart's pounding.

He grins. 'Darn wombats. There's not a fence in existence them little beggas can't wriggle under.'

He gets out, walks over to the fence and, with one mighty yank, pulls it back into position like nothing had ever happened. He dusts his hands and beams.

'Chuck your bikes in the back.'

Natasha stares at him in despair.

He grins. 'Don't worry about them ol' wombats, darl. They'll be back tomorrow sure as look at you.' He puts the ute into gear. 'You know, you wouldn't credit the trouble we've had with them wombats lately. Knocking fences down and chewing through wire. Never knew a wombat could chew wire, but it's been happening round here like billy-o.' He leans over to Natasha. 'My oath, if you didn't know better you'd swear the little beggas was doing it deliberately to annoy us.'

Natasha's shoulders sag. Terry chuckles. Little does he know the main wombat is sitting right next to him.

We roar off into town, narrowly missing a bus and two cyclists. Natasha's fuming.

When we get out at the pedestrian mall, she wheels her bike off at a hundred kilometres an hour. I have to run to catch her up. It's just as well we're walking because she's so furious she'd be running people over.

The Yarradindi Emu World posters now have an extra strip pasted across them saying: 'Plus Surprise Bikie Wedding'.

' "Dropped off the frame . . ."!'

'I don't s'pose they expected someone to be smashing up their statue, Natasha. It's not what people normally do.'

She stops next to the street sign saying 'Bunce Close'. Someone's changed it to 'Bums Close'.

She says, 'Never mind. Plan B.'

'What's Plan B?'

'Plan B is we find incriminating evidence. We break into Syd Pocky's house.'

'Are you crazy!'

'If anyone finds us, we'll say it was you wanting to go in and see your friends the Pockys.'

'Oh right . . . ! "Hi there, officer, I always visit my friends by crawling in through the kitchen window." And what about if Granny and Syd turn up? Or Terry? Or Crusher? You do know he's a trained killer?

'Do it, or I tell Suzie.'

'You dur-brain. I am not breaking into people's houses.'

'Well, don't. Dump Suzie.'

First I'm a vandal. Now she wants me to do break-and-enter.

'I'm not getting myself arrested.'

'You could already be arrested. You just smashed up the Big Emu. I'll say it was all your fault.'

That's it. I'll kill her. I'll get her round that fat throat. I grab at her.

She jumps on her bike and starts pedalling like crazy. I'm after her. I'm grabbing for her hair. She's screaming. I'm nearly level.

Suddenly I hear a car tooting behind us. It's the Captains and Suzie in a silver Mercedes the size of a container truck. I'm within centimetres of getting Natasha, but I can't let Suzie see me assaulting her accompanist. I drop back. Suzie and the Captains overtake, waving. I wave cheerily and beam through gritted teeth.

Natasha gives a whoop of triumph, yells, 'Sucked in!' and rides off towards the vet's.

Greenie moron.

As I come towards our place, there's a rustling in the bushes. It's Jet, wearing her shiny pink plastic backback.

She's seriously ticked off.

'Where have you been? I've been waiting here for hours.' She folds her arms. 'I got a proposition.

126

Five bucks, and next time I come to Big Kids, Little Kids I'll wear ribbons and pretend you just taught me to spell "constitution".'

'Get nicked.'

Then I realize she'll dob me in to Suzie.

We settle for a dollar. I feel exhausted. I s'pose vandalism takes it out of you.

Our shop's full of Cannibals discussing the Grand Opening and all the work they've been doing up at the emu farm. Dad's been flat out arranging the bikies' convoy.

In the kitchen Mum's giving Daisy her dinner and Granny's standing in her new wedding dress. Crusher's pinning up the hem with his giant hands. She looks like she fell into a giant meringue. Crusher grunts a cheerful hello through a mouthful of pins and explains how the blue trimming on the dress is bringing out the colour in Granny's tattoos.

Mum looks up from Daisy's mashed banana. 'Well, Gloria, it's up to you and Syd what you say at the ceremony. You can make promises about the future. You can celebrate all the good things that happened in the past . . .'

Crusher suggests that all the Pocky grandchildren throw rose petals as 'Elvis's Greatest Hits' pumps out through the PA system. I can just imagine Clint Pocky throwing rose petals.

He's more likely to do a moony at the bridal procession.

I sneak off to my room as they get distracted by Granny trying on her bridal veil. I flop on my bed. I can't believe I just helped destroy the Big Emu.

Syd, Crusher, Granny, Dad and all the Cannibals leave for a late-night working bee on the emu farm. I hear them revving their bikes and shouting. There's going to be another working bee up at Yarradindi Emu World tomorrow, plus the final rehearsal for the repeat wedding.

I drop into a deep sleep. I have a nightmare that Terry and an army of Pockys are chasing me through the shopping mall with axes because I told our Principal that Clint Pocky hadn't done his homework. It's incredibly realistic. I wake up in a cold sweat. It's three o'clock in the morning.

For a minute I'm relieved it's only a dream. Then I remember what I did to the Big Emu. If Terry and the Pockys can come at me with axes about Clint's homework, what will they do if they find out I personally took a hammer to the Big Emu's left drumstick and Natasha wants me to break into Syd's house?

And there's still my biggest problem. What am I going to do about the Captains? What if Caroline Dillinger's right, and Suzie and Dan are about to go out together? I stare into the darkness.

128

I'm woken by yells and revving Harleys. I look out of my window. The Cannibals are back. They're dropping in for decaf cappuccinos before they head off for more work at Yarradindi Emu World. They're working like maniacs. Terry and Crusher have joined them. They're both in emu leather hats. Terry's T-shirt reads: 'Don't be a lout, let Pocky fix your grout'.

Syd yells out a friendly greeting. Little does he know I chopped his Big Emu down to the wire. I head down to breakfast. Every surface in our kitchen is covered with giant emu eggs as Mum and Granny experiment with recipes. It looks like some creature from outer space has had a nesting frenzy.

As I help Daisy with her cereal, I rack my brains for ways to get rid of the Captains. Crusher's just arrived with Granny's finished wedding dress. Mum's hiding it in Dad's wardrobe. Syd's not allowed to see it before the ceremony because it's bad luck.

I go and help Dad in the shop. I mix a carrot-and-soy milk smoothie for a big bloke with a nose like a strawberry. Terry's telling Skull and Lily how he and Crusher have just finished the Big Emu Mark III after it fell down due to wet concrete.

Meanwhile Dad's trying to stop Syd spending more and more money on the emu farm. Syd just shifts his emu leather trousers and tells us his latest road-widening plans. To cope with the expected mobs of tourists at the opening, three of Terry's mates are going to turn up with bulldozers today and gouge a six-lane road up the hill to the farmhouse. The Fryes are going to love that.

Forget the Fryes, think of the Captains. What can I do? It's hopeless. I put a tofu burger in the microwave, open a new carton of soy milk and find myself face to face with Dan.

He looks at me through miserable eyes and croaks, 'Tell me more about Chippy.'

17

'Chippy, Chippy. Well. What more can you say about ol' Chippy?' I stare desperately around the shop for inspiration. I catch sight of Dan's anxious face. He really does care about Suzie. This isn't fair. Why isn't he a ratbag? I can't even hate him properly.

He shifts on his stool. 'You see, what I don't understand is why she never talks about him. Have you noticed that?'

'Yes, I have and it's because . . . There's a simple reason for that, Dan, it's because . . .'

Because what? Because what? I'm drowning. Dan's staring at me with his big honest face. My mind's gone a total blank. I clear my throat to play for time.

'You see, it's because . . .'

He interrupts, 'Because, I guess, he's just too . . .' his voice catches, '. . . special to talk about.'

There's a silence broken only by Skull belching.

Dan raises mounful eyes. 'Be honest. D'you reckon I've got a chance with her?'

I look at his huge, muscly shoulders, his film star face. I remember the blazer loaded down with badges. Telling Dan he's not good enough is a porky too big even for me. But I'm trying. My mouth opens and closes like a fish.

Dan watches me, sighs and gives a tortured laugh. 'I thought so. No need to say anything.' He gets up. 'Thanks, mate. I appreciate your time.'

And leaves a tip.

Well, I can't help it if he's a ruddy saint. I angrily wipe down the cappuccino machine. I refuse to feel guilty. I chuck the cloth in the sink, turn the tap on full blast to rinse it, turn back to wipe down the counter and find myself staring at Jet. This is all I need.

She leans her facial piercings over the banana cake. 'I've got a suggestion for you.'

'I've got a suggestion for you. Nick off.'

'That girl. Suzie. I just heard. Last night, big Dan from St Joey's was talking to her outside her house. For ages, right till her mum made her come inside. They reckon this morning he's going back to help her learn her lines. If you don't do something soon, you can forget it.'

If he spends that much time with Suzie he's going to ask her about Chippy.

'What you offering?'

She tilts her face up.

'Five bucks and he's cactus.'

'Five dollars . . . ! I already paid you last night!'

'I'm saving for a tongue stud.'

There's no choice.

'Two. I'm broke. Best offer.'

She sniffs, ponders, hitches up her pink plastic koala backpack and grunts, 'You're on. Shift your butt.'

'Where are we going?'

'To Suzie's.'

To Suzie's? My stomach leaps.

Jet smiles evilly. 'We'll put her off Dan for life.'

I stare at her. She reminds me of a late-night movie I once saw on TV where a little kid was being driven by Evil Forces. Maybe she'll lure me to Suzie's house, then turn green and tear my insides out. Who cares? If it gets me into Suzie's house, it's worth the risk. Outside, Brad from Big Kids, Little Kids is standing by his BMX.

'What's he coming along for? I can't afford to pay him as well.'

'You don't have to. We got a deal.' She smirks. 'He's page boy at his auntie's wedding next week. He's wearing . . .' she sniggers, '. . . a kilt.'

Brad snarls, 'You say anything at school . . .' His voice cracks.

Jet stares at him, straight-faced, says, 'I won't say a word,' then winks at me.

She really is scary. In a few years she'll be running the local mafia. She's probably already running the local mafia. We're going to Suzie's! This is what I've dreamed about.

Jet jumps on her bike. We shoot through back streets, cross over the shopping mall, and suddenly we're outside Suzie's. My heart does a backflip. Jet rings the doorbell then turns to me.

'OK. This is the deal. Brad and me are cute little kids. Act like you're our uncle. Brad, you know what ya do?'

Brad nods.

Jet takes my hand and puckers her face into an angelic expression. What in the world is Jet going to do?

Suzie opens the door. My heart's pounding. Dan looms up sadly behind her, then sees me and beams in welcome. It's obvious from his face that he still thinks he's in competition with Chippy.

That's a relief.

Jet lisps, 'Hawo, Thuzie. Ian was taking me and Brad to the park. And I know it's naughty, but I weally wanted to see you . . .'

Suzie's face softens. So does Dan's, the big dork. His kindness is driving me up the wall. I wish we could get this over with.

Suzie beams, 'Of course, Jet, come in. That was nice of Ian to take you and Brad to the park . . .'

Jet leans up to Suzie and whispers loudly, 'Yes. Ian is my big fwiend. He teaches me weading. I weally like you, but my favouwite, my weally big favouwite is . . . Ian.'

Suzie leads the way into the living room.

'You'd never guess, Dan, but before Brad and Jet came to Big Kids, Little Kids, they were having trouble with their reading.'

Jet adds, 'I was naughty because I couldn't wead the big words. Ian teaches me the big words.' She turns, open-eyed, to Dan, 'Will you teach us weading?'

Oh-oh. Now I understand. She's going to do to Dan what she did to me in Big Kids, Little Kids. But Dan brightens up. Partly he wants to look good in front of Suzie – but mostly, nice bloke that he is, he just wants to make the little kids happy. I wish I could warn him.

Suzie rushes off and gets some kiddies' books. We all sit round the table. Jet arranges it so I'm next to Suzie and Dan's furthest away from her.

Suzie beams round at everyone. 'Now. Brad and Jet will read in turns. You first, Brad.'

Brad stutters through two sentences. Suzie showers him with praise. Then it's Jet's turn. Here we go. I don't know exactly what she's going to do, but she's going to get him. She reads a few words, then pretends she can't read the word 'ought'. Suzie smiles at Dan encouragingly.

A big smile spreads across Dan's flawless face. He says kindly, 'That's "ought", Jet.'

Jet blinks.

Oh no . . .

Dan says, '"Ought" – you know, like, "You ought to clean your shoes."'

Jet looks at her shoes. 'My thews aren't dirty.'

Dan smiles warmly. 'It was just an example.'

Jet's lower lip wobbles. She wails, 'He's being mean about my thews!'

Dan chuckles, then panics. 'Now don't be silly . . . !'

Jet wails, 'Now he says I'm dumb!'

Dan's frantic. 'No, I said you were silly, not dumb, I . . . !'

Suzie jumps in earnestly. 'Dan, to children with low self-esteem like these, it means the same thing. You may think they're dumb . . .'

He's desperate. 'I don't think they're dumb . . . !'

Jet's screaming, 'He said I'm dumb!'

She signals to Brad, who yells, 'He kicked me!'

Brad's screaming in pain. Jet's sobbing uncontrollably. I'm trying to shut them up. Jet's amazing. She's even getting real tears out. Poor old Dan's trying to apologize. Every time he says anything, Jet turns it into another insult. Suzie explains to Dan how sensitive children like Brad and Jet are, then she goes off to get them a chocolate.

Dan hurries after her to try to explain. As soon as they're gone, Jet leans over to me and whispers, 'Check out that TV! These guys are loaded.'

Now they're coming back. Jet whispers something to Brad.

Brad says, 'Dan's gotta take me home to show he doesn't think I'm stupid.'

Suzie gasps. Dan's big, open face winces with pain at the very idea. 'Brad, mate, I don't think you're stupid.'

I feel terrible. 'Na, look, Dan, ignore him. He's just putting it on.'

But Brad starts sobbing and saying Dan's just like everyone else and thinks he's a loser. Jet joins in with protests. Finally, Dan smiles sadly, gives a manly shrug, gets up and says, 'I think I'm going to have to take the little guy home. It's just . . . well, it's being an only child. I'm not used to little kids.'

He's such a saint you could thump him.

Jet and I stay for lunch at Suzie's. First off, I'm guilty about Dan, but I can't keep it up. I'm on a cloud.

I stare round the table at Suzie's perfect family. There's her glamorous, beautiful mother, who's a leading doctor, famed for helping the poor. There's her kind, handsome father, who's a solicitor, famed for giving free legal advice to all the charities within a radius of fifty kilometres. There's her cute little brother, Harry, who's staring up at me with total admiration.

Even their Labrador trained as a guide dog for the blind but had to retire because of a kidney condition.

I'm a bit worried that Jet will blow her nose on the tablecloth or something, but she doesn't. She's perfect. She chatters on cutely about how I'm helping her with her reading.

Then Suzie chatters on gorgeously about our work with Big Kids, Little Kids. The only problem is that she then gets on to how she and I are going to take Brad and Jet to the Grand Opening of Yarradindi Emu World tomorrow.

I try to steer her off it. I suggest a whole range of other activities, but it's no good because the whole of Yarradindi is going to be there. Now her mum chips in and offers to give us all a lift.

I finally manage to switch the subject to how I'm looking after the Fryes' animals so the play can go on. Suzie praises me to her parents. I smile modestly and say it's nothing. Suzie gives me her gorgeous smile and says it's nothing to me because I love animals. She tells her perfect mum and dad how good I am with animals. She goes on about my love for Bobby the wombat and the bats. Harry asks if I want to become a vet.

It's happening again. It's because she's smiling at me.

I say I might become a vet.

They all 'Ooh' and 'Ah'.

I say I will become a vet.

They 'Ooh' and 'Ah' some more.

I go berserk and say I want to become a bat vet. The best bat vet in the world. I can't stop myself. I say that becoming the world's best bat vet is the most important thing in my life.

Now Suzie's dad's on about Great Vets in History. Suzie's mum interrupts about vets in Ancient Rome and Suzie comes in with a story about some man who discovered a cure for small-pox by checking out cows' pimples.

I want to change the subject, but these people know so much about vets it's unbelievable. They just won't stop. Harry explains how dogs used to die horribly of distemper with their tongues hanging out.

Jet secretly raises an eyebrow and sticks a finger in her mouth to puke. That's it. I have to get her away before she shows me up. And I have to get myself away before I tell them I plan to be the best vet on Mars or something.

I say, 'I'm really sorry, but Jet has reading practice.'

Jet stands up, lisps a thank you, and adds that it's so nice to learn all about blisters on cows' udders because they never talk about interesting stuff like that at her house.

Luckily, because they're all Clones, none of them pick up on the sarcasm. Suzie's dad gives Jet a chocolate. Suzie's mum gives her a book called *My Big Guide to Science*. Suzie gives her a ruler with multiplication tables on it.

Jet says, 'Oo! Fank you, Thuzie,' and secretly shows me a teaspoon she just pinched. I snatch it, stick it in a pot plant and shove her up the hall. Suzie and her family see us to the front door. As we come out, Natasha Frye's standing by my bike.

She says, 'I thought you'd be here.'

Suzie introduces Natasha to everyone.

Suzie's mum says, 'Ian's just been telling us how he's going to be a vet, Natasha. He's been telling us how much he loves your bats.'

Natasha doesn't miss a beat. 'Yes, he loves them so much he insisted on coming to help with them today, didn't you, Ian.'

Checkmate.

I grin brightly.

Jet hoists her pink koala backpack, waves cutely

at Suzie and whispers, 'For the Grand Opening it's two bucks.'

She pedals off.

Natasha hoists her Save the Whale backpack, waves cutely at Suzie and whispers, 'We're breaking into Syd Pocky's.'

18

Oh no . . .

Natasha's shooting along on her bike. I'm trying to catch her up.

'Natasha, get real. I'm not breaking into someone's house.'

'Suzie's going to love it when I tell her you're not really planning to be a vet. A vet! That's priceless.'

I'm starting to panic. 'But what do you want in there? There's nothing in there. The Pockys don't keep records.'

'We'll see about that.'

We're getting closer to Syd and Granny's. I get visions of Crusher going for my pressure points. We head through the pedestrian mall and pass Gould Street. Someone's changed it to 'Gooly Street'.

I jump off my bike and block her. I'm frantic. 'Natasha, you don't understand. If the Pockys catch us, they'll never beat up a girl, but me – they'll go mental . . .'

'Shut up, Ian.'

She rings the bell. Ripper starts barking, but there's no answer.

She smiles grimly. 'OK, we're going in.'

She sounds like some kind of war film. She's off round the back of the house, checking for open windows. I scuttle after her, frantic.

'What if somebody comes?'

She's standing on a rockery, fumbling with a window. She tries a tiny window right above it. It opens.

'Shut up and get in this window.'

'You get in. Why me?'

'You know the way to the front door to let me in. I don't.'

I hesitate. This is a crime. Ripper's barking his head off.

'OK, I will ring Suzie.' She gets out her mobile. She punches in the number.

'No! No! I'll do it.'

What choice have I got? This is a nightmare. My heart's pounding again. Any more outings with Natasha and I'm going to have a heart attack. I scramble up the wall and stick my head in through the little window. Way below is an ancient dunny. It's got one of those old-fashioned water cisterns with a chain, stuck high up on the wall. There's a big pile of wrestling magazines in one corner. In another is half a motorbike. The blood's pounding in my ears. Ripper's now barking like a maniac.

I gulp and shove my arms and top half through the window. But it's so tiny that getting my legs in is impossible. I'm hanging face down from the waist. The toilet is right underneath. I need something to grab on to, but there isn't anything apart from the dunny chain. I feel like I'm swimming in mid-air.

'What are you *doing*?'

'I'm stuck, you dummy.'

Natasha curses and shoves me violently. I shoot part way through the window, head first.

I yell and grab the toilet chain to break my fall. The dunny flushes as loud as Niagara Falls. I'm now hanging by the chain with my bottom half still stuck outside the window. I'm looking head first down the toilet pan. I'm getting a buttock's eye view of the toilet. My heart's thumping so hard I can hear it. If I let go of the chain I'll go straight down the pot.

Natasha's furious. 'Why did you flush the toilet?'

I shriek, 'Stop pushing me, you bloody idiot!' The water's still streaming noisily into the pan. Ripper's going ballistic.

'Stop mucking around, Ian.'

She shoves my feet hard. I yell and frantically grab the toilet seat with my free hand. I'm now doing a sort of half handstand on the Pockys' dunny seat, still hanging from the chain. There's a cracking noise and a jolt from above me. I look up. My weight's pulled the old cistern almost off the wall.

I have to let go of the chain. I can't. I'll go straight down the toilet. I could get wedged in there and drown.

There's another crack from the cistern. If that falls on my head, it could kill me. I have to let go of the chain.

Natasha shouts, 'Move, Ian!' and shoves hard. I yell, let go and snatch wildly at the toilet seat. I'm now doing a handstand on the Pocky's toilet and my feet are still out of the window. My mobile drops out of my pocket, plops in the dunny and goes cruising to the bottom.

The toilet door opens. I see an upside-down view of Terry Pocky, with Ripper barking his face off. Terry stands in the doorway in amazement. I twist my head. He's got his Discman earphones plugged in his ears. He's wearing a plaited leather necklace with an emu claw. His T-shirt says: 'Don't be a fool, Let Pocky clean your pool'.

His face clouds with fury. This is it. He's going

to beat me to a pulp. He takes his earphones off. He comes over and glances down the toilet.

I'm going to die.

I gabble, 'No! You see, the thing is . . .'

'Don't say a word, Ian. I know exactly what happened. Clint took your mobile and chucked it down the dunny. Little begga did exactly the same thing to me last week.'

I stare, then nod, dumbstruck.

'Come on, we'll get you out.'

He hauls me out of the window and sets me upright.

'S'pose you rang the doorbell and I didn't hear you.'

He gets my mobile out of the toilet, dries it on his T-shirt and hands it to me.

'Let it dry out. If it's still not working in a day or two, I'll take it apart and fix it.'

That'll really finish it off. He hands it to me. Lovely. That's just what I need next to my face, a phone that's been in Syd's dunny.

The front doorbell rings. It's Natasha. She starts into some excuse. Terry stops her.

He says, 'Don't worry, I know exactly what happened.'

I cut in, 'That's right. He knows how Clint took my mobile and chucked it in the dunny, so I came in to get it.'

Natasha's mouth drops open for a split second then clamps shut.

Terry says, 'You bet I do, and I can promise you he'll regret it. As for you, young lady, your name is . . . ?'

Natasha flashes him a sugary smile. 'My name's Caroline. Caroline Dillinger. And I would love to hear all about your emus.'

19

She barges straight in. Caroline Dillinger?

Terry's thrilled. He's even more thrilled when she explains that she and I are doing a science project on emus. He says he wishes his own kids took such an interest. He explains he's the only one here because he has to fix the washing machine.

I hiss out of the corner of my mouth, 'Caroline Dillinger?'

'I can't tell him my real name, dummy. He's fighting with my parents.'

We head into Syd and Granny's living room. The wild pig's head still hangs over the fireplace. Today it's got an umbrella hanging from one tusk. The room's full of model motorbikes, along with endless school photos of assorted Pockys. Terry hands me a magazine with a picture of an emu and the title *Big Bird Monthly* and goes off to get us some tea.

The second he's gone, Natasha's ripping open drawers and rummaging through cupboards.

'Natasha, stop it, you stupid idiot.'

'Why isn't there any stuff here? Why aren't there any photographs or records . . .'

'But what is it you're after?'

She spins round. 'Proof! I've got to show they're being cruel or they're capturing emus from the wild. If I don't get that place closed down before the opening . . .' She stops. She's white as a sheet. She looks weird. What's going on?

'What? What's going to happen if you don't get it closed down?'

'Here you go. Tea for three.' Terry's back. My heart somersaults, but Natasha instantly beams, 'I suppose you're planning on getting a lot of emu chicks, are you, Mr Pocky?'

Terry gives a sheepish smile. 'Well, we hope so. Been a bit of a hitch . . .'

He explains that none of the girl emus are interested in the boy emus, and Bruce Willis seems to have a particular problem because the girls keep running up and attacking him. Natasha says maybe he's using the wrong aftershave. Terry looks at her in complete bewilderment, then gets it and roars with laughter. He says maybe he should buy Bruce some aftershave. Natasha says maybe deodorant's better, maybe Terry should spray a bit in his armpits every morning. Or maybe that should be 'wingpits'. Terry hoots.

They're getting on like a house on fire. Even Ripper thinks she's terrific. She's cool under pressure, I'll say that for her. But why does she have to get Yarradindi Emu World closed down? And why did she go all weird like that? We go out to the kitchen to top up our tea.

A puddle of soapy water is floating out from under the laundry door. We rush into the laundry. It's the washing machine that Terry has just fixed. Terry says that the foreign goods you get these days are total rubbish. At that moment a shelf above the washing machine falls down. Terry says that the foreign shelf fittings you get these days are also rubbish.

The budgie squawks and says, 'Blue's a lucky begga!'

Terry fixes the machine, puts his screwdriver away and says, 'Well, I'm gonna have to throw yous out because I'm off to the farm.'

Natasha looks at him wide-eyed. 'Are you really going to see the emus, Mr Pocky?'

Terry beams. 'Sure I am.' He turns in the doorway. 'Course, if youse are interested . . .'

I could cry. Not the farm.

Natasha grins. 'We'd love to come.'

He grins back. 'It's like that with emus, isn't it? Once you know a bit about them – you're hooked.'

He's off out the door.

This is a disaster. 'Are you nuts?'

She's savage. 'Can't you see what a great chance this is? If we go out there as Terry's guests, we can get into the farmhouse. There might be incriminating documents in there.'

'What!'

'Don't you care about emus being turned into mincemeat?'

'I care about *me* being turned into mincemeat! All the Pocky kids'll be out there. They'll know you're not Caroline Dillinger.'

'Fine. I'll tell Suzie you lied to her.'

She's out to the ute with Terry. What can I do? I curse her and follow. Terry jams in a thrash music CD, gives a triumphant blast on the cow hooter and we set off at a hundred kilometres an hour down the main street. I slump down in my seat. Pedestrians scatter. The traffic lights at the end of the street are orange. Terry shouts, '*Woo*-ha!' and puts his foot down. We roar through on the red.

The ute's throbbing to the music. Terry yells about skydiving. He and a bunch of others are planning to jump out of a plane and form a twenty-person formation star over Yarradindi in the near future. He reckons skydiving's cool. There's no sensation of falling and people only die very occasionally. What am I going to do if Clint and Dylan Pocky are there? And what about Crusher?

We screech into the entrance to Yarradindi Emu World on two wheels. The new Big Emu is covered in swirls of red spray paint. It's been vandalized. Don't tell me . . . ? Yes, Natasha's smirking.

Terry slams on the brakes, stares, shakes his head and grins.

'Those ruddy kids! Still, it's only natural. At their age me and Crusher graffiti'd three carriages of the Melbourne Express in twenty minutes! I tell you what, Old Crush's work – *bewdiful* . . . !'

Natasha' s mouth drops open. He beams at her, rams his foot down on the accelerator and we shoot off up the hill. As we bump along past a heap of rusted cars we hear ear-piercing screams. Two upper primary Pockys are suspending a third above a crater filled with muddy water.

Terry leans across and yells, 'Adventure playground!' then adds, 'That's the thing about the bush, Caroline. They make their own entertainment.'

We arrive at the farmhouse and the emu pens. I can't believe how much has been done. It's going to be ready in time. Near enough, anyway. The Emu Education Centre's up and having its doors and windows installed. There are fences and sheds and brand-new concrete paths. Strings of flags have been hung up to give a party feel.

Further down the hill, a big concrete-mixer truck

is pumping out a fat coil of concrete. A mob of old men in black shorts and navy-blue singlets are raking and dragging it into place. I'm just wondering who they are when I realize they're the Cannibals without their leathers. Dad's down there, too. He waves.

Terry grins. 'Looking pretty good, but. Countdown to blast-off!'

Just across from us, another bunch of assorted Cannibals and adult Pockys are unloading toilet bowls and washbasins for the new toilet block. You can tell that it's a toilet block because it's got a sign saying 'MEN' on one side and 'WOMEN' on the other. The 'WOMEN' sign has got a painting of an emu wearing a bonnet. The 'MEN' sign has got a painting of an emu wearing a footy shirt with a can of beer under one wing. Crusher's just putting the final touches to the beer can.

The most amazing thing is the number of emus. There are heaps of them now. Terry starts rattling off their names. There's Madonna and Leonardo DiCaprio and Jennifer Lopez.

Syd comes lurching up on a bobcat.

'Running late a rehearsal aaaah! Emu a swaller Crushas keys a ute, a silly begga! Waita come outa other end, aaaaah!'

Terry roars with laughter, 'Don't ya love emus? They're that curious. Knew one once – swallered a packet of cement mix!'

As Terry gets out to talk to Syd, Natasha leans over and whispers, 'Right, now's our chance. We've got to get into that farmhouse.'

'We'll be seen.'

'We make an excuse.'

'But if any of the Pocky kids see you.'

'Shut up. Come on. Now.'

She's hurrying across to the emus. I reckon the best thing to do is help her, then get out as quickly as possible. My heart's pounding again. This is leading me to an early grave.

'Act casual,' she mutters. 'Just walk alongside the fence towards the house. When we're there, we'll wait till no one's looking, then duck inside.'

We scuttle along by the fence. I'm staring round wildly for Clint and Dylan Pocky. The only warning I'm likely to get is a rock landing on the back of my head. The thing is not to attract attention.

Oh no. Bruce Willis. He's right down at the other end of the enclosure we're walking next to, but he's seen me. He runs up, drumming. He's joined by another emu. And another. Now a whole mob of emus is keeping pace with me on the other side of the fence. They're all making weird drumming noises. I'm shooing them away, but they keep after me.

Natasha gasps, 'Hey. Look at the emus. They're following you.'

She's fascinated.

'I think I've heard of this, Ian. They think you're the dominant male.'

Terrific. The one time in my life I'm the dominant male and it's with a bunch of emus.

She goes on, 'Hey, maybe you're some sort of . . . emu whisperer.'

'Get nicked.'

'No, seriously. Maybe you are. Some people have a way with horses, maybe you're the same with flightless birds . . .'

Terry and Granny have come up. Granny calls out, 'Hey, Ian, them emus really like you!'

Bruce throws back his head and lets out a blast of drumming. Terry and Granny roar with laughter. Now Bruce is ducking and bobbing his head.

Terry leans over to her. 'Ian and his girlfriend are doing a project on emus, Mum.'

Great. Now Suzie's going to hear some garbled story about Natasha being my girlfriend.

I butt in. 'Oh no, Natasha . . . I mean, Caroline's not my girlfriend . . .'

Granny chuckles. 'Just good friends, eh? I heard that one before.'

'No! She's just doing the project with me. I just got lumbered with her.'

Terry looks a bit put out and whispers, 'Fair go,

Ian. She's a lovely girl. I hope you're not leading her on.'

'No way! She couldn't care less about me!'

At which point Natasha gives a strangled cry, throws herself in my arms and buries her head in my chest.

20

Oh, what? I shove her away, furious. I get one glimpse of the astonishment on Terry's face before I see why she did it. Clint Pocky's roaring up the hill on a motorbike. He mustn't see her face.

I yell, grab her back and clamp her to my chest so Clint can't see her. As soon as the motorbike engine fades into the distance, I shove her away and look around. To see Terry, Granny, Crusher and Syd, all wide-eyed with amazement. From their point of view we've been pashing on in full view of them and fifty emus.

I say, 'Oh. Ha. I'm sorry. You see, Caroline . . . Caroline *used to be* my girlfriend . . . We broke up and . . . and . . .'

Natasha murmurs, 'I'm sorry I did that, Ian.' She turns to Granny Pocky and says, choked, 'You see, sometimes . . . I remember the past.'

There's a chorus of pitying sighs. Syd gargles that boys of my age are silly beggas because we'd rather punch someone up the throat than show our emotions.

He should know, being grandad to the school's best throat-punchers.

Terry shakes his head. 'See, it's like Bob Westie says, "Show me a boy of fourteen, I'll show you aggression."'

Bob Westie's the Pocky family counsellor. Bob's a former wrestler, which is just as well since the Pocky kids' previous counsellor ended up having a nervous breakdown and going off on a solo canoe expedition to South America. When the kids get restless Bob just gets them in a half-nelson.

I yell, 'Bye, everyone!', grab Natasha's hand and drag her off.

Sixty Cannibals including Dad come roaring up the hill on their bikes, rehearsing the bridal procession.

I yell over the din, 'Stop pretending to be my girlfriend!'

She yells, 'What else d'you think we should have done? Let Clint Pocky see us?'

'You didn't have to say that stuff about remembering the past.'

'I had to explain why I hugged you. Don't think I enjoyed it, Ian. I've had better cuddles from a sick wombat.'

'Yeah, right – a sick wombat's about the only

thing that'd want to cuddle you, you weirdo!'

Terry and Syd come round the corner, overhear, and look at me like I'm a monster.

I march her down the hill. 'OK. We're getting out of here before Clint Pocky sees us.'

'No way. I'm going back to get in that house.'

There's a sudden roar of engines. Natasha and I both turn round – and stand, staring in amazement. Way down the hill, at the entrance to Yarradindi Emu World, are two gigantic excavators, side by side. They've smashed their way through a fence next to the Big Emu and are slowly but surely gouging a wide track in the grass next to the dirt road.

Terry comes up beside us and says, 'Beautiful sight, but. Poetry in motion.'

Natasha gasps, 'They're digging up the bilby crossings. Mum'll kill them, she . . .' She stops mid-sentence. She's staring down the hill.

I follow her gaze. The fat woman with the potato-sack pants has just come out of the Fryes' barn with a bunch of those Greenie Psychos. They're shouting and pointing at the bulldozers.

Natasha gulps. She's all white and weird like she was at Syd and Granny's. The next thing, she's pelting off down the hill and talking away nineteen to the dozen to old Spud Bum. I watch, fascinated.

What's she up to? They go into the barn. So

Natasha's in with the Psychos. I don't like this at all. Natasha doing stupid things to the Pockys on her own is one thing. But Natasha joining forces with Spud Bum and her Psycho pals is another. I have to see what's happening in that barn.

I scuttle down the hill and up to the half-open door. I look through the gap by the hinges. The Psychos are sitting cross-legged in a circle – and Mrs Frye's talking to them.

I should have known. She's going on about how they're going to wreck the Opening Ceremony, particularly Syd and Granny's repeat wedding.

The plan is that as the tourists are arriving, one bunch of Psychos will be protesting peacefully down at the Big Emu, just walking about with placards. The other bunch of Psychos will be hiding with Spud Bum in the barn. The Psychos down at the Big Emu will keep protesting peacefully as the wedding parade arrives, led by Constable Platt, in his car for traffic control purposes. But once the convoy has arrived outside the farmhouse, ready for the ceremony, all hell will break loose.

I feel my mouth drop open. At Mrs Frye's signal, the Psychos down at the Big Emu will start yelling and smashing up the Big Emu to attract Constable Platt. Of course, he'll whizz down to the gate.

When he's safely down there sorting it all out,

Mrs Frye will give Spud Bum and the rest of the Psychos the signal to come storming out of the barn with paintball guns. They'll zap Granny and Syd with red paint and disappear back into the wilderness before Constable Platt has time to arrest anyone.

Red paint! All over Granny's new wedding dress! This is frightening. Someone could get killed. What can I do? I could tell the Pockys. Then Natasha would be cactus, she'd dob me in to Suzie, Suzie would lose her pianist and I'd lose any chance with Suzie. The same thing would happen if I told the police or my parents.

But what if Syd and Granny end up in jail on a murder charge for running over some whacko who thinks they can talk to wallabies? What if Suzie gets hurt in all the fighting?

What if Natasha tells everyone I was helping her?

What do I mean, 'if'? She will tell everyone I was helping her, the whacko ratbag!

Now Mrs Frye's talking about how they'll arrange things. They'll communicate via mobile phones. None of them have ever used mobile phones before because they disapprove of the transmission towers and they reckon mobile phones roast your brains.

Seems to me their brains are already roasted.

The plan is that Mrs Frye will be up at the farm behind an emu shed with a mobile phone. She'll use this to talk to Spud Bum and the Psychos with paintball guns down the hill in the barn. Spud Bum and her followers have to wait until Mrs Frye gives them the word before they come out because Mrs Frye reckons, quite rightly, that without the element of surprise the combined Pockys and Cannibals will throttle every last Psycho in ten seconds flat.

Mrs Frye is instructed to go off and buy mobile phones.

The meeting's over. They're all getting to their feet. I'm standing there in shock.

Which is a totally dumb thing to do, because as Natasha gets up she sees me.

Bum. I jump up and pelt downhill towards the entrance to Yarradindi Emu World. There's a huge roar as the Cannibals drive back down the hill again, rehearsing the grand procession. Granny's right at the end, in the sidecar of a giant Harley driven by Skull. They all wave at me.

As I get to the road, I hear a car tooting. It's Mrs Frye in the ancient Land Rover. She pulls over, beaming.

'Hello, Ian. Want a lift into town? You're exactly the person I need.'

21

I stare into Mrs Frye's demented face. I can't refuse
a lift, or she'll suspect something. I smile brightly
and accept. I'm just about to get in when I hear a
screech of rage. Horace the bat is hooked, upside
down, on the handle over the passenger-seat door.
Mrs Frye explains that he loves coming along for
the ride. Horace chirps viciously and snorts a lump
of snot at me. Mrs Frye goes off into peals of
girlish laughter and crashes through the gears.
We're off.

I've never seen Mrs Frye so cheerful. The trip's
a nightmare. Horace swings from the handle, snorting gunk, trying to nip me and chittering savagely
at passing motorists. Every time we stop at traffic
lights we cause a sensation.

Mrs Frye wants my advice on mobile phones.
She's so dim about them it's unbelievable. She
thinks they run on torch batteries. I have to explain
about plugging them into the electricity socket to
charge them, and how you can pay by the month or

buy cards. At that moment a car comes round the corner, goes into a skid and ends up half off the road. The driver leans out of his window and yells, 'Why you got a flamin' monkey in the car?'

Mrs Frye snorts with fury, winds down her window and shouts, 'It's a flying fox, fool!' Then she adds, 'Meat-eater!'

We turn into the main street. A lady approaching in a Volvo takes one look at Horace and nearly crashes into us. Mrs Frye jams on her brakes, swerves and yells a volley of abuse. Horace is swinging like a furry pendulum, chittering furiously in my face. We screech to a halt outside the mobile phone shop. Mrs Frye puts on the brake, turns off the ignition, hooks Horace on to her pullover and says, 'The standard of driving in this town is a disgrace.'

She makes me come into the shop to give advice. I can't escape. The salesman starts sniffing, realizes Mrs Frye's got a bat hanging from her cardigan and comes charging towards us. He's about to chuck us out when Mrs Frye announces that she wants two high-quality mobiles. He stands about a metre away from us and hands the mobiles to me to pass on to Mrs Frye.

This is embarrassing like you wouldn't believe. It's not only because every time Mrs Frye gets a different model she asks which buttons you press and how you talk into it. It's also because every time she brings a mobile phone anywhere near Horace, he chitters and tries to kill it. Mrs Frye starts shouting at him to stop. He chitters louder.

The salesman leans over and asks her please to keep it down because her bat is upsetting the other customers. Horace swings out and tries to nip him. Mrs Frye asks the salesman what he's got against endangered species, then adds that his phones are garbage because they're too small for her face and the bit you speak into doesn't stretch round to where your mouth is.

All this reminds me that my own mobile's wrecked and I'll have to face Mum and Dad going full-ape when I tell them. I'm just working out what excuses I can make when Horace snorts a lump of snot on a three-thousand-dollar sound system as Mrs Frye's buying her phones.

This is just the break I need. In all the shouting and chaos that ensues I sneak out, unnoticed. The last words I hear are Mrs Frye saying she'll report the phone salesman to the Parks and Wildlife people for threatening to injure a protected species. The salesman says she'd better do it quick, because Horace'll be dead if she doesn't get him out of there. I scuttle down the back streets to our shop. All this running's set off my bad ankle again. I feel like I'm living in a video game called 'Mad

Conservationists', where I'm being chased for ever by people who discuss the law with wallabies.

As I open our kitchen door, I'm face to face with Granny Pocky singing, 'You Are the Wind Beneath My Wings' (with a karaoke backing) in front of Terry, Syd and Mum. To kick off the ceremony, Syd and Granny are going to sing songs to each other in front of the crowd. This will happen just after the arrival of the bikies' guard of honour and just before the Pocky toddlers arrive to chuck rose petals over the happy couple.

Granny's really getting into to it. The crocodile in her cleavage rolls and leaps as she does all the arm movements. Syd's watching with admiration. Granny finishes with a big flourish and dive of the crocodile. We all clap. Syd whistles, gargles and roars, 'Aaaah, bettera Bette Midler, a clevera begga.'

Syd and Granny hug. I feel a stab of guilt. I've got to warn them, but I can't.

Syd sees me and says, 'Aaah! Lovely girl a Caroline Dillinger a lucky begga aaaah!'

I realize, the last thing he saw of me, I was clamped in a passionate clinch with Natasha. Granny adds that I was mad to dump her. She's made for me.

Mum says, 'What? Ian, have you got a girlfriend!'

Here we go. 'No, I have not!'

Dad comes in from the shop. 'Ian? There's a girl here to see you.' He drops his voice. 'Good-looking as well. Good on you, mate!' They all cheer. But I'm so stoked I don't care. Suzie's come to see me. It's because of that lunch. She likes me. She's come to invite me out. If only I had time to change my T-shirt. I stride in, sucking in my stomach.

But it's not Suzie, it's Natasha. She's holding out a mobile phone. I'm choked, then furious. Bloody Natasha! Why can't she stay out of my life?

'It's my dad's. He never uses it. Have it till I can find some way to get you a new one.'

'Are you nuts? People'll think I stole it!'

'Please, Ian . . .'

'Oh, I get it! You're trying to bribe me not to dob you and your mum in for planning to wreck the Opening . . .'

'That's right.' She cuts me off. She's weirdly quiet. She looks at me sadly. 'Ian, you have to help me. You're my last hope. The point is, if the police catch my mum causing any more trouble . . .' her voice catches, '. . . she'll go to jail.'

22

I thought nothing the Fryes did could surprise me – but jail!

We head to the beach for privacy.

It turns out Mrs Frye's been caught by the police heaps of times for attacking people she reckons are abusing animals. She used to work with Spud Bum (whose real name is Angela) and the Psychos, who are so crazy that even the most demented of Greenies won't have anything to do with them.

So, Mrs Frye has got caught doing all kinds of terrible things. She got caught slashing the tyres of all the people who worked in a meat-packaging factory. She got caught punching a policeman who tried to get her off the front of a bulldozer threatening the habitat of the endangered Smaller Slimy Bell Frog. She's always getting fined, which is one of the reasons (on top of all the animal bills) that the Fryes are always broke.

It finally came to a head a couple of months

ago. She was spray-painting graffiti over the sheds of a man who ran a battery-hen farm. He caught her and they had a fight. She sprayed red paint all over his trousers and pulled out a big lump of his hair by the roots. He took her to court.

And this is the really serious bit.

The judge said she had to stop making a nuisance of herself, or else. He sentenced her to six months in jail, but said she didn't have to go as long as she behaved herself and didn't get into any more trouble for a year.

She agreed. She faithfully promised Mr Frye and Natasha that she'd give up protesting. She promised never to see Spud Bum or any more Greenie whackos of any description whatsoever.

Things were going fine.

But then the Pockys started building Yarradindi Emu World. Mrs Frye got angry. Knowing what her mum was like, Natasha rang up the local Council and the Parks and Wildlife people to get the Pockys shut down in case Mrs Frye grew so angry that she did something and got herself arrested. But they all said the Pockys were entitled to open an emu farm. So next, Natasha tried to put the Pockys off by cutting their fences and turning on the taps of the water tanks so they'd run out of water. But the Pockys didn't notice. Meanwhile Mrs Frye was getting angrier. The Pockys started ploughing their bikes all over their wetlands. Mrs Frye got even angrier. The last straw was the time I was at Yarradindi Emu World, when the Pockys were blowing up tree stumps.

After that row with Terry, Mrs Frye went straight back to the house and telephoned Spud Bum and the Psychos, who, unknown to Mr Frye, she'd been allowing to use their old barn for meetings. Mrs Frye told Spud Bum and the Psychos that she'd help them sabotage the Grand Opening by letting them stage an attack from the Fryes' shed, even though she couldn't get involved herself in case she got arrested. It was all to be top secret. Except that Natasha overheard the call.

Natasha blinks back tears. 'I couldn't let her get drawn into something like that. It was just too risky. I had to do something fast. I thought, if I could shut down Yarradindi Emu World *before* the Grand Opening . . .'

'. . . Your mum wouldn't get arrested.'

'That's why I wanted you to spy on the Pockys. I thought maybe I could find evidence that the Pockys were being cruel to the emus, or maybe breaking the law by catching emus from the wild or something. That's why I got you to help me break into Syd and Granny's place. I thought I could take the evidence to the RSPCA or the Parks and Wildlife people.' She sighs. 'It was bad enough when Mum was just letting Angela lead the paint-ball attack. Now she's actually leading it herself. There's no way she won't be arrested. And the terrible thing is, she doesn't care. I've got to stop her, Ian. I can't have my mum in jail.'

'Can't your dad help?'

She folds her arms anxiously.

'That's the worst thing. He's already worried sick about all the bills for the animals and Mum's fines. You've seen how he bottles up all his anger. He's really on the edge of cracking up. If Mum goes to jail, I really think he'll have a nervous breakdown.' She stares at me, worried. 'You're the only one who can help me.'

I can see what's coming.

'I am not helping you wreck the Opening Ceremony!'

She leans over earnestly. 'You don't have to. I've had this idea. It just came to me tonight.' She pauses, 'You know how you're an Emu Whisperer?'

Not that again. 'Don't be dumb . . .'

She's triumphant. 'Bruce Willis will follow you anywhere, and the other emus will follow Bruce Willis. Now, forget the whole idea of you spying on the Pockys or getting into the farmhouse. You just sneak up to Yarradindi Emu World tonight, make a fuss of Bruce Willis and lead them all down into the wilderness area. It's so big the Pockys'll never get them back out, so there won't be any emu farm – so there won't be any Grand Opening for Mum to wreck and get arrested over.'

'Yeah, right – and what happens when Crusher sees me leading off a hundred emus?'

'But my mum'll go to jail!'

'It's the best place for her! You can't go around pulling out chunks of people's hair and wrecking emu farms.'

'You can't go around persecuting innocent hens.'

This is insane. An Emu Whisperer. Pied Piper to a bunch of pop-eyed emus. I head back along the beach. She's running after me.

'I'll tell Suzie. I'll tell the Pockys you broke into their house. I'll tell your mum and dad.'

I spin round and yell, 'And I'll tell the police about your mum. I'll get them to be there at the Grand Opening so they can arrest her.'

Her mouth drops open. This is fantastic. I've got her.

'You wouldn't.'

There's a wobble in her voice. I feel bad.

She pounces. 'Please help me, Ian. *You* don't want Syd and Granny's wedding wrecked. Neither do *I*. I don't agree with the emu farm, but it's the Pockys' right to run it if they want to. I just have to protect my mum and dad.'

I stare at her desperate face. Jail. No wonder she's worried.

She jumps in. 'Just go up to the emu farm tonight and get Bruce to follow you. I'll help you get Suzie. I'll keep Dan away from her at rehearsals. I'll keep saying how cool you are and keep bringing you into the conversation.'

It's tempting, but who knows whether she'd keep her word? This is the girl who shoved me through Syd Pocky's toilet window and made me chop up the Big Emu.

She sees I'm wavering and goes for it. 'OK, the deal is this.'

No way. She's not dragging me into another disaster. I've still got to face Mum and Dad going ballistic when I tell them I've wrecked my mobile. I'm not getting tangled up with Crusher and a mob of dopey emus.

'No, Natasha.'

'Please.'

'Read my lips. No.'

I hurry off. She's devastated, but too bad. I can't get involved.

I suppose I already am involved.

No! None of this is any of my business. An emu whisperer, for heaven's sake. Forget Natasha and her parents. Forget Syd and Granny. My business is going out with Suzie. I've got to make her feel about me like she did at lunchtime. Lunchtime! It feels like months ago. I can't have some Greenie disaster at the Grand Opening sending me back to square one with Suzie.

Which reminds me, I've really got to stop Suzie going to the Grand Opening. It was bad enough when all I had to worry about was Terry showing her the mozzie bites in his armpits. Now there's going to be World War Three, not to mention the possibility that Natasha will tell her I'm a liar, just to get revenge.

I have a quick memory of Suzie beaming gorgeously at me over the lunch table. I smile to myself. *That's* what all this is about. I cheer up. She really did seem to like me. I'll ring Jet and get her to swap tomorrow's meeting with Suzie to the park.

Back at the shop, Dad and Skull are working out the Cannibals' procession route by lining up tomato sauce bottles and forks across a table. Terry looks up, sees me come in and says, 'Mate. Listen to your heart.'

Syd's anxious because he's got a poison pen letter threatening to wreck the Opening unless the Pockys set their emus loose. I stop in my tracks. It's obviously the Fryes or the Psychos, but I can't say anything. Terry says him and Crusher will step up the armed patrol. Syd shakes his head, shifts his emu leather pants and gargles anxiously that everything has to be perfect on the day for Granny.

Granny hasn't been well lately. She put her back out lifting the sidecar of a Harley Davidson, and she's been worried about Crusher, who's been a bit lost since he left the commandos. The wedding is really going to cheer her up.

Nothing must go wrong.

I hesitate over the cappuccino machine. I have to warn them.

Stay out of it!

I sneak up to the phone in the hallway and ring Jet. Her voice is hushed and irritable.

'I'm in the middle of a job!'

I'm not even going to ask.

'Tomorrow. We're going to the park instead of the Emu Farm.'

'S'pose that was Suzie's idea, was it? Or is Natasha's mum gonna cause trouble?'

'No, it's not Suzie's idea. Anyway, how come you know all this stuff?'

'Get real, everyone knows. Mrs Frye's been marching up and down the shopping mall for weeks with that dumb sign about emus. Plus she's in trouble with the cops. She's always getting fined and stuff. That's why Natasha left her old school. It was some special private music school. She gave up her music so they could sell the piano to pay the fines.'

So that's why Natasha came to our school so suddenly.

Jet interrupts my thoughts. 'You'll have to give Suzie some reason for changing your mind. What's your excuse for not going?'

I hadn't thought of that.

Jet says, 'Tell her I'm frightened of emus.'

There's muffled shouting and a shriek. Now she's running.

She shouts, 'Wait! Tell her I'm *allergic* to emus! Meet you at the gates to the park, eleven o'clock! Three dollars!'

There's what sounds like a police siren and she hangs up. Great. Surrounded by criminals. At least I can ask Suzie's dad to be my lawyer.

I ring Suzie. I go into a rave about how we can't go to the park because Jet's allergic to emus. I say how feathers make her sneeze. I say how even the thought of feathers makes her sneeze.

Suzie's sympathetic. She says, 'That's OK, Ian. I'll just go with Dan. He asked me this evening.'

23

I cover the phone and swear. Why doesn't she just *like* me? Why do we have to go through all this craziness? I try to back-pedal. I just say that we'll get Jet some allergy pills so we can all go along together. Suzie says that's fine, but Dan's coming anyway. She says he wants to tell her all about his plans to set up a Big Kid, Little Kid scheme at St Joey's.

I bet he does. From very close up.

I've got to be at that Opening with Suzie now he's there. I ring Jet and tell her Suzie wants to go to the Opening. There's shouting in the background. A man's voice is yelling.

Jet swears and bellows, 'When you gonna dump that big Barbie?'

'She's smarter than you, dork brain.'

'She's a pain in the bum. Eh, you don't know anyone who wants to buy a set of Vee-Dub windscreen-wipers, do you? Good as new?'

'No, I don't.'

'OK. See you in the shopping mall at ten. A dollar rebooking fee. You planning to make a move on her?'

'None of your business.'

'For three dollars extra Brad and me'll keep Dan away from her. You can get her alone for a romantic moment. Up there on the hillside.'

I can't resist.

I hang up. Terrific. On top of everything else, I'm broke. Just as I'm standing by the phone, Bogle rings up on his new, home-made mobile and raves on about how he's proved scientifically that people don't recognize you when you whisper because he just rang his mum and she didn't know who it was. He says that now he can ring all the people he hates and say insulting things in whispers. He's planning to start tonight. I point out that if he's going to do that he'd better withhold his number because it's just come up on my phone. There's a silence. For a genius, Bogle is one serious goose. For a split second I consider asking him to make me a mobile but, knowing Bogle, it'd be a major drama.

I get rid of him.

If only I could get rid of Natasha and her stupid mother and just concentrate on Suzie. I chuck myself on my bed. I remember Mrs Frye rattling on about mobiles. What a dur-brain. She won't even be able to use the stupid mobile. She couldn't even work out which way up it went.

I wish I could just lock her up somewhere. Maybe I could lock her in one of the sheds. That's no good. She'd get out unless I was there to guard it, and how can I be guarding whacko Mrs Frye at the same time as being with Suzie? I can't be in two places at once.

Wait a minute.

And then it all falls into place. I can't believe it. I pace round the room, running it over in my mind. If it works, I get to stop Mrs Frye wrecking the Opening, I get Natasha off my back, and (*yes!*) I get free, uninterrupted access to Suzie!

I sneak down the hall and ring Natasha.

'Ian? Are you going to help me?'

'OK. I'm not going to lead Bruce and the other emus into the Wilderness Area, but if I stop your mother wrecking the Grand Opening will you promise never to tell Suzie I'm a liar?'

'Absolutely.'

'And will you promise to keep Dan away from Suzie like you said?'

'I swear. At every rehearsal. And I'll bring you up in the conversation and say how cool you are, and how you're so terrific with the animals. Which you are – nobody ever likes Bobby or Horace . . .'

'And will you promise never to ask me to help

you shut down the Pockys or vandalize stuff or do anything like that ever again?'

'Yes.'

Here comes the crunch. I'll finally get Natasha Frye off my back.

'And if I keep doing the animals for you until Suzie's play, after that, will you stay out of my life completely?'

There's a pause. I hold my breath.

'I will.'

'See you in the bat cages in twenty minutes. Bring your dad's mobile and your mum's new ones.'

She's there, waiting for me, with the mobiles. I check over my shoulder.

'Can you impersonate your mum on the phone?'

'I s'pose so, why?'

'OK. Isn't your mum and old Spud Bum's plan all based on talking to each other on mobiles?'

'Yes.'

'And Spud Bum isn't going to move until she gets the go-ahead from your mum?'

'Yes.'

I laugh out loud. 'They're both totally stupid about mobiles. What we do is, we offer to preset their phone numbers for them. We arrange all the presets. When your mum thinks she's ringing Spud Bum, she gets through to me on your dad's phone. When Spud Bum hits the preset for your mum, she gets you. We keep them trapped with excuses. We keep saying stuff like, the police are coming or there's an emu in the way of the paintball guns. It means I can be with Suzie except for when your mum rings my mobile.'

'But they'll recognize our voices.'

'We don't use our voices.'

Thank you, Andy Bogle.

'*We whisper!*'

I explain that Mrs Frye and Angela Spud Bum won't recognize our voices as long as we whisper. I set out the order of events. The Grand Parade is at eleven, with the wedding at eleven-fifteen. After the ceremony, Syd and Granny are planning to leave for a second honeymoon, led by a convoy of Cannibals and Pockys, with Constable Platt heading the procession.

Obviously, we can't keep Mrs Frye and Spud Bum away from every one of the Pockys for the whole day.

But if we can just stop them wrecking the wedding ceremony, we should be able to stop Mrs Frye being arrested, because Constable Platt won't be there. In other words, all we have to do is stall the attack for the fifteen minutes of the wedding ceremony. After that, Syd, Granny, the Cannibals, heaps of Pockys and – most important of all –

Constable Platt will all be gone. Bottom line – it doesn't matter what happens after that.

Natasha's frowning. 'It won't work. They're bound to ask why we're whispering.'

The bats are chittering and swinging wildly, upside down, all over the open bars of the roof. I narrowly miss getting wee'd on. They really do store it up and wait for me.

'Say that there are people around so you've got to keep your voice down.'

I step sideways and miss a stream of wee.

Natasha raises her eyebrows. 'You're getting good at that.'

'Just as well.'

Mr Frye appears nearby with a bucket of meat for the eagles, talking to himself. He hasn't seen us, but we can't risk being overheard. We head off to Noddy's fence to work out the details. Tomorrow morning Natasha will keep her mum away from the emu farm for as long as possible. She'll do this first by slowing Mrs Frye down when they're preparing the animals' breakfasts. After that she'll invent problems with the animals. At ten-thirty or so, I'll turn up with Suzie, Jet and Brad.

She shakes her head.

'But that's where the problems start. I won't be able to keep Mum away for the whole morning. And what about Angela?'

'I'll keep an eye out for Angela. If she looks as if she's about to attack, I'll text you and you can ring her pretending to be your mum.'

'And say what?'

'I dunno. Say there are plain-clothes police about. *I know!* Say there's a news team from Yarradindi TV station on the way, and if she holds off spattering Syd and Granny until they arrive, the story will go out on TV across the whole country. Maybe across the world.'

'But whatever you tell them, people like Mum and Angela aren't just going to stand around while Syd and Granny get married. They'll go for it. They'll attack.'

She's right. It's dumb. It'll never work. For a second I think about forgetting the whole thing, but I have to give myself the chance to get Suzie before Dan does, and that's not going to happen if there's a riot just as I'm trying to make a move.

I shrug. 'It's our only chance.'

For some reason she puts out her hand for me to shake. I shake it. It seems appropriate. Like, we're both doomed. I put Spud Bum's mobile number into Mr Frye's phone while Natasha does all the pre-sets on the two new ones. I head off.

I'm just opening the gate when Mr Frye appears from behind a shed. He's dancing with excitement.

'The shrikes, Ian. I've just seen them fly past the house. Three males. Quick! If we go now we'll hear what's going on.'

The last thing I want to do is sit in that mozzie-infested hide with a raving lunatic, but this guy's got so little to cheer up his life I can't refuse.

We slog across the paddocks with Mr Frye rattling on about what the shrikes were doing last year and the year before and how their behaviour at the moment is really exciting. He says the Pockys' floodlights and late-night concrete-pouring have been disturbing the night birds.

He beams and says brightly, 'But then again, the building work will be finished soon and we'll all be back to normal.' A muscle works in his cheek. 'After all, the Pockys are entitled to build on their own land. Even if they are building a total monstrosity and . . .' He stops himself, then grins through clenched teeth. 'But let's not think about the Pockys. Let's think about the shrikes.'

Boy, is he close to snapping. I can see what Natasha means. I say a few enthusiastic things about shrikes to cheer him up. He grins gratefully. How did I come to be spending my life with total lunatics?

We get to the hide and crawl inside. Mr Frye flicks a few switches and settles down to listen, beaming. 'They're there now. This is coming through live. This is a once-in-a-lifetime occasion, Ian. Take in every second.'

I make excited noises. I can feel the damp fungus soaking through my shorts.

There's chirping and warbling, then more chirping and warbling. I secretly check my watch. Then something weird happens. A very loud rustling sound blots out the chirping and warbles. It must be very close to the mike.

Mr Frye sits up. 'What's that?'

Something is being dragged. Then there's a click and a hiss.

Mr Frye is on his feet. 'That sounds like . . .' he's puzzled, '. . . a bottle being opened . . . ?'

There's more rustling very close to the mike, then glugging, then, unmistakably, a human burp!

Mr Frye leaps up in outrage. 'There's someone there! There's someone sitting under my tree, drinking!'

There's a click, then silence. We lean closer to the speaker.

Suddenly, a voice yells at two million decibels. 'And they're comin' down the straight! It's Merchant Service, Mystified, away from My Boy Bill, Hot Shot in fourth place . . .'

We clamp our hands over our ears. Every bird for miles flies up in the air, squawking with terror.

The needles on the audio equipment are going berserk.

Through the speakers an unmistakable voice bellows, 'Aaah, gerra move on a silly begga, aaah!'

'Mystified! Mystified! My Boy Bill is coming through . . . !'

It's Syd on fence patrol.

Mr Frye rushes out of the hide, then rushes back to shut the noise off, then rushes back out again. He's dithery with panic. It's suddenly silent, except for the departing birds screeching frantically as they fly off into the distance.

Mr Frye gives a low moan of despair. 'That's the shrikes. They've gone. Two years of work.'

Suddenly there's a long, low sound. It's Mr Frye growling. His face is contorted in fury. I've never seen him like this. He's going to explode.

He roars, 'That was a Pocky! That was a Pocky on my land! Disturbing my shrikes! I will not have it! I WILL NOT HAVE IT!'

He strides out of the hut. He's storming up the hill. I pelt after him. Crusher would have his carotids in seconds. Then he stops. He makes an enormous effort to control himself. He looks like steam might come out of his ears.

He says, through gritted teeth, 'I must set an example,' and stalks back to the house like a robot. I watch him go. Of course, he's setting an example for Mrs Frye. Little does he know she's already lost it. What a family.

I hurry off discreetly. Tomorrow's going to be a nightmare. I've got to get up the courage to take Suzie's hand at the same time as impersonating someone with a bum the size of Melbourne.

I try impersonating Spud Bum.

I hiss, 'Hello? This is Angela. Any problem, Jacinta?'

Not good. Not good at all.

Back in our kitchen, there's been a drama about Granny's wedding dress fitting into the sidecar of the Harley. It's too big and fluffy.

Crusher's remade it so that the skirt part is held together with Velcro and can be removed when Granny gets in. It means that Granny will be whizzing along the freeway dressed as a bride on top but with her normal black workman's shorts underneath and her skirt rolled up in a big green plastic rubbish bag on her lap. She has a couple of practices ripping the skirt off and putting it on again, kidding about. It's quite good, actually. It's a bit like a magician's act, except Granny's about fifty years too old to be the magician's glamorous assistant.

Daisy gurgles with laughter, so Granny does it again. Daisy roars. Terry comes in to tell Granny that he's picked up all of the Pocky men's wedding suits and he's going to take them up to the farm now, ready for them to get changed into tomorrow. There's so much work to be done that they'll still be doing the finishing touches tomorrow morning. As it is, they'll be working right into the night. Dad rings Mum to say he won't be back until after midnight. Good job I didn't agree to go up there and lead off Bruce Willis and the emus.

While Granny closes her eyes, Terry shows us Syd's outfit. It's a white suit with top hat to match. I get a mental picture of a big red splat across the front, and I gasp. Mum asks me what's wrong. I pretend it's just that I'm totally impressed with the suit.

Fifteen minutes. I just hope Mum doesn't drag the ceremony out.

I head to my room to plan making my move on Suzie. For a start, I have to take her hand. A wave of fear passes over me. I can't! But I've got absolutely no choice. Dan's definitely worried about Chippy, but not worried enough to be put off asking Suzie to go with him to the Grand Opening. And if the pair of them get on well enough at the Grand Opening, that's my chances finished. The question for me is, when do I do it? When do I take her hand?

I'll have to do it before the wedding. I can't do it

afterwards. I mean, *if* (and it's a big if), *if* we manage to hold off Mrs Frye and Spud Bum until after the wedding, they'll go ballistic with rage and wreck everything. There's no way I'll get a chance to be romantic if I leave it until then.

I stare at myself in the mirror. I think I'll get her to look out at the view over the valley. I'll have to make sure there's a boulder or something to stand on so I can stare into her eyes. The thought makes my stomach clench with fear. I tell myself to get a grip. I tell myself to believe I'm self-confident. I am self-confident. In fact, I'm so self-confident that tomorrow, Psychos or no Psychos, I will take Suzie's hand. I will find a romantic moment, take her hand, and Suzie McLaren, Super-Clone and most gorgeous girl in the school, will be, officially – can I even think this? – my girlfriend.

I catch sight of myself in the mirror.

I look terrified.

24

I have a night full of crazy dreams about trying to solve maths problems to do with wallabies. I wake up, knowing something terrible is about to happen. Oh yes. The Grand Opening. My heart sinks. How did I ever get myself into all this? Why did I say I'd help Natasha? How could I have ever thought I could impersonate Spud Bum?

I head for the shower, trying to calm myself down. The main thing, absolutely the main thing, is to make a move on Suzie. Just the thought of it makes me go all shaky. I can't miss this chance.

It's easy to get away after breakfast, since our house is in chaos. Dad's lost the leather gloves that go with the Cannibal outfit he's got to wear to be part of the convoy. Daisy's spilt orange juice over Mum's special outfit for the wedding and Granny comes in to borrow hairspray. She'd forgotten to buy any because all the Pockys were up until four this morning, working at the farm to be ready for the Grand Opening.

I get to the shopping mall half an hour early. I'm a bag of nerves. What if Natasha gets snaky and tells Suzie I'm a liar? What if Jet acts up? What about Dan? What if I've got bad breath?

Oh no, I've got bad breath!

I huff into my cupped hands and sniff. I can't tell. Can you ever tell?

'Hi, Ian.'

Suddenly it's Suzie. My heart somersaults. I suck in my stomach. She's got Harry, her little brother, with her. She's looking all distracted.

'Have you seen Jet? She ran off. She was acting all funny about the people in the hot-bread shop. I suppose she's nervous about coming with my family. I don't know what it is.'

I know what it is. I've seen Clint and Cunningham do it. There's a basket on the counter of the hot-bread shop. It's got bits of bread inside and a sign saying: 'Sample our delicious bread varieties'. They wait till no one's looking, then stick a dead cockroach in it.

Just then Jet and Brad come trotting round the corner. Jet demands a cuddle from Suzie and gets it. Brad demands a cuddle from Suzie and gets a kick on the ankle from me.

We set off in Suzie's mum's gleaming four-wheel-drive. Suzie's in the front. I'm in the back with Harry, Brad and Jet. Suzie's mum gives us a running commentary on the history of the main street of Yarradindi.

Jet finds a Walkman in the pocket of the seat in front of her and starts putting it in her backpack. I snatch it, put it back, and mime punching her in the head. A mobile is ringing and ringing. I suddenly realize it's Mr Frye's. I answer it. An old man says slowly, ''Ello? Yarradindi Meats 'ere. 'Ow many cows' feet d'ya want?'

It's some meat supplier for Mr Frye. I hang up in a panic. It rings again. The old man starts off identically, 'Ello? Yarradindi Meats 'ere.'

I hang up. It rings again. It's like a recording. I turn it off.

Suzie says, 'Who *is* that, Ian? Is it a prank call?' Luckily she gets distracted because her mum's asking for answers to a quiz on Yarradindi in the horse-drawn era. Just as Mrs McLaren says, 'And does anyone know what we call a four-wheeled open-top horse-drawn vehicle – and I don't mean "cart"?' the Big Emu comes into view.

There's a traffic jam. The Pockys were right. Everyone in Yarradindi's come along. I see Jesse and Melissa, the Principal, all the teachers, all the people from Big Kids, Little Kids, Pricey and Andy Bogle, Caroline Dillinger, everyone from Chess Club. Mrs Gonzales sees me and Suzie, and waves. We wave back. Being in Big Kids, Little Kids makes you a member of a kind of teachers' club. It's weird. I don't know whether I like it.

The Psychos are out in force, protesting. They're walking round the Big Emu, holding placards saying things like 'Protect the emu' and 'Yarradindi says no to Emu Burgers'. Spud Bum's up the front. Wallaby Man's up the back, wearing an emu mask. I crane my neck to see if Mrs Frye's lurking about anywhere. She isn't. Good. Natasha must be keeping her occupied.

We join the traffic queue snaking up the huge new track. It's festooned with strings of plastic flags. There's a big hand-painted billboard of Syd, grinning, with his fist held up to Bruce Willis's head and the slogan: 'For a Meal with a Punch, Eat Emu for Lunch'. At the top of the hill, Crusher, wearing his emu leather shorts, is directing traffic into the car park, which is next to the Yarradindi Emu World Emu Education Centre. The bouncy castle is still being set up under Terry's instructions.

Terry's wearing his emu claw necklace plus emu leather trousers and a hat. His T-shirt reads: 'Don't be a Nerd, Eat a Slice of Big Bird'. He's getting a bit hot and flustered because the bouncy castle seems to have a puncture, and, at the same time as sorting that out, he's also supposed to be getting the barbecue going for the free emu sausage sizzle.

As we get out of the car, he waves, stops a

tomato sauce fight between two primary-school Pockys armed with big red plastic tomatoes and whispers, 'Seen Caroline a while back, Ian! Now's your chance to make things up.'

Jet sidles up to me. 'OK. Brad and me'll see to Dan. You just get Barbie into a romantic situation.'

'What do you know about romantic situations?'

Brad sniggers. 'A lot more than you do, Pizza-face.'

He's probably right. Suzie comes back from talking to the Principal. On cue, Jet and Brad turn into happy toddlers, jumping up and down and squealing, 'Bouncy castle! Bouncy castle!'

Suzie smiles and shakes her head. 'Learning first, *then* bouncy castle. Oh look, there's Dan.'

In his street clothes Dan looks like a young god. He leans down and whispers, 'I know I haven't got a chance against Chippy, but . . .' He gulps. 'I've got to see her.'

There's a deafening *whoomph* and pillar of flame as Terry chucks kerosene on the barbie. A bunch of Pocky kids cheer.

The place is packed. Melissa's standing next to the toilet block, dressed in her St John's Ambulance Brigade uniform. I try to get Suzie to come and look at the view of the valley so I can make my move as soon as possible, but she insists that we take Harry, Brad and Jet to the Emu Education Centre.

We join the queue. The exhibition's called 'From Bird to Burger'. Harry takes my hand and starts rattling off his twenty-three times table. Jet does a rude sign behind his head.

Suddenly I notice Natasha across the paddocks. She's frantically waving her mobile and pointing at it. My stomach turns over in panic. Something's gone wrong. I'd forgotten my phone was switched off. I punch it on.

'Ian, I can't stop her. She won't listen to any excuses. She's over with the emus, trying to pick a fight.'

I look. Sure enough, Mrs Frye is standing with her arms folded next to Bruce Willis, looking furious. She's obviously waiting for someone to come along and say how cute the emus are so she can go into a rave against emu farming.

This is bad news. I thought Natasha could stall her at least until the convoy arrived.

'OK. I'll tell her there are plain-clothes police about. Back me up.'

I mutter an excuse to Suzie, push out of the queue and dash behind a shed where I can still keep an eye on Mrs Frye. Now we'll see if Bogle's right about people not recognizing your voice if you whisper. I take a deep breath and punch in her number.

Mrs Frye jumps with surprise as the phone rings, then starts fumbling around, trying to answer. She can't even work out how to answer it. She keeps pressing the wrong buttons.

Suddenly her voice booms, 'HELLO? CAN YOU HEAR ME?'

She nearly bursts my eardrums. Here goes . . .

I whisper hoarsely, 'Jacinta? It's Angela.'

Troy Pocky is looking at me with interest. Across the paddocks, Mrs Frye's staring at the phone like it's about to explode.

She bellows, 'ANGELA? SPEAK UP, I CAN'T HEAR YOU!'

At least she hasn't sussed it's me. I whisper, 'Stay hidden.'

'WHAT?'

I'm going to suffer permanent hearing damage here.

'Plain-clothes police! Stay hidden!'

'PLAIN WHAT? OH! RIGHT! JONATHAN!'

What?

'*Jonathan?*'

There's a pause.

'JONATHAN. ISN'T THAT WHAT YOU'RE SUPPOSED TO SAY AT THE END OF THE CALL?'

I twig. 'You mean "Roger".'

'ROGER, JONATHAN, SAME DIFFER-
ENCE. BE READY TO ATTACK ON MY
SIGNAL!'

What an idiot. I watch her back towards one of
the Fryes' sheds. I should have known she wouldn't
listen to reason. We're in deep trouble. There's no
time to waste. Mrs Frye could do something crazy
any minute, and when she does there'll be a riot. I'll
have to make my move on Suzie now, at the Emu
Education Centre itself. Perhaps I can get up really
close and take her hand. Just, sort of, casually . . .

Me holding Suzie's hand!

My stomach flips in panic.

I'm just pushing my way through the crowds
when I come face to face with Caroline Dillinger.

I'm opening my mouth for our usual exchange
of insults when she leans over me, smiles toothily
and breathes, 'Ian, I just want to say, I know how
hard this is for you.'

I blink. This is clearly some complicated bit of
sarcasm, but I haven't got time to work it out
because I need to get back to Suzie. I push past the
wedding present table.

Dan's lion-like head looms over the crowd. He
smiles bravely and lets me back into line. Jet's
telling Suzie how much her mum likes me.

Now we're inside the entrance to the Emu

Education Centre. It's full of battered posters of emus and decorated emu eggs. There's an emu gift table, plus racks of emu leather clothing with the Pockys' design label name, which is 'Emusing' and was thought up by Terry.

Syd marches up and down the line, offering emu meat kebabs and gargling at bewildered tourists.

The Principal goes past, telling someone how he hopes it doesn't rain because the windscreen-wipers off his Vee-Dub just got stolen.

The side of me that's next to Suzie is tingling with her closeness. I sneak a look at her dangling hand. Why don't I just grab it? *Yeah, right – supposing she pulls it away?* I'm so near I can smell that lovely fabric softener. Meanwhile she's deep in conversation with Jet, Brad and Harry about how male emus, not females, are the ones who look after the eggs. Dan's staring at her like a big, forlorn horse. I look at the hand. My heart's pounding.

Take it, you big nong!

I gulp. Right, I will. I'll reach out and grab it. I'll do it. On the count of three. My heart's pounding.

One . . . two . . .

'Yo! Done your science project yet?' It's Jesse, his plastic face beaming. He leans over to me. 'I'm doing a paper rocket, powered with baking soda.'

25

I feel like telling him to attach his rocket to his bum and blast himself into outer space. Instead I say, 'Hey, Harry, show Jesse how you can count in twenty-threes.'

Jesse gives a delighted shout and joins in with him. Cunningham thunders past, wheezing and doing armfarts.

That idiot Jesse. He's really put me off.

Now Pricey and Bogle appear.

'Hey, Rude-Man, got a place behind you?'

Dan smiles warmly and lets them push in. They squeeze between him and me and end up nearly as close to Suzie as I am. Brilliant. Now I've got to try to make a move on Suzie with Bogle breathing down my neck.

Time's ticking away. Mrs Frye could strike any minute, but there's nothing I can do. We file past a glass case containing a dusty stuffed emu. It's got wonky glass eyes and, for some reason, one of its legs has had every bit of feather and skin removed so it's just bones.

It looks horrible.

Various little kids are standing, open-mouthed. Syd comes up with a plate of emu kebabs, points at the emu and says, 'Aaaah Big Bird aleg off, showa skeleton!' The kids pout in horror and start sobbing that Syd's killed Big Bird. Syd tries to cheer them up by holding out the plate of emu kebabs and saying, 'Aaaah, eata Big Bird.'

Suzie's explaining to Brad, Harry and Jet that the stuffed emu isn't really Big Bird and they're not to worry.

Jet says, 'Weally, Suzie?' and gives me a look.

Suzie leans over me. She whispers in my ear, 'Isn't Jet coming along well? You've really built up her self-esteem.'

I'm all jelly because her breath's in my ear.

I gabble, 'Yes, she's doing really well . . . and . . . and I think coming round to your place made all the difference . . .'

This is it! Grab the hand!

My phone rings! *Let it ring!*

'. . . because I think seeing you, and . . . and how everyone really likes you even though you're so clever . . .'

Suzie says, 'Ian, I think that's your phone . . .'

I'm drowning. How can I get romantic with all

these people around? I gasp, 'You see, the way I feel . . .'

The stupid phone's still ringing. I swear silently and punch 'answer'.

'ANGELA, JUST TO CONFIRM MY POSITION . . .'

It's that silly old chook Mrs Frye.

'I'M NOW LOCATED BEHIND THE SECOND EAGLE SHED . . .'

I murmer, 'Good, yes. Stay there.'

Now Suzie's looking. Mrs Frye's raving on. I don't know how to get rid of her.

I shrug at Suzie, cover the mouthpiece and say confidentially, 'It's my granny.'

Pricey says, 'Your granny just called you Angela.'

'ANGELA? WHERE ARE THE POLICE?'

Suzie's anxious. 'Ian, why does your granny want the police?'

Bogle snorts with laughter. 'Angela? What does your mum call you? Priscilla?'

Caroline Dillinger passes by, smiles and murmurs, 'Be brave, Ian. Talk soon.'

I whisper, 'Thanks, Granny, call you later,' and hang up.

Suzie freezes in her tracks. ' Ian! Don't hang up! She's asking for the police. Why is she asking for the police?'

I stutter, 'No, you see, she just *thinks* she wants the police, she doesn't really want the police.'

'Nobody asks for the police without a reason!'

I'm drowning. 'Yeah, but she's a bit, you know . . . bonkers . . .'

Suzie gasps. 'So you hang up on her? You desert a poor, mentally handicapped old lady?'

I rattle on with excuses. Suzie's outraged and demands I ring her back. Dan nods and tells me that ringing back would be a good idea. Bogle and Pricey are calling me Angela. Am I going mad? Here I am, seconds away from holding Suzie's hand, and I'm suddenly stuck in an argument about my non-existent loony granny. I grind my teeth and frantically punch in Natasha's number.

'Hello, *Granny*!'

Natasha says, 'Eh?'

I say loudly, '*Granny*, don't worry about the *police*.'

Natasha's voice comes through urgently. 'The police? Where?'

For crying out loud!

I say through gritted teeth, 'No, Granny. I just phoned to let you know I care about you, now I'm going.'

Natasha hisses, 'OK, what's the problem?'

The only problem's you and your mother, you dumbo.

I snarl, 'No problem, Granny, we all realize you're a bit . . . mental.'

Suzie snorts in disgust, snatches the phone and says sweetly, '*Hello*, Granny, this is *Suzie*, a friend of *Ian's*.'

I snatch it back in case she twigs it's Natasha.

She grabs it back.

Now we're wrestling with the phone. I'm desperate.

'No. You don't understand. She's frightened of strangers. Suzie, please, please . . .'

Syd Pocky passes by, gives Suzie a disapproving look and says pointedly, 'Play around expect a trouble! Where-a Caroline a shameful begga, aaaaah?'

My shirt's wet with sweat. I must be reeking. I let go of the phone in case Suzie can smell me. She settles in for a chat. Natasha must have got the picture because now Suzie's rattling on about services available for the elderly and how she'll personally come round and shampoo Natasha's hair. I'm dying. Everything's going so wrong.

Jet makes faces at me to go for Suzie.

Like I don't want to!

Suzie finally hangs up, hands me the phone, smiles and says, 'There. See? A bit of kindness goes a long way with the seniors.'

Dan's melting. He says, 'Suzie, would you talk to *my* granny like that?'

My phone rings. I pounce.

An old man's voice says, "Ello, Yarradindi Meats 'ere . . .'

I hang up before Suzie offers to shampoo him as well. Luckily she's not listening because Dan's telling her about his granny's hip replacement. That troublemaker Natasha. I could kill her. Why did I ever feel sorry for her? She's a maniac.

Now we're out of the Emu Education Centre. Jet grabs my arm. 'Are you stupid or what? You had five chances in there. Now shift your butt and go for it. We'll get Dan on the bouncy castle.'

We have to pass by Terry at the barbecue. He gives everyone an emu sausage sandwich and stops me. 'Ian, I just seen Caroline on the phone. She looks worried. Can't you just *talk* to her?'

Now Jet and Brad have dragged Dan to the bouncy castle and Suzie's standing all alone, but Terry won't let me go.

'Another thing, mate. Troy reckons there's a plain-clothes cop called Roger up here. I think that's him, over there.'

He points to the Big Kids, Little Kids teacher from Yarradindi Primary, who's chomping into an emu-egg sandwich, his jawbone grinding up and down through his withered cheek.

I just get away from him when Caroline Dillinger comes round the tree, takes my hand and murmurs breathily, 'Ian, do you ever look at me and feel like running in the opposite direction?'

I am going mad.

'Clint's dad told my mum about how you really like me but pretend you don't. How you're rude to me because you really like me. I mean, I should have guessed by the way you insult me. But then, as Clint's dad says, boys are so immature. They're frightened of strong emotions, so they run away.'

She leans closer.

'You see, Ian, when boys of your age fall in love, they react with the only thing they know, and you know what that is?'

How can I get away? You don't tell Caroline Dillinger you think she's repulsive. You're liable to get your teeth pushed in.

'Fear, Ian. Fear of strong emotions. Fear of not being cool enough or good-looking enough. But you mustn't worry about that. I know you're short. I know you're a bit meaty and your ears stick out, but those things don't count. It's what's inside that counts. And inside, Ian, you are a beautiful person. So, because I know what it means to you, Ian.'

She leans closer.

'You can kiss me.'

26

Oh! Horrible! Caroline Dillinger all puckered up for a kiss!

My phone rings. I could weep with relief. I mutter, 'Caroline. I have to go. I . . . I can't stand the stress of being near you.'

I hurry off. This is insane. Caroline Dillinger's in love with me, Mrs Frye and her brain-dead mates are going to wreck the wedding. Worst of all, dopey Dan's going to get Suzie. I rush off towards Suzie and the others at the bouncy castle. The phone's still ringing. Which moron is it now?

It's Natasha.

'Emergency! You'll have to pretend to be both of them. You'll have to pretend to Spud Bum that you're Mum, and to Mum that you're Spud Bum . . . !'

This is the limit.

'Get nicked. I'm sick of you. Why can't you keep your end of the bargain.'

'I'm trying to. Mum's making me stand next to

her to help her with the phone. She thinks every time you hang up she's getting accidentally cut off. I can't impersonate Mum to Angela if Mum's standing right next to me, can I?'

'Yeah, but how can I impersonate both of them?'

'I dunno. Improvise. I've redirected Angela's calls from Mum's phone so she'll come straight through to you.'

'Natasha!'

She's hung up on me. If I ever get out of this stupid situation I'll kill her. Across the paddock, Terry and Syd are hurrying into the house to get into their wedding suits, ready for Granny.

This is it. I have to go for Suzie. It's now or never.

I strike up to her and blurt out, 'Suzie, er . . . there's this view over the National Park Wilderness Area just across there. I want Jet to see it, but I'm not sure if she'll be frightened. Can you come over and see what you think?'

Suzie smiles at me. That dazzling smile . . . !

I hurry her over to the view. I can hardly breathe. What if she sneers at me? In the distance I can hear the roar of the motorbike convoy arriving with Granny. I have to be quick.

We arrive at the view.

She says, 'Yes, it's really steep, isn't it? But if you

keep Jet well away from the edge, she should be OK.'

There's a silence. I spring on to a rock so I'm level with her. She's staring down at the view, her dark hair shining. My heart's beating all thick and fast. My knees are starting to shake. Her smell's making me giddy. Her hand's just hanging next to her. This is it. I lean casually against the fence. All I have to do now is reach out . . . like this . . . and . . .

Suzie turns, gasps with astonishment and says, 'Ian, the emus . . .'

I glance over my shoulder and nearly collide with Bruce Willis's beak. He's standing, pressed against the fence, along with about a hundred other emus. He's drumming romantically.

Suzie laughs. I pretend to laugh. Suzie laughs some more and tickles Bruce's head. I laugh desperately. What am I going to do? The noise is deafening.

Over the hill, led by Constable Platt's police car, comes a stream of huge motorbikes, two by two. Suzie runs off to look. I'm in shock. I just stand there.

The bikes have all got bunches of white ribbons attached to the handlebars. Right at the end of the convoy is Granny in the sidecar, with Skull driving.

Everyone cheers and applauds.

I'm about to head after Suzie, but I get a call from Spud Bum, who thinks I'm Mrs Frye. I shout, 'Emergency! Stay where you are!' and hang up. As soon as I've hung up I get a call from Mrs Frye, who thinks I'm Spud Bum. She tells me to start firing the paintball guns. I shout, 'I can't! There are police outside the barn!'

I see her running down the hill to look. Natasha's grabbing at her arm and pleading with her, trying to stop her.

We'll never stall her for fifteen minutes. Oh, forget her. Forget all of them. I've got to get to Suzie. I've got to be with her when the riot starts – because if I'm not, Dan will be. I try pushing through the crowds, but it's impossible. Syd comes out of the house with Terry and all the Pockys. They're all in white suits with top hats. In a few minutes they'll be covered in red paint. Gutsa flicks a switch on the sound system. Elvis blares out of the speakers at the noise level of a jumbo jet taking off. The flocks of birds go demented.

I try to go round the other way to get to Suzie, but the crowd's even bigger. Granny's getting out of the sidecar, adjusting the Velcroed skirt of her big meringue wedding dress. Syd's started to move from his side of the platform, a big grin on his face. Granny's started to move from her side of the platform, a big grin on her face.

Mum adjusts the microphone. She's saying Syd and Granny are having the ceremony to show the world their great love for each other.

Now I can't even see Suzie. My phone rings. It's Mrs Frye screaming at me.

I hiss, 'Stay put!' and hang up.

Now it's Spud Bum screaming at me.

I hiss, 'Stay put!' and hang up.

My phone's ringing and ringing. What am I going to say next? They're both so crazy they'll risk death anyway. This is the end. The Psychos are going to wreck the wedding. What's worse, they're going to wreck my chances with Suzie. I have to find her. I start pushing through the crowds. I'm shoving and jostling. I can see Dan's head. And Suzie's head.

Mum says, 'If anyone here knows any reason why these two people should not be brought together again in marriage, let them say so . . .'

Suddenly there's a garbled yell from up the hill.

It's not Mrs Frye.

It's not Spud Bum.

Who is it? The yelling and shouting continues. It's some crazy person.

It's Mr Frye. He's running towards the barn, bellowing. He's found the Psychos inside. He's hauling them out and ordering them off his land.

They're running out with their paintball guns. This is fantastic.

Mr Frye is going to stop the Psychos!

But suddenly, *splat!* Red paint hits Granny.

Splat! Red paint hits Syd.

Oh, no! The Psychos are ripping down Terry's emu fences. Syd and Granny are staring at each other, frozen. Terry and an army of Pockys and bikies start yelling and running to protect the fences. There's going to be murder.

My heart is pounding. What can I do?

Then, amazingly, Granny begins to laugh. She yells, 'Who knew I always wanted to play paintball?'

She gives a whoop, rips her skirt off and jumps off the platform, dressed in her bride's top and her black shorts. The audience bursts into applause.

Syd yells, 'Wharra joke a wedding, a silly beggas!'

Granny pounds straight up to the nearest Psycho, snatches his paintball gun and fires it straight back at him.

The audience is going crazy, clapping and cheering. They think it's all part of the show. Constable Platt is trying to get some order.

Now all the bikies are laughing and grabbing the Psychos' paintball guns and shooting back at them. The Pocky kids grab food from the barbecue and start throwing it at them. Spud Bum gets hit on the back with an emu egg.

The Psychos turn tail and start to run, bellowing. It's wonderful. I catch a glimpse of Noddy the kangaroo standing by the upturned refreshments table, munching placidly on a sandwich.

But Mrs Frye's screaming and struggling to escape from Natasha. Natasha's clinging on for dear life. Mrs Frye wrenches away, shoves Natasha to the ground, shrieks, 'I'll get you!' at Syd, and starts pelting down the paddocks towards him.

Mr Frye throws back his head, lets out a bellow of fury and starts running after her. Constable Platt's sprinting towards both of them, shouting warnings.

Natasha's jumping up, yelling, 'Ian! Help! Stop her! She'll get arrested!'

I run like crazy to cut off Mrs Frye before she gets to Syd. A roar of audience applause makes me turn around. Bruce Willis is running after me through the broken fence. The stupid crowd is going wild. They think this is part of the act as well. Now other emus are following Bruce Willis. Now there are six, now ten, now a huge mob. I suddenly realize: if I stop, they'll trample me. I shoot forward, yelling.

Across the paddocks I glimpse Mr Frye gaining on his wife. He's yelling and telling her she's an irresponsible idiot and if it wasn't for Natasha he'd let her go to jail. He's nearly got her. Suddenly, he leaps. All those years of chasing Noddy have given him amazing skills. He brings her to the ground in the most amazing rugby tackle.

The crowd roars.

But I've got my own problems. Now I'm pounding downhill at the head of a mob of emus. My legs won't stop. My lungs are burning. My ankle's going to give way. I veer left to try to shake off the emus. The emus veer left. I veer right, the emus veer right. Down on the road I see a tourist bus on the freeway. They're taking photos – Local lad out exercising the emus. We're down the hill, into the National Wilderness area. I'm pelting down a path. I can't keep this up. The path's running out. It's a dead end. It's all trees and dense scrub. I'm going to smash into a tree and get trampled. There are no low-hanging branches.

I scream and jump like I've never jumped before. I soar. I'm going to die.

I'm hanging on to a branch, gasping and sobbing, as the emus stream past underneath.

I dangle, swear, and drop to the ground. At least all those leaps for Suzie taught me something.

The first thing I notice is the smell. Then the chirping. Bats. I look up. I'm in a bat colony.

There are bats everywhere. There's a swooping

sound. A bat flies down and hangs upside down, looking at me. It chitters viciously and snorts a big lump of snot. It's just like Horace.

Wait a minute. It *is* just like Horace. They're all identical to Horace. They've all got Horace's weird, bent nose that Mrs Frye thought was a deformity. It's a bat colony of Horaces! It's a new breed!

Natasha comes pounding up the path, gasping, 'Ian, are you all right?' She stops in her tracks. Her mouth drops open.

I say, 'Yeah, look, they're all Horaces!'

She's shaking her head, pointing. She looks like she's seen a ghost. I turn to see. She has seen a ghost. Standing in the middle of the clearing, snarling at us, is a Tasmanian Tiger. Except they're completely extinct.

Terry and Syd come roaring up on a four-wheeled motorbike, bellowing. Terry's waving a rifle.

'Quick. Outa here. These blokes'll kill you!'

He's aiming the rifle at the Tasmanian Tiger.

Natasha's rushing up to them. 'Stop! These animals! Do you know what they are?'

'Too right I do, Caroline. Bloody mongrels, that's what they are. Bite ya soon as look at ya. I told you they was dangerous. I bin warning you lot all along about the animals round this place. I usually come down here once a month with me rifle and pop off a bunch of 'em to keep down the numbers.'

Natasha is shaking, 'You mean . . . there are more than these?'

'More? There's bloody millions, darl! All shapes and sizes. Always has been. Ya never see half the beggas anywhere else. They just hang round being a nuisance in 'ere.'

I look at Natasha. Natasha looks at me.

The Pockys have got a whole forest full of endangered species. Except they're not endangered. They're tough as guts. Because, of course, they're all Pockys.

As we're standing there in shock, Mr Frye's mobile rings. An old man's voice says slowly, ''Ello, Yarradindi Meats 'ere. I'm just ringing back to tell ya – get nicked.'

And that's how the Pocky Family Australian Wildlife Safari and Animal Refuge came into being.

And how, incidentally, I became Captain of Conservation.

27

Suzie got the Principal to give it to me on the basis of my heroic behaviour and discovery of the Lost World of the Pockys. Suzie thought I deliberately led off the emus to stop them dying of distress during the paintball fight. I couldn't really explain that it was an accident. The badge got handed out during Assembly. Since I always wanted to be a Captain I can't complain.

It turned out that about ten extinct or endangered Australian species were alive and thriving on the Pockys' property, plus twelve new ones. Of course, every naturalist in the world wanted to come and see. So they all did, and they were really impressed.

They gave all the new animals long Latin names that included the word 'Pocky', which was totally right because the reason all the animals survived was exactly because they were Pocky versions of the real thing. Which was also, of course, why all the animals the Fryes kept rescuing were so horrible.

It's like I always think. If a meteor hit the earth and there were five survivors, four of them would be Pocky kids wandering round during the sixty years of darkness doing armfarts.

Once Syd and Granny realized they were sitting on the world's most valuable wildlife reserve, they decided to give up the idea of farming emus and open their property to the public as an Australian safari park. Which was just as well really, because the only emu that came back from the wilderness was Bruce Willis. He followed me. You could say he was the one who found it. Every time I go to the Safari Park, old Bruce comes up for a pat. I've learned to live with it.

Crusher designed and made all the uniforms for the staff to wear. Syd employed Mr Frye as Chief Warden because none of the Pockys could remember the animals' official names.

So Mr Frye gave up his job at the local Council to work for Syd full-time. Syd pays him so well that the Fryes were able to afford to do up their wildlife refuge. Mr Frye's training Crusher to look after animals. Crusher's really good at working to a timetable, from his years in the army.

One of the nicest things is that Noddy turns out to be a Pocky animal, so instead of threatening to put him to sleep for being so horrible, the Parks and Wildlife people have put a special protection order on him because his whole sub-species of kangaroo is naturally horrible, and it has nothing to do with being badly brought up. So he roams free. He's struck up a friendship with Bruce Willis.

Mrs Frye has had the weirdest change of all. She and Horace went on so many TV news programmes to tell people about the animals that she became a bit of a celebrity. Now she runs her own wildlife TV interview show for our local TV station, talking to famous people about which endangered species they really like.

People who don't know how demented she is think she's really interesting and amusing. Horace always brings the house down by hanging quietly from her cardigan and going for people or spitting gunk at exactly the right moment.

Mr and Mrs Frye made it up after Mr Frye's amazing rugby tackle. According to Natasha, they saved face by agreeing that the tackle was all for the best, because if Mrs Frye hadn't run at Syd I wouldn't have led off the emus and found the marvellous Pocky Wilderness. In fact, I get the feeling that the more time goes by, the more Mrs Frye is convinced that she was the one who found the Pocky animals in the first place.

As soon as the Fryes got money again, Mr Frye bought Natasha a piano. You wouldn't believe how good she is. She did the drama performance for

Suzie and the Captains. They came second in the State. I still feel a bit guilty about Dan. He gave up trying to compete with Chippy and took his broken heart on an exchange trip to China. He's spending a term learning Mandarin and astrophysics.

Bogle's building a solar- and wind-power system to run the school's heating. Pricey's doing the welding. It's going quite well, except for when Pricey accidentally welded a big chunk of the machine to a metal desk leg. Chess Club has been disbanded because a whole lot of Primary School boys started getting some weird thing about chess affecting their rude bits.

I expressed surprise.

And Caroline Dillinger came up to me at school and explained that while she'd always known I secretly loved her, she actually had a boyfriend, so I would have to be brave.

I said I'd try.

And that's about it. I haven't yet managed to make a move on Suzie. But I'm working up to it. Weirdly, I'm spending a lot of time with Natasha. She's really stoked because she's just got into the finals of some big piano competition in Germany. Even if she loses, she gets to meet all these important people in the world of piano playing.

Of course, she's practising like crazy. When Suzie's off at lunchtimes doing leadership seminars, we often have our sandwiches together. Sometimes I listen to her play.

It's lunchtime on the day before Natasha leaves for Germany, and the first bell's just gone for the end of lunch break. I'm telling her some funny stuff that happened during History when we had this guest speaker in, because she's in a different group.

She says in a matter-of-fact way, 'Ian, you forget. Not everyone's as smart as you.'

'Smart? As if. I got fifty in Science last week.'

She starts packing up her music. 'I'm not talking about memory tests. I'm talking about smarts. You know. Quick-thinking, someone who can suss people out.'

I cut in, straight-faced. 'A good liar.'

She shrugs. 'Your lies didn't seem to hurt much. You got the Pockys what they needed. You got my dad and mum what they needed, which means you got me what I needed. You looked after our animals. That's not bad going.'

'I only did it to get in with the Clones.'

I could bite off my tongue. It sounds terrible, talking about Suzie like that. She's kind and thoughtful and lovely, she's not some sort of robot.

'What are the Clones?'

She suddenly gasps and grins. 'It's Suzie, Jesse and Melissa!' She chuckles. 'That's really funny,

Ian, that's really perfect. You see, that's what I mean – you're really perceptive. Who else at school could think of something like that?'

I've got to set things straight. 'Yeah, but Suzie's not some robot or anything . . .'

She grins warmly. 'Of course she isn't. And she's really lucky to have you. I bet you have such a heap of laughs. Hey, what about that time you got stuck down the toilet?'

I chuckle as I help her pack up her stuff. 'You shoved me. I could've drowned, you know. What a way to go. What would they have said at my funeral?'

'And what about you having to feed Bobby all the time? He's horrible, and you were so nice to him.'

'He needs a good kick in the endangered goolies.'

She bursts out laughing.

Now I'm laughing too. 'And then you made me chop up the Big Emu. I couldn't believe it.'

'I'm sorry. I was so desperate about my mum. And I was half crazy because I'd got my dad to sell our piano to pay Mum's fines and I thought I had to give up music for ever. I knew you were the sort of person who wouldn't let me down.'

'You're joking. I was dying for an excuse!'

'I'm not saying you liked it. I'm saying you stick to your commitments.'

I snort, 'Give me a break – what are *you* after? I'm not breaking into any more houses for you, you know.'

She chuckles as she closes the lid of the piano. 'No, I'm serious. You do. What about when you and those Year 7s were scrubbing graffiti off the gym wall?'

'Eh?'

'You remember. Just after I came to this school. You and Suzie were helping a bunch of Year 7s to scrub graffiti off the gym wall, right?'

'Right.'

'It was a really hard job and it was obvious you were only doing it to be near Suzie. Fair enough. But then Suzie went and left you on your own with the Year 7s.'

'So?'

She shrugs. 'So, it would have been the easiest thing in the world for you to have ducked off or to have bullied the Year 7s into doing all the work. But you didn't. You kept doing your fair share. And I thought, there's a decent person. So when it came to choosing someone to help with the animals . . .'

'And to do handstands on people's toilet seats!'

We pack up, laughing again. What an insane

few days. She's smiling. She's really good-looking these days, now she's happy.

I say, 'Why *did* you offer to play the piano for Suzie?'

'To stop myself going crazy, really. I was missing the piano so much. I was totally stressed out about Mum.'

She looks at me.

'Ian. Look. Thanks.'

She kisses me on the cheek.

I smile. 'Hey – any time you want a good bit of vandalism. And good luck in the competition.'

'Think of me tomorrow. The train leaves at four-thirty.' She pulls a face of panic.

I squeeze her shoulder. 'You'll be fine.'

I head off, grinning. She's OK, Natasha. I've noticed her going round with Bogle a bit lately. It'd be cool if they got together. We could go out as a foursome. And I'm glad she's doing her music. I really admire her, trying to give up her music to save money for her parents, but they didn't really want that, and it would have been such a waste.

Life is good. I arrive next morning at Suzie's place. Her mum's just arranging a big bowl of flowers on the table. Her dad passes through and waves me a greeting. He says he's photocopying me an article in the paper about new uses for recycled tyres.

Harry comes in and shows me the latest Lego model he's made.

Suzie and I do a whole heap of homework together, then have a really sophisticated lunch with posh salad and lovely cheeses (at home I'd be grabbing a sandwich between serving old ladies vitamin pills and listening to the Cannibals talking about their varicose veins). After lunch it's more homework. Suzie shows me a really easy way to memorize equations in maths. She reckons it's really easy to get high marks if you know tricks. She reckons I can easily top my maths group, and then, if I put in the work, move up to a higher one.

Not bad!

I'm stoked about what Natasha said. She thinks I'm really smart. I mean, I don't believe it, but Natasha's no fool. I guess Suzie must think I'm pretty cool as well, since she's inviting me over. Not to mention her fixing it so I'm Captain of Conservation.

Next week I have to do a special speech for the whole school on landfill. Sounds as boring as watching paint dry, but I'll stick in a few jokes.

We get on to our music appreciation project. Music makes me think of Natasha, which makes me think of the time Natasha and I were trying to get into the farmhouse at Yarradindi Emu World and everyone thought she was Caroline Dillinger.

224

I chuckle. Suzie asks me what I'm laughing at. I make up something lame about the book I'm reading. She blinks and smiles politely. That's one of the cool things about Suzie, she's so elegant. She never does a big belly laugh or anything.

Not that I'd mind if she did.

Actually, it would be quite good if she did, because then I could do a belly laugh as well. And crack rude jokes. I mean, I don't want to crack disgusting jokes or anything, but, for example, I'd be embarrassed to mention Bobby the Wombat's goolies to Suzie. It'd be gross. I have to be really witty and sophisticated, like her dad.

Her dad cracks these really clever jokes. Like at lunch he told us this really funny story about how dumb people confuse the words 'lay' and 'lie', and so really what they're saying is that they lay eggs.

Or something like that.

After we've done our homework, I have afternoon tea with the whole family. I'm exhausted! Suzie's mum explains how she's working with victims of car accidents who have to build up their confidence to drive. Suzie's dad says rehabilitation's a very important thing for car accident victims.

I love it how Suzie's parents treat you like an adult. I love these really intelligent conversations. I drift off. I think of Natasha laughing. Funny how she assumed that Suzie and me would have a lot of laughs, because our relationship isn't at all like that. Shame Natasha's going, really. I'll miss her.

Suzie pours me some more tea. She says that after tea we'll go and look at some more maths equations, so I can practise her memory trick. Her dad chips in with other memory tricks I can use, this time for History.

I'm getting a bit tired of homework, so I say, 'Maybe tomorrow.'

There's a silence. Suzie's family look at each other. Her dad blinks. 'You have to build on this sort of thing, Ian. You can't achieve without work.'

Suzie smiles. 'Honestly, it won't take long.'

Her mum says, 'Yes, Ian. Come along. You do want to be smart, don't you?'

But I am smart.

They launch into ways I can get smarter. Even little Harry joins in with some method he's got for learning his tables. I stare round at them. I feel really weird. And surprised. And . . . kind of angry. Or am I hurt?

Because I *am* smart. And I'm funny. And perceptive, and I can be relied on. I'm not some kind of robot you can re-program to be exactly what you want.

I suddenly realize what I am to Suzie, and to her family.

I'm a project.

28

Well, sorry. I'm not a project. I'm me.

Wait on. That's rude – I mean, these people are really nice. I'm in a daze. Suzie's mum's offering me carrot cake and telling me about how she memorizes people's names so they'll feel she really cares about them. Suzie's dad's complimenting me on being Captain of Conservation and saying it's only the start. Harry's saying he'd really like to be Captain of Conservation and would I come and talk to his Primary School class.

But a voice inside me is saying I don't want to be Captain of Conservation just because my girlfriend rigs it for me. I don't want to change people or be changed myself. I don't want to spend my life struggling to get a hundred per cent in History for the sake of getting a hundred per cent in History.

I want to struggle for what *I* think's worthwhile. With the people *I* think are worthwhile. And with people who think I'm worthwhile as well, who like me for myself. People I can laugh and relax with and talk to, like Bogle and Pricey and Natasha.

I feel so mixed up and angry. And then there's the weirdest thing. Because suddenly, in the middle of feeling so angry and dark, the mention of Natasha is like the sun just came out.

I think of Natasha's face all lit up, talking about her music. I think of that stupid fluffy hair of hers and when it got stuck in my watch strap after the sheep's eyes went flying and we had to be chopped apart. Those sheep's eyes!

'What are you smiling at, Ian?'

I feel flustered and guilty. And I suddenly realize why she's asking me the reason I'm smiling. It's because with Suzie I never smile. I stare at her scientifically. It's not just that she wants to change me.

She's boring.

This is insane. Suzie, boring? I look at her perfect face. I've been wanting her for so long. I'd have done anything to get her. I did, but now . . . It's not her that I'm thinking of.

It's Natasha.

Wait a minute. I must be going crazy. Natasha is insane, an idiot Greenie, somebody who drives me up the wall.

But she isn't. She's . . . she's really . . . interesting. And good-looking. I mean, seriously good-looking.

Not like a model or anything. Not like Suzie. It's like she's good-looking as part of a whole bunch of other things, and...

Stop this! This is stupid! I am *not* interested in Natasha. Suzie's telling me the trick to remember French verbs. Suzie's mum's suggesting I come with their family to the art gallery because my parents don't have time to take me. What a nerve! Who's she to criticize my parents? My parents are cool. But my mind keeps turning on Natasha. I have to see her. I have to see if I'm right. But she's getting the four-thirty train. I'll never catch her.

I mumble an excuse and hurry out. I jump on my bike and pedal like a lunatic. My legs are burning. Of course Bogle's after her. She's fantastic, how could I not have realized it? She's good-looking and smart and funny – she plays the piano like a genius – and what about the way she was doing all that stuff for her parents? I come round the final bend.

The Land Rover's gone. I stare blankly at the empty drive.

A voice says, 'Hello, Ian. If you're looking for Natasha, she's round with Bobby. Be quick, because we've already missed the four-thirty train. Horace's ear infection played up again and . . .'

I'm pelting towards Bobby's pen. Where is she? She's next to Bobby's enclosure, with her back to me. My stomach somersaults. I stop in my tracks. I have to be wrong. This is crazy. I can't be feeling this way about *Natasha*.

She turns and beams at me.

She is absolutely lovely.

'Hi, Ian. Can't stay away from Bobby, eh? Help me feed him – I know how much you enjoy it. Open the gate.'

I'm staring at her like I've never seen her before. I open the gate. It swings back and her hand accidentally touches mine. It's like an electric shock. She rattles on about how she's just heard from the people she and Mrs Frye are staying with in Germany.

I can't look at her. My heart starts pounding.

'Ian? Your hands are shaking. Are you OK?'

When I was about eight someone bet me I wouldn't jump off the top diving board. You stand on the edge of the board with the pool way below, like some tiny, oblong jewel. Fear eats every part of you. No going back.

I swallow hard, 'Can I write to you?'

There's silence.

Don't say no, don't laugh.

She coughs and says, very briskly, 'Of course you can write to me. I was expecting you to write.'

'No. I mean. Write to you . . .' here goes '. . . like, seriously.'

There's more silence. She's straight-faced. She coughs again. 'What about Suzie?'

I mumble, 'Suzie's over. I mean, it never started. Look, Suzie wanted to change me, she wanted to turn me into a kinda . . . cut-price Clone and I finally realized I wanted to be my own person and . . .'

I take a deep breath.

'. . . I wanted to go out with *you*.'

I tail off. I try to meet her eyes. She won't look at me. She's blinking very quickly. Our eyes meet.

She says softly, 'Ian, you're not . . . this isn't a joke, is it . . .' She stops. She's all pink.

I gabble, 'No, I'm serious. I'm way-set serious. I suddenly realized how well we got on together. I mean, not at first. I hated you at first.' I give a panicked laugh. 'I mean, it's a bit hard to like someone who's making you smash up people's stuff and break into their homes.'

Silence again.

I rattle on desperately. 'But of course, I understand now why you did it. With your mum. You had to . . .'

I stop. She's staring at me, frowning. *What does that mean?* Now she's looking away and refusing to meet my eyes. *What does that mean?*

My voice comes out all strangled. 'So, er . . . do I write?'

She nods and looks down. 'Yes.'

I'm drowning. I can't work out what she's thinking. Does she like me? Is she about to start laughing?

I clear my throat. 'And . . . and . . . you like me, then?'

She's silent. She's blinking again. She looks at her feet and gives a nervous little laugh.

'Like you? Ian, I'm totally *stupid* about you. Didn't you realize?'

She looks at me anxiously. I feel like a light's turned on inside me. I feel like jumping in the air. I don't know what to do.

I give a kind of gasping laugh. 'Well, no. It's a bit hard when you're having your head shoved down a toilet.'

She bursts out laughing. 'Look, stop going on about that. I only did it once. *And* you deserved it. Hanging there, *whingeing*.'

'Whingeing? You nearly drowned me.'

'Oh garbage, you big wuss, you were perfectly OK.'

She is fabulous. We start to wrestle. I threaten to shove her in the wombat poo for lack of respect. She threatens to shove me in the wombat poo for threatening to shove her in the wombat poo.

I say, 'Respect that wombat poo. That wombat poo's your bread and butter!'

She packs up. I take her in my arms. It's so natural I can't believe it. I'm staring into her lovely eyes.

There's a round of applause. It's Terry, Crusher, Syd and Granny. They're in their new Yarradindi Australian Safari uniforms.

Granny waves and yells, 'Good on yer, Ian!'

Syd gargles, 'Aaah! Caroline-a girlfriend again, a lucky begga aaah!' He's never got the name thing.

Terry yells out, 'Bewdy, Ian! I always knew you two were made for each other.' The T-shirt under his jacket reads: 'Don't be a Low Life, Visit the Wildlife'.

Mr Frye shouts, 'Natasha! Time to go!'

We hurry into the house to get her stuff. She's going to write. She'll be back on the twenty-third of May. The time between is like a looming hole, but I can take it. The question is, will she find someone else on the trip? All those musicians. All glamorous and German. As we come out to the Land Rover to wait for her parents, I'm grabbed by panic.

I say, pretending it's a joke, 'Don't go finding any bloody musicians . . .'

She looks at me seriously. 'Stop it, Ian. Stop always assuming other people are better than you. You're wonderful. You're gorgeous. You're so good-looking – those fantastic eyelashes!'

I choke with amazement and delight. She thinks I'm gorgeous? Is she mad?

A smile lurks on her lips.

'Mind you, I have been brought up with wombats.'

I'm trying to take it all in. I've got a girlfriend. The BEST girlfriend. Who thinks I'm wonderful and gorgeous and clever, so I don't have to lie or fake or change or pretend to be something I'm not, ever again.

She says, 'What are you grinning about?'

What can you say? I look into her lovely, smiling face. I'm so close I can see each freckle, each eyelash. I can feel the heat coming off her cheeks.

Everything goes silent. Then, without saying anything – without having to say anything – we lean together. I close my eyes.

I kiss her.

And if you've never kissed the person you've just realized you love and who is wonderful and who loves you back way beyond anything you ever dreamed you could deserve, let me tell you, that first kiss is like flying to the moon. Better. You're on the highest mountain, with a whole new country laid out in front of you, bright and perfect and gleaming. I'm the happiest I can ever remember being.

My heart soars.

(And hey – the second kiss isn't bad either.)